CLIVE ALLEN
UP FRONT

MY AUTOBIOGRAPHY

CLIVE ALLEN
UP FRONT

MY AUTOBIOGRAPHY
WITH JAMES OLLEY

First published as a hardback by deCoubertin Books Ltd in 2019.

First Edition

deCoubertin Books, 46B Jamaica Street, Baltic Triangle, Liverpool, L1 0AF.

www.decoubertin.co.uk

ISBN: 978-1-909245-96-9

A CIP catalogue record for this book is available from the British Library.

Cover design and typeset by Leslie Priestley.

Printed and bound by Jellyfish.

To Lisa,

We've grown up together,
you have experienced everything
– the highs and the lows.
You are an incredible wife and
mother to my children.
You are one of the most selfless
people I know and
I wouldn't have achieved half of
what I did without
your love and support.

This is for you.

Contents

CHAPTER ONE

Changing Lanes

SUNDAY 14 MAY 2017. TOTTENHAM BEAT MANCHESTER UNITED 2-1 IN THE FINAL GAME PLAYED AT WHITE HART LANE. A FAREWELL CEREMONY TAKES PLACE AT FULL-TIME.

I NEVER THOUGHT I'D LEAD THE LINE AT WHITE HART LANE ONE more time. Around 50 former players and managers had been invited to walk onto the pitch at full-time and there was genuine confusion about how we would be organised.

Several club legends included in the parade had spoken to club officials beforehand, demanding to lead us all out. The organisers had a real dilemma as a result and decided the only fair way to do it was in alphabetical order.

We were welcomed into a joyous atmosphere. Spurs deserved to beat United and Mauricio Pochettino's side ended the season unbeaten at home in the Premier League. High on a mix of euphoria and nostalgia, the crowd went through a back catalogue of songs as I waited in the tunnel before a video began playing on the big screen.

Sir Kenneth Branagh introduced and narrated a short film depicting some of the greatest days in the stadium's long history since the first match on the site back in September 1899.

Various images from the 2,533 games played at the Lane were selected, including from the 1960/61 double-winning season, the European Cup Winners' Cup run of 1963, Diego Maradona's appearance for Ossie Ardiles's testimonial and great goals from some of the best: Glenn Hoddle, Paul Gascoigne, Gareth Bale and Harry Kane.

The booming PA took over with a military-style drum-beat provided by the Tottenham Hotspur Marching Band, specially assembled for the day and located just to the left of centre on the pitch.

'Please. Welcome our former players who graced this pitch at White Hart Lane flanked by a guard of honour from our academy.

'Our first man scored a record 49 goals in 1987, double footballer of the year… striker CLIVE ALLEN!'

The crowd cheered as I made my way out onto the pitch, waving and smiling to all four corners. What a moment. I'd barely taken ten strides when the PA continued.

'Talented and industrious, 370 games over eight years, FA Cup winner in 1991, midfielder… PAUL ALLEN!'

I reached the centre as my cousin Paul took his applause and walked to the other side of a central plinth from which world-renowned tenor Wynne Evans would later sing.

'The scorer of the first goal in that legendary double season of 1961, striker, LES ALLEN!'

With a crutch in his right arm, Dad made his way across the grass as the roll-call continued. Darren Anderton, Steve Archibald and Ossie Ardiles came next.

Ossie walked across the pitch and Dad took his place alongside me. The club's greats continued to file out and as 30,000 fans sang about Ledley King having one knee yet being better than John Terry, the rain began to fall and umbrellas were passed along the line to those of us already in the middle. Dad held his own umbrella, as did I. The weather did nothing to dampen the spirits, although it tried.

The names kept coming as the rain got heavier: Teddy Sheringham, Ricky Villa, Chris Waddle.

'Ladies and gentlemen, the great players who graced this pitch thousands of times between them. The Kings of White Hart Lane!'

The emotion of standing next to my Dad and my cousin while being described in those terms overwhelmed me. I looked across at Paul. He smiled back. I looked at Dad. Nothing.

CHAPTER TWO

Born Into It

'IT'S BETTER TO BE A HAS-BEEN THAN A NEVER-WAS.' THIS WAS MY Dad's mantra from as young as I can remember.

I was six years old when I realised he was famous in football. He played in the Queens Park Rangers side which beat West Brom to win the 1967 League Cup Final and it was the first event I can remember attending as a family.

Prior to that, he was part of one of the most iconic teams in Tottenham's history and people stopped him anywhere inside a mile of White Hart Lane.

Dad scored 27 goals in Spurs's Double-winning season of 1960/61 and played alongside the legendary Jimmy Greaves for a short while before moving to QPR in 1965.

He was an old-fashioned inside-forward, playing off the main striker. I remember he had a good touch with excellent awareness of what was going on around him. He wasn't the quickest but he had a fine goalscoring record, 61 in 137 appearances, made all the more impressive by not operating as an out-and-out striker.

In subsequent years, I have talked to some of the old boys I work with at Tottenham on matchdays about him. John Pratt, a former midfielder who made over 400 appearances for the club before later returning as a coach and then assistant manager, told me Bill Nicholson described Dad as his most dangerous player in the Double team.

For the great man to say that about my Dad in one of the best teams in Tottenham's history is quite an accolade.

Greaves ultimately replaced Dad in the starting line-up, prompting a move to

QPR, where he ended his playing career. He also briefly managed at Loftus Road during the 1969/70 season. It seemed across London I couldn't go anywhere as a kid without anyone telling me what a great player he was.

Of course, I was proud of that. Everyone liked him and he had a powerful, consuming influence over me, particularly in my formative years.

The daily guidance of a top sportsman helped me understand the commitment and focus required to make it as a professional.

But I slowly became aware of the Allen family tree's reach, spreading much wider across football. My uncle Dennis played for Charlton before spending almost a decade at Reading. Everybody loved Uncle Den. He always let us kids – my Dad had six siblings who all had children of their own, so family gatherings were quite something – do whatever the respective parents said we couldn't do.

When I was 11 years old, I watched him play for Belgian side Oostende at Colchester in a pre-season game towards the end of his career. A family group of about 20 went to support him but he didn't need it. Den was a rugged centre-half, a good footballer but very tough. He was naughty. I would have hated playing against him.

There were two guys sat on a wall in front of us, shouting abuse at him, thinking he was Belgian and therefore wouldn't understand what they were saying. Den kept smiling in their direction and early in the game he launched into a tackle right in front of them, completely wiping out Colchester's right-winger.

These two lads were up in arms and he just winked at them. He made a similar tackle later on which drove them madder still. We all stood up in support but Den focused on these two lads, baying for the referee to send him off. He went over to the touchline and right in front of them, turned around and pulled his shorts down.

The women in the Allen clan all had their hands over their eyes in disbelief but I thought it was brilliant. All the boys did. He was our hero after that.

Football clubs can be strange places, particularly at youth level. You are introduced to more people than you can ever remember. A constant need to prove your ability can trigger inhibitions which become hard to shake. Every now and again, you might catch a glimpse of a first-team player to set your heart racing in awe and admiration.

None of that applied to me. I'd been fortunate enough to be immersed in club culture from a very young age. I once went to a match at Loftus Road in a QPR kit given to me as a Christmas present before knocking a ball around with family friend Terry Venables and Rodney Marsh prior to kick-off. I was lucky.

I got the right advice in key moments. Aged 11, I was playing for Gaynes School Under-12s in Hornchurch against Dury Falls. Dury's coach was Dave Spurdle, who doubled up as selector for the District side and while I was just looking forward to playing, Dad sat with me a few days before the game to stress its importance.

'This is your chance,' he said, 'and I know how you can guarantee yourself a place in the District side. Score six goals.'

It might sound like undue pressure to put on someone so young but it sharpened my focus. We won 8-0, I scored the six goals ordered and was selected for the District side.

An obsession with goals is something you have in your DNA. It is a measure by which you can determine individual development and that is a rare thing in team sport. The way I was brought up, it wasn't about the one you scored but the next one. Harry Kane has got it. Having worked with him during my time as a coach at Spurs, I know that first-hand. I could never have foreseen Harry would have the career he has today but you could always see the fundamental attributes that could make him a goalscorer.

Practice makes perfect. You have to drill yourself to know what type of finish you are attempting the split-second a chance comes your way. How can you be most efficient in scoring? Power, precision, contact on the ball. I played in the street kicking the ball against the kerb, striking it into a small goal for hours and hours. I'd smash it over the fence, run off through the bushes to get it, bring it back and start again.

I was playing competitive football aged six – for an Under-10s side – and wanted to be out there every moment I could. Over time, you become confident that you can strike the ball properly with either foot from different angles or at different speeds. In my peak years, this was probably my best quality. Nowadays I struggle to hit a golf ball properly and that doesn't even move. I suppose it is a lot smaller.

I very rarely got nervous, even when I was young. My mindset was: 'This is where you want to be, this is what you want to do for a living. Go and make it happen.'

It helped me when I was older. Old Trafford, Highbury or Wembley – millions of people wanted to be in my shoes but I was there and had put the hours in to make it count. In high-profile situations, amateurs worry about what can go wrong but professionals focus on the chance to succeed.

I could put myself to sleep easily. If we were an hour away from the ground I could sit on the bus and nod off. In a way, it was like meditation and became a routine over time. I still can do that today.

Because you get labelled a goalscorer, you are expected to score in every game. I could come off scoring in a 4-1 defeat and although I hated losing, there was something I could take from it. It wasn't satisfaction but I could process the defeat internally by telling myself I'd done what I was supposed to do, once at least.

There was probably some jealousy towards me growing up with people thinking I was only progressing due to my Dad, but it made me more determined to make it on my own terms. To be my own man.

As I began progressing through my teenage years, I became aware of how unique it was to be part of an extended football family. Only my older brother Andrew decided to pursue another passion in his life: cars. He was a good all-round sportsman in his youth and got a job working in design at Ford upon leaving school.

When representing District or County teams, I'd hear people say 'Oh, he's an Allen' or 'His Dad was a player'. Carrying the family name became something to overcome. My cousins Paul and Martin had the same hurdle.

Like my younger brother Bradley, Paul and Martin were always going to be players. There was never any doubt about it. Harry Redknapp has said to me many times that being brought up in the Allen family environment was like being born with the skills and mentality to make it as a professional footballer.

Paul was so industrious and competitive, an incredible athlete from a young age. People have told me how in his first training session at West Ham, Billy Bonds crushed him in a tackle, picked him up and said: 'You'll be alright for me, son.'

Paul would dust himself down and go again. He was fearless in the way he approached the game. Martin had a similar mentality. If anything, he thought he was a better player than he was but that's not a bad thing. You need that inner confidence in difficult moments, especially when dealing with expectation created by the name on the back of your shirt.

Bradley perhaps had an impossible task on his hands in that regard, following Dad and me. My son Olly and Martin's son Charlie were the same. Bradley had some great attributes but maybe his lack of physicality stopped him from reaching the very top, although he went on to play in the Premier League for QPR, once scoring a hat-trick against Everton.

We all knew the pros and cons of being an Allen, but each of us wanted to follow our own path. We were all on a mission and had to be blinkered, all while recognising and respecting the fact that we were part of a highly unusual football family.

Occasionally I had to bite my tongue. My mates would talk about famous players they'd seen on television or read about in newspapers when I knew what they were like in real life. Talk didn't interest me too much anyway, I was just focused on trying to make it.

I progressed from the District side to England schoolboys, which gave me early exposure to big stadia like Wembley and Celtic Park and football icons such as Brian Clough, who had been brought into the England set up by Ron Greenwood.

During a 1978 tournament in Las Palmas when I was 17, I got one of his typically harsh lessons. I was wearing moulded soled boots during a game and had fallen over a few times in the first half. 'Put on some boots with studs,' he said, 'and if you fall over again, I'm taking you off.' I didn't dare fall over after that. He was often unorthodox – holding one pre-match team-talk out there in the blazing midday sun – sometimes brutal, but almost always right.

The game that stands out from my early years, though, was aged 14 for London Schools against Bristol Schools at White Hart Lane in October 1975. Bristol had turned up with the same colour shirts as us so we had to borrow a Tottenham kit. Suddenly I was wearing a Spurs shirt and playing as a centre-forward at the Lane. Against a Bristol team containing a young Gary Mabbutt I scored a hat-trick in a 5-0 win.

You can see why, looking back now, it felt like my destiny to play for Tottenham. I'd progressed well enough to receive offers from four clubs when considering whether or not to turn professional aged 16.

My maths teacher at Gaynes wanted me to stay on and take A-levels. He argued if I was good enough now to play football professionally the same would be true in two years and I could pursue it with academic qualifications, which may prove useful at some point.

However, I was adamant I wanted to leave and take up an apprenticeship. But where? Tottenham, Ipswich, Manchester City and Queens Park Rangers were my options. I didn't really support a team. I loved football but I couldn't nail my colours to the mast. I don't really know why. Perhaps that's one of the reasons I ended up moving around so much.

Because of my father's connection with Spurs, they were close to my heart, but I just didn't feel I had a chance of playing at Tottenham given the size of the club and likely competition for places. I also didn't want to leave home, which ruled out moving to Suffolk or Manchester. Dad had left QPR by the time I had the chance to sign for them but he was still speaking to various clubs on my behalf. It was like having my own agent.

He'd left Swindon Town after two years as manager and had the time to help me make the right decision.

However, West Ham were one club that wouldn't contact my Dad about me. They had rejected him as a 15-year-old and he subsequently went to Chelsea to start his career.

Yet they did approach his brother, Ron, about Paul, who is a year younger than me. Clearly, some issues remained between Dad and West Ham but that's football. In any case, I don't think I would have joined the Hammers because even if they had made an offer, my Dad would have advised against taking it.

QPR had finished runners-up in the First Division in 1975/76 and many of their players were over 30 years old. I was training at QPR and had those experiences with Terry Venables and Rodney Marsh as a youngster. I'll always have a soft spot for them.

I believed I'd have more of a chance to break through there and my Dad agreed. After I signed Terry told me about what a bright future I could have.

I started in the youth team and soon graduated to the reserves, but the first team had dipped to the extent that by early 1979 – just six months after I had left school – I was beginning to train regularly with the first team.

Had I stayed in school and left aged 18, it would have been so much harder to pursue a football career. I always believed I was good enough if I got the chance so I wanted it as soon as possible. I had tunnel vision to becoming a footballer – the thought of doing something else never entered my head – and fortunately it happened.

There's a different process in place now whereby young players have a better opportunity to study if they are that way inclined. It comes down to the individual. It is hard to do because you have to be 100 percent focused to make it as a player.

I remember going to day release college once, on a Thursday. I think it was an accountancy course but all I really remember was being completely bored. I understood the importance of it but I didn't want to be there. I never went back because I couldn't afford to miss Thursdays at QPR – that was when they prepared teams for Saturday matches.

Whether I was playing for the youth team that weekend or possibly looking to be involved in the first team, I had to be there for two reasons: one, to be training with the group and, two, to make an impression on those making the decisions in whatever team I was aiming for.

I certainly wasn't given any special favours because of my Dad. In fact, I assumed I'd have to work twice as hard for any sort of recognition and spent hours practising my finishing with coach Theo Foley.

Theo wouldn't call me Clive. He preferred 'Son of Les', a phrase he used in my presence for years after I signed.

Dad took more of a backseat at this point, but we'd already endured some difficult times. Our relationship was particularly strained when I was around 13 to 15 years old, before I went to QPR as an apprentice.

Dad treated me like a young professional and sometimes I came home in tears. My Mum, Pat, would always ask me what was wrong and her sympathetic, calming influence was a counter-balance to my Dad's relentless cajoling. I confided in her.

'This is the way he is,' she'd say. 'He is not being hard on you – he wants only the best for you.'

'But he's never satisfied. I never hear anything but criticism or where I've fallen short.'

Round and round the conversation would go, neither of us shifting from our respective points of view. A hug would usually bring it to a close.

Signing professional terms is a huge moment in anyone's life but I hadn't achieved a level he was happy with.

After joining QPR, he told me: 'Right, it is now down to you.' He still watched my games though, and if he thought I hadn't played well, he wouldn't have to say anything. I knew. One look would say a thousand words.

On the one hand, this gave me the drive some parents would suggest a child needs to succeed. But placing these demands on a teenager blurs the lines in a father-and-child relationship. Childhood should be about freedom of expression but this is also a period in a young player's potential career which demands discipline and sacrifice. Applying the requisite pressure without alienation or stifling natural growth is extremely tricky.

I had an insight into what was needed to make it at the top level and without it I might not have achieved anything. Standards were instilled in me at a fundamental level. I had to score the most goals in a training session. I had to be the quickest in the sprints. In the back of my mind, my Dad's words drove me on: unless you push yourself every minute of every day, you will fail.

The senior players also left me under no illusions about what was required, even if the first team was struggling at the time. I played for the reserves in a practice game against the first team and inside the first five minutes, David Webb absolutely nailed me with a tackle from behind that left me in a heap on the ground.

Just like Paul's experience with Billy at West Ham, the message was clear: there are no favours here. I swept the dressing rooms, picked up their kit and took those physical lessons they gave me because those are tests you had to pass to progress.

I knew the rough treatment was coming because Dad had prepared me for it. 'Don't answer the pros back,' he'd say. 'Don't take liberties, they are challenging you to see if you can handle it.' It was just part and parcel of a young player's education and nothing specific to me at all. Those who didn't cope didn't progress.

I made a good impression and broke into the first team towards the end of the 1978/79 campaign. My simple target, which applied throughout my career, was to average one goal every two games. At the top level, this was the benchmark for a consistent goalscorer.

I was introduced slowly with a series of substitute appearances, one of which produced my first senior goal in a 3-1 defeat at Aston Villa in March 1979, while in another I found myself facing the fearsome Norman Hunter at centre-half as we lost at Bristol City. I took a few heavy challenges that day.

When I came on against Chelsea, Ray Wilkins whispered into my ear 'good luck son, many more appearances I'm sure,' a nice touch that stuck with me.

John Hollins was great in helping me to settle in to the first team. Stan Bowles was a wonderful player to play with, one of the best passers of the ball and his creativity was one of my main routes to goal.

My full debut came in April against Coventry. The pitch was dreadful – almost as much of a distraction as the visitors' chocolate brown away kit – and it felt just like another game. I was nervous but it was where I wanted to be. We were 1-0 down but I managed to equalise from just outside the box and went on to score a hat-trick – a moment which announced my arrival as a QPR player.

Collectively, however, it was only a brief respite from a truly dismal end to the season – the solitary victory from our final 12 league games, form which meant relegation to the Second Division.

Tommy Docherty replaced Steve Burtenshaw as manager and turned to youth, chiefly by partnering me with Paul Goddard in attack.

That was great for both of us because there wasn't just one youngster having to go in and prove themselves. We may have been a young partnership but we'd played together for a while from the youth team to the reserves and developed a good understanding which helped us thrive.

I scored 30 goals in the 1979/80 season as we finished fifth in the Second Division. I devoured every opportunity I was given to play. This was what I did, what I wanted to do throughout my career: score goals. My Dad had instilled in me the need to seize the moment – deliver your best and move on to the next. I got into a rhythm which I suppose many young players aspire to, but I expected it.

However, throughout this period there was never a moment where I felt like I'd made it. I was constantly proving myself. My form was attracting attention from some of the biggest clubs in England but I was never bothered about it. You can't get distracted.

It was easier back then, of course, with much less media scrutiny. Many players get sidetracked with all the trappings of fame nowadays. It takes an incredibly strong mentality to stay dedicated, shun the immediate gratification a modicum of success can bring and keep that drive to apply yourself on a daily basis in order to improve.

Across the 1978/79 and 1979/80 seasons, I scored 34 goals in 55 games in the Football League, FA Cup and League Cup.

Yet, regardless of how many goals I scored in a game, Dad would remind me of the wasted chances.

Tottenham legend Bill Nicholson once collared him in the dressing room as he relaxed after scoring five goals in an FA Cup game against Crewe.

'I don't know why you are looking so happy,' he said. 'What about the ones you missed?'

The Nicholson influence was there before I was old enough to recognise it. Dad would defend me in public, particularly with the press, but in private it was different.

It has always been complicated. I'm grateful for his guidance but pained by his parenting. Whenever I pushed back or felt I was winning a particular argument, the same line would halt me in my tracks.

'It's better to be a has-been than a never-was.'

CHAPTER THREE

Arsenal – Million Pound Mystery

SIXTY-TWO DAYS AFTER ARSENAL MADE ME FOOTBALL'S FIRST million-pound teenager on 12 June 1980, I was sold to Crystal Palace without playing a competitive game.

You couldn't have made it up. The Gunners had played 70 matches in the 1979/80 campaign – a remarkable effort but one which ended in agonising disappointment by losing the Cup Winners' Cup Final to Valencia on penalties and the FA Cup Final to West Ham.

Those two cup runs had generated revenue the club wanted to reinvest in the squad to give them that final nudge towards winning silverware. They were looking for a statement signing.

It all began with a phone call shortly after the end of the season. Queens Park Rangers manager Tommy Docherty told me over the phone that the club had agreed a £1.25million fee to sell me to Arsenal.

'You are going to a great club,' he said. 'I have [manager] Terry Neill and [coach] Don Howe in the office with me. I would like you to speak to them.'

Terry chimed in: 'It has all been agreed and I would like to meet you down at Highbury.'

I was about to go on holiday to Corfu with my girlfriend Lisa, yet 24 hours after Tommy's call I was marvelling at Highbury's marble halls and the impressive bust of legendary manager Herbert Chapman with my Dad and Arsenal chief executive Ken Friar.

The trophy cabinet was a sight to behold, reinforcing the size of the club and opportunity before me.

We then sat down to discuss terms and I asked to think about the offer overnight. In truth, there was no real decision to make. QPR wanted the money and the step up for me was something every teenager would have wanted.

The next day, I signed a four-year deal with Arsenal and the newspapers turned up for interviews.

'We don't do things lightly here,' Terry told reporters. 'Our supporters deserve the best and that is what I believe we have given them by buying Clive.'

As I got in the car to go home, my Dad was unusually quiet. I didn't know at the time but years later I learned Bill Nicholson had watched me play on several occasions during the 1979/80 campaign.

He'd spoken to Dad about me, privately. All Dad said to me during that period was: 'Remember, wherever you play, you never know who is watching.'

It was yet another measure of instilling high standards in my conduct at all times, but I also believe he thought Spurs were going to come in and make an offer for me before Arsenal did. A Canadian side that played in the North American Soccer League, Vancouver Whitecaps, had reportedly made a seven-figure bid but Tottenham never came calling.

Maybe they weren't convinced about paying so much for someone so young. It was a huge deal for Arsenal – their previous transfer record was just £440,000 for England international Brian Talbot. It was a huge deal in the game too.

Transfers were getting bigger but I was still only the fifth player in history to change clubs for more than £1m after Trevor Francis became the first 16 months earlier. Trevor, Andy Gray, Steve Daley and Kevin Reeves had all achieved much more in the game than I had but Arsenal were clearly banking on me realising the potential I'd shown to that point.

The press had a field day, with some claiming the game had gone mad. My media duties included a bizarre photoshoot with Page 3 model Jilly Johnson, who had her arms wrapped around me wearing only a swimsuit and high heels, while I stood there in my full Arsenal kit.

Regardless of the hype and expectation that came with the transfer fee, I couldn't wait to get started. I reported back in the middle of July to Arsenal's London Colney training ground. Pat Jennings, Sammy Nelson, Pat Rice, Alan Sunderland and Frank Stapleton all introduced themselves and made me feel welcome. Liam Brady was about to move to Italy but he also made a point of saying hello.

John Hollins was a friendly face from our Rangers days together. Pre-season was tough but productive under Don and before too long we left to go on tour.

From the first game, things didn't feel right. Arsenal had founded their success on a 4-4-2 system with Sunderland and Stapleton up front but I was asked to play wide-right in a 4-3-3 shape against Glasgow Rangers in our first pre-season friendly.

It wasn't a role I knew too much about, having played as a central striker under Tommy at Rangers without too many defensive responsibilities.

Playing on the wing was totally different. To be honest, I was still trying to hone my skills as a centre-forward and so to go to Arsenal and to be told I was playing wide-right was a big ask.

I was taken off at half-time and we lost 2-0. Dad told me: 'It doesn't matter where you play, you have still got to perform.' But I was surprised by the whole thought process from Terry and Don.

Next up was Sir Alex Ferguson's Aberdeen. We lost 2-1 and I barely got a shot at goal. I was thinking about that lack of goalscoring opportunities on the journey back from Scotland but, to my surprise, Don was more interested in discussing how I'd sometimes not tracked the opposing full-back, allowing him a free run down our right flank.

Arsenal had paid all this money for me because of my ability as a striker and yet here Don was coaching me defending. It made no sense.

A few days later we went to Belgrade for a four-team tournament comprising local sides Red Star and Partizan along with Vasco da Gama of Brazil.

I played the first 50 minutes against Vasco in the same wide role before being substituted.

Don was withering. 'I'm taking you off so you can sit down and watch how we do it,' he said.

I sat out the next game altogether for the same reason. It clearly wasn't ideal pre-season preparation, but the newspaper headlines we landed to when arriving back to London that Sunday knocked me for six.

Splashed across the back pages was the suggestion I was about to be sold to

Crystal Palace in a swap deal for Kenny Sansom. We all know the papers don't get everything right so I shrugged it off as best I could and reported for training at Colney the next day. In all honesty, I didn't think it was genuine but I wasn't angry about anything being leaked to the press. I was programmed to interpret it as merely something else I had to deal with.

I was getting changed when Don came over and told me not to bother. Alarm bells immediately went off in my head.

'Terry wants to see you at Highbury,' he said, before turning his back on me and heading out with the rest of the boys. I stood there as the noise of their pre-training chat gradually disappeared, replaced by silence.

My mind began racing on the car journey. Why didn't Terry just tell me the stories were nonsense at the training ground? After all, the start of the season was less than a week away and every session was vital in order to hit the ground running.

I called my Dad on the way. He told me just to hear Terry out so I headed straight to his office upon arrival, passing through the marble halls I'd admired just a few weeks earlier.

'Sit down, Clive,' said Terry. 'Look, this isn't the way I wanted it to come out but those swap stories about you and Kenny... there's something in it.'

I was speechless.

'After looking at the team in pre-season, Sammy Nelson's knee injury and the goals we've conceded, we feel we need a left-back and Kenny is our preferred choice.'

The man who had sold Arsenal to me as a club where I could make my name was now telling me, in his words, I was 'surplus to requirements'.

How could that be? Even if they needed another defender, how could Alan and Frank suddenly cope with the goalscoring burden on their own given they felt compelled to spend so much on me in order to help?

I think my response surprised Terry. Maybe it even surprised me. I suppose I had nothing to compare it to as a 19-year-old. In that moment, I realised my Dad had prepared me well to remain professional.

'But I don't want to leave,' I said. 'I have signed a contract to play for Arsenal and that's what I want to do. It wasn't that long ago you were telling me I was an important part of the future of the club. Now I'm not needed.'

There had clearly already been dialogue between Arsenal and Crystal Palace about a transfer, maybe even between Terry Neill and Terry Venables directly.

'Well, if you stay,' said Terry, 'you won't play in the first game of the season at West Bromwich Albion on Saturday.'

He was trying to push me to join Palace.

'Fair enough,' I said. 'That's fine by me. If, as manager, you give me permission to speak to Terry Venables, I will. But as far as I'm concerned, I'm an Arsenal player and I want it to stay that way. But sooner or later, if I decide to stay after speaking to Terry, you will have to play me in the first team. It is your head that will be on the block if you have paid all that money for someone to play them in the reserves.'

There was surely no way he could argue with that. Without disagreeing, Terry stood firm and told me to speak to Venables.

The next day I met Terry at a hotel in west London.

'What's the matter with you?' Terry asked, beaming from ear to ear as he entered the room. He'd known me from such a young age that it didn't take much for him to realise something was up.

'Why aren't you smiling?'

I explained my head was still spinning from the night before.

'I don't have to sell Crystal Palace to you,' he continued. 'You either want to play for me or you can stay at Arsenal. It's up to you.'

'Where are you going to play me?' I asked.

'Down the middle, up front,' he replied.

That was just about all I needed to hear, but I asked for the night to mull it over. I was staying with my girlfriend Lisa to hide from the press because speculation was rife. Would I be considered a failure if I left Arsenal without playing a game? Would my reputation be damaged? What was really going on here?

My future at Arsenal was pretty bleak, and here was a manager who knew me, understood me and was offering to play me in my preferred position. Terry certainly made me feel wanted.

I met him again at a London hotel and signed for Crystal Palace before going to the training ground at Mitcham to meet my new teammates.

Goalkeeper Paul Barron was also with me, having joined as part of the deal, and one look at the playing staff filled me with optimism: Vince Hilaire, Jerry Murphy, Billy Gilbert, Peter Nicholas – these were young players dubbed 'the Team of the Eighties' after surpassing all expectations in their first season back in the First Division.

I signed on the Wednesday and started against defending champions Liverpool in the first game of the season that weekend.

And just like that, Arsenal was consigned to history. They invested a lot of money in buying me as a young talent and I would have liked the opportunity to prove them right. I don't regret signing for them but, in a way, perhaps I've held it against Arsenal ever since.

There were so many conspiracy theories doing the rounds at the time. One claimed QPR chairman Jim Gregory wouldn't sell to Terry in the first place so I was parked at Arsenal to eventually get me to Palace.

That made no sense. I could have been injured in pre-season and transfers of that size could be complicated enough between two clubs without introducing a third.

Another theory suggested Palace were short of cash and the only way they could do any business was to trade their prized asset, Kenny Sansom, with a team that wanted him and his sudden availability triggered a late change of heart at Arsenal.

But, again, I could have been injured at any point and I could always have flat out refused to move. Furthermore, couldn't Kenny and I play in the same team? If they wanted him that badly, I'm sure Arsenal could have found the money.

I haven't spoken to Terry Neill since and I won't because nobody can change what happened.

Within two months, he had gone from taking me around the club – in front of a television crew – telling me what a future I had, to deeming me 'surplus to requirements'. You have to question that kind of judgement.

Terry later claimed in a 1985 book entitled *Revelations of a Football Manager* that the forward combination of Alan, Frank and me 'didn't look right'.

'Don and I realised there would be a lot of criticism if we unloaded Allen to Palace before he had played a single league game for Arsenal but we had to be positive and make a judgement in the best interests of the club,' he said.

But he must have had an idea of how the three of us could play together? If you are planning to bring in a striker, you think about whether he would play as part of a three or work as a two with one particular player.

Nobody told me during the negotiations that I would play on the right.

I thought I would be coming in to compete for one of the two central striker positions in place of Alan or Frank. But we never played two strikers in the games we played so they must have had a pre-existing plan to change things. In which case, how can you reach the definitive conclusion it won't work after a few warm-up games?

I guess I just wasn't the player they thought they were acquiring, which I find very difficult to understand because they'd obviously watched my games beforehand. To have an idea that it wasn't going to work from a few pre-season games is just bizarre. I don't accept what Terry wrote as being the legitimate reason.

He also refuted the idea he'd bought me 'as a puppet' because QPR and Palace wouldn't do business and I'd like to believe at least that much was true.

Whatever really happened, the whole situation was bizarre but completely out of my control. I suppose I was lucky in one sense that this all happened back then before the explosion in modern media. There was a lot of press interest but if something similar happened today, there would be an almighty 24-hour media storm going on for days and days.

At the time, I just wanted to get my career going. If it wasn't Arsenal, it would be somewhere else.

Looking at the positives, one long-term benefit was that I never felt fearful of moving clubs, entering another senior dressing room or changing my environment. For all I later achieved with Tottenham, I feel my experience at Arsenal sparked the making of me as a man.

Another consolation was that I received two significant signing-on fees in one summer for my troubles.

The regulation of the day stated players got a signing-on fee worth up to five percent of the transfer fee, paid over the course of their contract. For my move to Arsenal, that was worth £62,500.

I'd signed a four-year deal so they paid me the first quarter of that on arrival but having decided to sell me, the remaining three payments were due immediately.

The cap on signing-on fees was abolished shortly after my transfer to Arsenal so by the time we sat down with Terry to discuss joining Palace, we could actually have negotiated anything.

We were so naïve. He just said 'five percent' and it was done. We didn't have an agent with us – if we had, we would doubtless have got more.

My contract was worth £500-a-week – the same figure I was on at Arsenal. As the dust settled on my move to Palace, it hit me I'd just earned £130,000 in signing on fees.

'You know you've just won the pools, son,' said Dad.

Money wasn't the driving factor for me. I just wanted to play. But just as I felt things would settle down, it wasn't long before my number was up once again.

CHAPTER FOUR

Crystal Palace – Growing Up

I HAD TO GROW UP FAST AND CRYSTAL PALACE'S 1980/81 SEASON made me do just that. If there was a checklist for everything a player could experience in their career, I would have ticked off almost all of it in a single 12-month period before I turned 20 years old.

Terry Neill had made me inherently distrustful of managers and so I took particular comfort from working for a family friend like Terry Venables.

Bonham Road in Dagenham had become known as a hotbed of footballing talent. My Dad had grown up there with Dennis and Ron, as had Venables and Ken Brown, a defender who would go on to make more than 500 appearances for West Ham.

The families frequently socialised together and later, Dad signed Terry for QPR and made him captain.

We'd moved to Hornchurch by the time I started playing football. So, after being spotting by QPR scout Ron Howard playing for Havering District aged 13, I was invited to train there and would see Terry with my Dad on matchdays. Even at a young age, I was drawn to his character. He was always welcoming with an infectious personality and loved to talk football.

There was a natural connection because of that but as a young player, he knew what made me tick.

After taking over in 1976, Venables guided Palace from the Third Division to the First in a meteoric rise. They even topped the table at the end of September 1979 and although that stay was short-lived, an eventual finish of 13th was then the highest-ever league placing in their history.

Optimism was high and I turned up to the training ground at Mitcham with genuine hope for the season ahead.

We lost to Liverpool – no disgrace in that at Anfield – and Tottenham before our first home game of the season against Middlesbrough. I scored a hat-trick and we won 5-2. Terry said he was delighted for me – but that I should have scored six. Where had I heard that before?

I suppose it was his way of keeping me hungry but I began to feel it was a shame he wasn't more ruthless with the team as a whole. We needed a good kick up the backside but he was too close to the players to give them the tough love they needed. Many of them had come through the ranks with him.

It got a lot worse in September. The month started well enough with a League Cup win against Bolton before we lost to Coventry, a game I'll always remember for the wrong reasons.

We were losing when the referee gave us a free-kick just outside the box, on the left edge of the area.

The ball was rolled to me and I tried my luck from 25 yards. It flew into the top corner, hitting the stanchion and bouncing back out as I ran off to celebrate. Except the referee waved play on. I couldn't believe it. Several of my teammates ran to confront him and after consulting both linesmen, he ruled no goal. They all missed it.

It was the best strike of my entire career. In cricketing terms, I middled it. In tennis, it came right out of the sweet spot. It absolutely flew in.

I knew straight away that it was a goal. The referee kept saying: 'It didn't go in. It didn't go in. It hit the woodwork.'

Terry said afterwards he was 'disgusted by it' as the goal would have put us back in touch in a game we ended up losing 3-1.

Part of me for a while thought I might be remembered for what became known as 'the goal that never was' rather than the ones I scored.

What I do know is that decision destroyed our season. It became the second loss in a run of seven consecutive league defeats – Palace's worst sequence of results since 1925 – and Terry's future was suddenly under the spotlight.

I was on the England Under-21's plane flying back from Romania when my

Palace teammate Vince Hilaire came and sat next to me.

He told me Terry was leaving and going to Queens Park Rangers.

'How do you know that?' I asked.

'One of the reporters told me.'

True enough, when we got back to England, it was announced Terry had departed. My reaction at that stage was 'What is happening to me? What's going to happen next?'

Long-time Palace coach Ernie Walley took over as a caretaker and dropped me almost immediately. The first team went to Norwich for a match while Vince and I were sent to Hereford for a reserve match. I wasn't happy, to say the least.

The insinuation was obvious: I was to blame for the poor start to the season. Yet I was among the leading scorers in the First Division in a struggling side and any striker will tell you how hard that is to do.

I think in hindsight he dropped me to stamp his authority on the managerial position. But it left me at rock-bottom.

Was it me? The manager who bought me for more than £1m had swapped me for a left-back, the manager who signed me for Palace had walked out and now the new guy had dropped me altogether. We finished November second-bottom and there was yet more turmoil, this time off the pitch.

Malcolm Allison took permanent charge after getting sacked from Manchester City and while Ron Noades was on the brink of buying the club from Ray Bloye, Terry raided Palace to take John Burridge, Terry Fenwick and Mike Flanagan with him to QPR, where he was the new manager.

I needed a pick-me-up. The money I'd earned in such a short space of time was of little consolation, but it had least given me some security in my personal life. It was something I didn't have a lot of with regards to my career on the field at the time.

I had a solicitor and a bank manager who made sure that I did things right. I bought a house and got a mortgage.

But midway through this misery of a season, I bought a brand-new car, a German-built Ford Capri 2.0 S, black with a white stripe down the side. The insurance was £500 and my Dad went absolutely mental because although I could afford it, he felt it was an example of unnecessary largesse.

It was a boy-racer car but I was 19 years old. I never even used to drive it. I had a sponsored car which I drove to and from training, probably angering my Dad even more over the £500 insurance for the Capri. I sold it to Mike Flanagan a couple of years later. He had it for ages.

In December Malcolm put me back in the team and I scored twice in a 4-1 victory over Norwich, ironically enough, to give him his first win in charge.

But by that stage, the damage had been done in terms of my relationship with many of the other Palace players. At one time or another, four of us travelled from the east side of London – Mike Flanagan, Gary Goodchild, Neil Smillie and me. We never really felt like we were accepted, and it certainly wasn't an atmosphere that was conducive to success. When Mike left for QPR in December 1980, things got worse.

Ernie had worked with the club's youngsters, bringing a lot of them through the ranks. He wanted to play those he knew and I paid the price for it. Terry was too soft on them, Ernie effectively told them in his team selection that it wasn't their fault. There was no dialogue with Ernie, either – his management style was to act like a sergeant-major.

Malcolm was an excellent communicator but his ideas were a bit odd. It is good that a manager is always thinking about the game and ways to improve the team but he was imaginative and eccentric which can be divisive traits in a manager.

He had me in midfield for a couple of games at one point but that didn't last – it just didn't play to my strengths. Then he wanted our central defenders to play out from the back, something that is commonplace now but at that time in the Football League, it invited needless pressure and contributed to poor results.

Everything came to a head at the turn of the year. For the first time, I asked for a transfer. It was after a game at Middlesbrough in which we were beaten 2-0 and I missed a penalty. In the dressing room afterwards, a few of the lads made comments under their breath, but deliberately loud enough for me to hear. They were blaming me for losing.

I'd never done it before but I reacted furiously. Angry words were exchanged and although it didn't come to anything physical, I made it very clear I'd hardly missed on purpose and perhaps the senior players should also take some responsibility for what was going wrong.

The problems ran far deeper than one missed penalty. All through their careers, they'd been told what good players they were and Malcolm followed Terry's lead in praising them to the hilt even when we were losing.

They couldn't handle a downturn after years of success, which along with two first-team promotions had included two FA Youth Cup successes in consecutive years and some fine performances in the Football Combination, the reserve-team competition of the day.

The divide grew wider after that. I wasn't frozen out completely but nobody went out of their way to talk to me. They were incapable of being self-critical. I knew I had faults – it never took long for my Dad to point them out – but these Palace players resided in a bubble impervious to criticism.

Things got crazier still. Malcolm lasted just 55 days, as Ron Noades completed his takeover and wanted his own manager at the helm. He appointed Dario Gradi.

Results didn't pick up. We failed to win any game in February and by March we were 11 points adrift of safety and staring relegation in the face.

My mood hadn't improved. A transfer failed to materialise – there was a lot of speculation but I never spoke to another club and nothing ever got close – so I just became focused on getting to the end of the season and finding a way out.

I had an explosive moment with Dario on the training ground. We were playing a training game and I smashed one in off the crossbar.

'Play on!' shouted Dario.

I stopped in my tracks. 'What?'

'Play on!' he said again.

'What are you talking about? It went in!'

A heated exchange followed where we shouted at each other pretty intensely. Was it another jibe, this time about the Coventry game? Was that my fault too? He sent me in from training and told me I'd have to come back in the afternoon to go running alone.

I came back and did what he asked.

At the end, I said: 'Look, I'll do this every day if you want but it won't change my view on what's happening here and the situation. I'm being blamed for everything.'

That was the first time I properly stuck up for myself. I think it was the only time I was ever sent in from training.

Dario became my sixth manager in nine months. He was like a schoolteacher. He let the players get away with an awful lot – more than he should have really given how badly we were playing – but the situation was too far gone to salvage when he came in.

I repeated my transfer request and this time it was accepted. Lisa was invaluable to me during this period. She had left home to train as a physiotherapist at Guy's Hospital and was in the midst of her studies. We'd meet two or three times a week for dinner and talk about everything and anything. Lisa never seemed down about it and her desire to stay detached from football gave me the removal I needed.

In April, we recorded our first victory since December with a 3-1 win over Birmingham but it only delayed the inevitable. Palace were duly relegated, winning just six matches with a points tally of 19, one of the lowest ever for a First Division season. I ended the season as the club's top scorer with 11 goals – a reasonable return in the circumstances – but it counted for very little.

It was never the same once Terry left. Few clubs would have survived the sheer turnover of personnel at all levels. We were due to go on a close season tour but I had no interest in doing so. I'd spent many weeks in the reserves and whenever I did appear for the first team, the rot had set in. We were losing every week and it was a demoralising place to be. My self-belief had taken a real knock but Dad kept drilling me on the need to be professional. Whatever game I was playing in, I had to train right, prepare right and give my all.

'There's always someone watching you,' he said, stirring memories of Bill Nicholson in my mind. People check on a young kid in moments like that to see what character they have and how it affects them.

Dad had done the same thing himself as a manager, checking on people when the chips were down. It was something I always remembered.

In a way, it just taught me what football was going to be about. The whole lesson was concentrated into one year – and what a difficult year it was. It should have been a massive season for me after moving to Arsenal, but instead my career went into a tailspin.

There was a lot of negativity. I had a price tag around my neck and that got mentioned every time I scored, failed to score, or was left out of the team. 'Million-pound teenager has been dropped' or 'Million-pound teenager has scored'. I had to learn how to deal with it.

I always watched *Match of the Day*, win, lose or draw. I'd read a Sunday paper after the game but I never really took it in too much.

I needed another fresh start and thankfully Terry Venables was on hand again to provide it. He knew better than most what I'd gone through.

I was at Havering squash club when the phone rang. Terry wanted to see me and within a couple of days I re-signed for QPR in a deal worth £400,000.

I didn't care about the price drop or any implications people would draw from it. I was just happy to be back there. And, equally, I was back with Venners. QPR had a completely different atmosphere and Terry was a new man – it was only seeing him work at Loftus Road that really brought home just how much pressure he had been under at Palace. It affected his mood, his decisions – now he was more the genial character who would go on to emerge as such a strong figure at Barcelona.

He knew how driven I was and what my goals were. He loved the game and always asked questions of his players. In turn, I would ask questions of him and he liked that. That's why most players loved him: he was always thinking of a new training session or a specific innovation to help improve your game. I felt totally comfortable with him.

He often used to say to me: 'I love you when you score goals. You become electrified.' He knew what goalscoring meant to me and the effect it would have. He helped develop different aspects of my game, the positions I took up, because we were always asking questions of each other. He was the best coach I played under.

For me, whether QPR was the easy option or not, it was what I needed at the end of that year.

I think I was still the same person but it was almost like I'd taken a gap year from developing, bunkered down in a malaise of football's making.

But everything about QPR made me feel like home. I was happy and I was going to play. I was full of confidence as a result and in a place where, finally, I could seriously kick on.

CHAPTER FIVE

QPR – Road To Wembley

SOME PLAYERS HAVE TO WAIT YEARS FOR THE CHANCE TO RIGHT the wrongs of the past but all mine came straight away in one remarkable FA Cup run.

Re-joining Queens Park Rangers was a blessed relief after what happened at Arsenal and Crystal Palace but I knew by now controversy was never far away in football.

Rangers chairman Jim Gregory and manager Terry Venables had decided to install a plastic pitch at Loftus Road, much to the chagrin of many other clubs.

The old pitch lurched between a quagmire and arid, dead ground as grass struggled to grow during a succession of harsh winters. Senior officials cited the surface as a sizeable obstacle to promotion.

Moving to an artificial 'Omniturf' pitch initially appeared a radical step but it was the product of the club's fact-finding mission to the United States, where plastic surfaces had already permeated several American sports.

Terry quickly got on board. In 1972, he had co-written a novel with author Gordon Williams entitled *They Used to Play on Grass* which predicted football would one day no longer be played on grass and furthermore, he also saw it as a way of speeding up his players' movement and sharpness because it would increase the pace of the game, a view many managers eventually came to share. However, the plastic surface was initially opposed by the Football Association.

The Football League had accepted the change but Jim threatened to pull QPR out of the FA Cup in the 1981/82 season if the FA continued to kick up a fuss. Eventually they relented and thank God they did.

Although, I didn't feel like that initially. The plastic pitch posed its own problems. After the very first game we played on it, against Luton Town, my Dad said: 'I'm not coming to watch that again. It's not football.'

He did come again but not very often. And I could understand why: it was, in some respects, a different game. Initially, teams – including us – played like they did on grass and had to adapt quickly.

When you dropped the ball, it bounced higher than where you dropped it from. You could get away with a lot less as a player and it finds out those with bad technique.

Adjustments in terms of style had to be made, too. You couldn't play a ball into space. The ball had to be within a yard either side of the player you intended because otherwise it would just shoot off the surface and out of play. Weight of pass was absolutely vital. Hopeful long balls were always hopeless.

Shooting was different, too. We learned to favour dipping shots that bounced in front of the goalkeeper. It wasn't a perfect surface – the ball could skip off low or bounce high. There were so many times a low shot bounced off the surface and hit the roof of the net.

Over time, what became known as 'Rangers's 'Magic Carpet' was a massive advantage to us, chiefly because Terry assembled a team that could play well on that surface.

We were all ball-players, quick and technical in the way we passed and moved. Our two centre-halves, Glenn Roeder and Steve Wicks, were comfortable in possession. They didn't have to play it long, they had the confidence to work it short. Malcolm Allison would have approved.

I wasn't the most physical player but technically I always felt I could deal with the ball.

There was a lot of controversy at the time and I'd say it now: it was an unfair surface. We could manipulate it how we wanted, primarily by putting varying amounts of sand or water on the pitch.

Teams would come and train on it on a Friday afternoon and it would be slow, dry and sticky. But then on Saturday morning, the ground staff would flood it and it would be slick, wet and fast.

We didn't train on it a lot – mainly because it was brutal on the body – but whenever Terry wanted us to we did in matchday conditions so we knew it inside out.

I've still got after-effects from it today. There will be lads who've got bad knees or hips from playing on that pitch so often. It was like playing on concrete.

Eventually, it made me a better player but initial progress was slow. Indeed, we lost that opening game to Luton and by Christmas 1981, I'd scored just four goals. That was terrible by my standards, especially in the Second Division. Instead of averaging one goal every two games, I was nearer one in six.

The trials and tribulations of the previous 12 months were, in hindsight, affecting me more than I realised at the time. The fans had been great with me but I was trapped in a cycle of struggling to score, working harder in training but failing to score again, only to work even harder. I was pushing myself more and more because it was all I knew.

The turning point came in the boot room at Orient in October. It was another difficult game for me in which I hadn't scored and, to make matters worse, I missed a penalty at 1-1, which as a result ended up being the final score.

Terry took me off. He was probably putting me out of my misery as much as anything but although I recognised he had to do the best thing for the team, I was still frustrated as it looked like I was being blamed for the whole performance.

After the game, Terry sat me down, one-on-one.

'What are you going to do to get out of this rut?' he asked.

'Work harder,' I said.

'You know what?' said Terry. 'I don't want you to do anything other than the normal sessions. No additional finishing, nothing. You aren't in good form. All you are doing is reinforcing the bad habits.'

It felt completely alien to me but was worth a try. I didn't find it easy, no striker does. It was horrendous not to work on it because you feel like you are being lazy. I'd go to the gym or see Lisa and just think I should be on the training pitch.

But the adage is right: one goes in off your backside, then the next chance comes along, you take it and away you go again. Then you practice and put the work in because your timing comes back. Good habits are reinforced.

Terry's advice was great and I used it years later as a coach. The best thing in that situation for a striker really is to go away and switch off. Let your instincts return and stop second-guessing yourself.

The breakthrough for me came in the FA Cup third round. It is a competition that has always meant a lot to me and even today I'd argue it is the best club cup contest in the world.

It is a cliché but there is magic about it. Some of it has been lost by the influence of the Champions League in big clubs' thinking but it has a fantastic unpredictability.

You never knew what was going to happen, certainly back in my playing days. Everybody was up for it, with no exceptions. It was a space where dreams could soar, where players and clubs could escape the reality of their league form. The Final was always the biggest game of the season and Wembley had a real aura about it. It was a boyhood dream to play in one.

The first time I went to Wembley was in 1967, aged six, when my Dad played in the first League Cup Final at Wembley: Third Division QPR against First Division West Brom. We went on a bus with the family. I had tonsillitis and fell asleep at kick-off. I woke up with QPR 2-0 down just after half-time, during which there was an incident my Dad talked about for years afterwards.

Clive Clark was playing for West Brom – having been transferred from QPR – and he was loving life after scoring both first-half goals. Both teams were in the tunnel about to go out for the second half and he shouted down the line: 'Well, lads, that's the easiest £100 bonus we've ever earned.' £100 back then was a lot of money.

QPR's Mark Lazarus shouted back: 'Well, don't forget boys, Jim has put us on £500 a man to win now.'

He hadn't. It was all psychology but the idea was to sow a bit of self-doubt in their minds. A few of the West Brom players audibly said to each other: 'How much?'

Nobody will ever know how much of a factor it was but QPR came back to win 3-2. I remember going to the team banquet briefly that evening before my grandparents took me home and I saw the cup. I fell in love with the idea of cup glory there and then.

Later, in 1980, I bought my first VHS recorder so we could watch together as my cousin Paul become then the youngest player ever to play in the FA Cup Final, for West Ham against Arsenal.

I wasn't able to go to the game but capturing his appearance for the family archive was my responsibility: I bought the recorder from Tottenham Court Road on the Thursday and spent two days practicing using it so I could get it right. I recorded the whole day from breakfast time when the coverage started.

I watched it that day and then the following week Paul came over and we relived it, thankfully a happy experience as Trevor Brooking scored the only goal for the Hammers in a 1-0 win.

The FA Cup Finals of the 1970s and 1980s were often fiercely contested. Ipswich versus Arsenal in 1978 sticks out in my mind because I was in Poland at a European Championships with an England youth team and we all listened to it on the radio because we couldn't get television pictures. Ipswich were underdogs yet they dominated the game. Still, they had to work so hard for the breakthrough, eventually provided by Roger Osborne 13 minutes from the end giving them a 1-0 win. Those experiences cemented my love for the FA Cup.

This time we'd been drawn against Middlesbrough at home in the third round. They were a First Division team but we were favourites because by now the 'Magic Carpet' was a real advantage to us. I missed the game through injury and we drew 1-1.

The replay was a real old-fashioned cup tie, blood and thunder, end-to-end stuff. I was fit enough to play. I didn't score but Warren Neill made his debut and got the winner as we won 3-2 in extra-time.

That win – on grass, remember – gave our season a fresh purpose. In the fourth round, we faced Third Division Blackpool and were lucky to escape Bloomfield Road with a 0-0 draw. We should have lost.

The replay was completely different. It was probably our best performance of the season to date and I scored four as we won 5-1. I needed those goals badly – four in one match was a massive confidence boost.

I even had chances to get a fifth goal but wasn't able to. Afterwards, Dad reminded me of that day in 1960 when Bill Nicholson told him he should have scored six.

I think we are the only father and son pairing to have scored four in an FA Cup tie but we would definitely have been out on our own if I'd scored a fifth.

Next up was Grimsby at home and a 3-1 win. Suddenly, QPR were in the last eight and all eyes were on the draw. I remember it happening almost in slow motion.

'QPR are at home...', which immediately gave us a real chance, '... against Crystal Palace.'

I knew in that instant it was the biggest game of my career to that point. All week in the build-up, I had complete tunnel vision in training. I'd be lining up against so many players who had made me a scapegoat and treated me with contempt.

In those situations, you have to keep a clear head and not let everything that's happened influence you but it wasn't easy. It was a big game independent of me: a London derby, the quarter-final of the FA Cup.

I tried to play down the personal subtext publicly and Terry protected me to some extent in his pre-match press conference but he knew how desperate I was to win.

There was no conversation with the Palace players beforehand, warming up or in the tunnel. The game itself was feisty. I hadn't had many opportunities and one goal was going to win it for either team. It was still 0-0 with a few minutes to go when we won a corner.

I jostled for position and as the ball travelled it came down slightly behind me, but I managed a half-volley which flew into the far corner. The feelings of relief, joy, vindication overwhelmed me. It was 12 months of turmoil blown away in one moment.

I went mad, running half the length of the pitch to face the Palace supporters, doing the most stupid celebration removed from anything I'd done before in my life. I denied it at the time but I admit it now: I was goading them. You don't think about anything else in moments like that.

There was a riot at the end of the game when we were in the dressing room. I didn't really think anything more of it, instead dreaming of getting the chance to play in an FA Cup semi-final, but on the Monday morning Terry called me into his office and told me there were people who thought I was responsible for the trouble.

'We've got to go the cop shop. Shepherd's Bush police. You need a brief?'

I did. I'd never needed legal advice for anything like this before. Off we went in the afternoon. I was nervous.

'Look, don't worry,' my solicitor said. 'They can't really do anything but give you a slapped wrist.'

The police put forward several allegations and told me there was a possibility I could be charged for inciting a riot.

I was also hauled before the FA and given a lecture, reminding me of my position of responsibility and not to abuse it again. The whole experience was an ordeal at the time as I felt I was being punished for doing my job, but in hindsight

I understand why they said what they did.

I wasn't charged by the FA or the police. My solicitor was right: slapped wrists, along with a reminder to 'be more aware of my actions because they can provoke extreme reactions'.

It was an over-elaborate celebration for me and not something I'd normally do but players are human and there was an extreme set of circumstances behind it.

The celebration was also a natural reaction on behalf of the team I was playing for and the possibility of reaching an FA Cup semi-final. That it came against Palace was all the sweeter. I didn't feel I had to change my behaviour. If anything, it was closure.

The semi-final threw up a tie against West Bromwich Albion, but the real kicker was the neutral venue: Highbury.

The ground where a year earlier I thought I would walk out as the first million-pound teenager in football and try to establish myself as one of the best in the First Division only to never kick a ball there.

Nowadays, the semi-finals are played at Wembley and I don't agree with that. I can understand the reasons why the FA take it there but playing at a neutral ground away from Wembley is special in itself and a gradual escalation in the climax of the competition.

Villa Park, for example, was always a special place to play: I scored my first league goal, an FA Cup semi-final goal and a hat-trick on the opening day of the season all at that famous ground.

Taking that neutral, non-Wembley step away means the FA Cup loses something. There are so many stadia that could host a game of that magnitude now.

Back then, I was delighted at the opportunity as suddenly I had another chance to address my recent past.

As the cup run unfolded, Terry used to take us to Brighton to train and Plumpton races to relax. It became a superstition and although the trips were nothing too grand, they were both an extra incentive and something which made us feel we were on the brink of a special achievement.

The game was typically tense. The stakes were so high that free-flowing football was at a premium. West Brom were a very powerful, strong side.

Terry was always of the belief that if we played our game, we could beat anyone and focused his team-talks accordingly. So it was particularly noticeable that in his final instructions, he spent a long time detailing Bob Hazell to mark Cyrille Regis. 'If you do that, we win the game,' he said.

It was a scrappy game on a blustery day played on a pitch ravaged by a season's play: bobbly, dry and uneven all over. The winning goal was probably in keeping with the football that day but I didn't care one bit.

West Brom defender Alistair Robertson found himself in possession just inside their area with about 15 minutes to go, the score at 0-0. He was six yards away from their goalkeeper. It looked like that's where the ball was going but I remember thinking 'he's going to try and clear it' and closed him down as a reflex.

His attempted clearance struck me flush on the kneecap and went like a bullet back past him into the net. In front of the North Bank.

It was both a complete fluke and one of the best goals I've ever scored. A few thoughts went through my head after the game. Should I have been at Highbury with QPR at all? Could I have been there with Arsenal? I reflect on it now and wonder whether it was written in the stars. Palace, then Arsenal – my demons were being banished one by one.

And so to Wembley to play Tottenham in the Final. It was a strange week. We had a couple of days at the Selsdon Park Hotel to prepare. Spurs were the FA Cup holders and hot favourites, even though their Argentinian duo Ricky Villa and Ossie Ardiles withdrew from the squad due to the Falklands War, which began in April 1982.

Ossie went back earlier than Ricky but both sat out the cup final for safety reasons and while that was a bitter blow for them and Spurs, selfishly speaking it was a major boost to our chances; they were both fantastic players and only a year earlier Ricky had scored what remains one of the most iconic FA Cup Final goals in history, jinking his way through the Manchester City defence to score the winner in a 3-2 replay victory.

Spurs finished fourth in the First Division that season, 16 points behind champions Liverpool, while we ended just two points off promotion from the Second Division in fifth place. The team had settled into a reasonable rhythm without really threatening to go up, despite how close we finished.

I turned 21 years old on the Thursday before the Final and Venners let me go to a party the family had organised at a pub near my home in Hornchurch. I went for an hour or so along with teammates Glenn Roeder and Mike Flanagan before heading back to the hotel. Turning 21 is a milestone in anyone's life but I only had thoughts about Saturday.

The FA Cup Final build-up is something to experience in itself. Television coverage would begin at the hotel on the Saturday morning and continue all the way to 3pm kick-off. I'd watched Paul go through it all with West Ham and now it was my turn. You were in a bubble but there was an itinerary of what would happen which helped with trying to keep your emotions in check.

I hadn't done a great job of that in truth but I was okay by the time we got to Wembley. I was walking around the pitch about 80 minutes before kick-off when a television producer collared me and asked for an interview.

Bob Wilson began the conversation live on air.

'How are you feeling at this moment?'

'Very nervous,' I said, 'I've just seen the family. I've just shed a few tears just to unwind a little bit. I got a bit het up on the coach coming up but I'm alright now.'

'Well I'm not one to give you advice Clive but what I'd like you to do at this moment is take these earphones because if you put them on, we can link you up with your father in the BBC gantry.'

I thought he was still on the bus with the family.

'Hello?' I said.

'Can you hear me?' said Dad.

'Yeah,' I said, as I involuntarily began rocking from side to side.

'It's great isn't it?' he continued.

'Yeah, it's magic.'

'It's different to the Bush,' he said. 'You've got plenty of room to move about out there today.'

'That's right.'

'I hope you make the most of it.'

'I hope so too. Thanks a lot.'

There was then a long pause. It felt like an eternity. The camera focused on Dad's face, which looked a little screwed up. I couldn't see it at the time because there was no monitor but I could hear in his voice he was struggling to deal with it. It was so uncharacteristic and not something I'd really seen from him before, catching me off guard.

'Hello? Are you still there?' I said.

'Yep.'

'I've just seen all the family, gave them a wave,' just talking to break the silence. 'They all look well, nice and relaxed. So… I wish I felt the same way. I'm just a bit het up now but raring to go.' My voice started to break.

'Once you get out there, there will be no problems.'

'No, I know. I'm dying for that at the moment. I just want to get out there and play.'

'Good luck.'

'Cheers, thank you.'

I took the headphones off and went straight to the dressing room. The whole thing was a stunt and it completely threw me. I was on the brink of tears again.

Venners walked in and could see something was up. I told him I was fine but in truth it was a really emotional situation. I lost control for a few moments. The BBC got what they wanted but I'm not sure players should be exposed to something like that so close to kick-off.

A couple of days earlier, I'd been on a tour of Wembley with my cousin Paul for a television piece but that was fine – the timing gives you appropriate distance mentally from the match and, obviously, the dynamic between Dad and I was very different.

That said, I don't think it affected my performance, which as it turned out, was effectively ended after two minutes.

I chased Tony Gale down the touchline, lunged for the ball and rolled my left ankle. It was something I'd never normally do so early in a game but I think a combination of factors came into play: the adrenaline of the occasion, wanting to get a touch to feel like I was in the contest, making my mark as early as possible.

I hobbled on but knew straight away I was struggling. I kept jogging about but I could feel it swelling up like a balloon within five minutes. Whenever the ball came my way, I'd take a touch and lay it off – keep it as simple as possible. Anything else was beyond me.

'Are you okay?' Terry asked from the touchline.

'Yeah, yeah,' I said, as convincingly as possible.

'Are you sure?'

'Yep.'

I wasn't coming off. It was the FA Cup Final. I wasn't coming off at half-time, either. I went for a scan using Wembley's X-ray machine, which concluded it wasn't broken. Instead I had cracked the capsule which was why it filled up with fluid. They strapped it up as tight as they could and I went back out.

I shouldn't have done – and it would never happen today. I was a passenger. I got about three or four minutes into the second half and Terry said enough was enough.

I walked off with tears in my eyes. It was very hard to take. I played for two minutes and for the rest of it I couldn't perform. I didn't even have a half-chance. I should have come off for the good of the team but you just don't feel like surrendering in that way. I was devastated because even at 21 years old, you start to think you may never get another chance. I paid a price for it because my ankle was probably never quite the same again, if I'm honest. But I don't regret it.

The 90 minutes ended 0-0 but Glenn Hoddle put Spurs ahead in extra-time. The lads did tremendously well to force a replay as Terry Fenwick equalised five minutes from the end.

My roommate Glenn Roeder was suspended for the second game and I was injured. Scans confirmed I'd suffered ligament damage.

As is Terry's way, he kept us both part of the squad, me despite my leg being in plaster.

An hour or so before the game, I went out to look at the pitch in crutches and as I hobbled out, Brian Clough caught my eye when he was about to finish a television interview.

Once it was over, he walked up to me. I thought he might be coming over to chew the fat having managed me in England's youth teams. I really should have known better.

'You shouldn't be out here,' he began. 'Get in, you are injured. If you were part of my club, I wouldn't let you come out here on crutches and have people see you.'

That was Cloughie. I tried to make my case but he was having none of it. It hurt me at the time and even now I don't think he was right. I can understand his thinking but I was just trying to stay part of the group and it is something a lot of managers do now with injured players.

I watched from the bench as we fell behind to another Hoddle goal, this time from the penalty spot. John Gregory hit the bar, Mike Flanagan went close and Bob Hazell played brilliantly but it wasn't to be.

Glenn Hoddle had some nice words for me afterwards: 'Don't worry, your day will come. You will be a winner at Wembley someday.'

A season of redemption ended with another chapter to re-write. My leg was in plaster and I spent the summer thinking about what might have been, why I dived in so early.

Glenn's words meant a lot to me. Little did either of us know, the next chance I'd get at Wembley would be as his teammate.

CHAPTER SIX

QPR 2 – Super Hoops

LISA AND I WERE MARRIED IN BRENTWOOD ON 3 JULY 1982 AND I GOT into trouble almost straight away.

I had requested permission from Queens Park Rangers to go away for three weeks immediately afterwards on honeymoon to Mauritius.

At the time of asking, pre-season details weren't confirmed but the club were relaxed about the situation and granted my request; we'd been engaged for 18 months and had things mapped out long in advance so I hardly sprung it on them.

In fact, they had a reminder a few weeks before the end of the season. Lisa and I went to see Father Mel, who was due to marry us (Lisa is a Catholic, I'm not). We sat together with the priest.

'Look, I can't tell you about married life because I've never been married,' he said. 'But I am a Tottenham supporter. Any chance of a cup final ticket? I'll happily marry you if so.'

I looked at Lisa and she burst out laughing. Football really is inescapable. I told a couple of club officials about it and they shared in the joke. He got his ticket and performed the ceremony.

Our honeymoon was great – a time to be with Lisa and put losing at Wembley, my whole career in fact, into perspective – and just the personal time I needed after a difficult end to the season.

Upon getting back to London, I called QPR's chief scout, Arnie Warren, to ask where I needed to be and when, only to be told the team had already gone to Sweden. Arnie said they decided to change the original schedule and go on tour earlier than planned.

The club claimed they tried to contact me but I never heard anything. Aiming to make up for lost time, I flew straight out and as it happened, a friendly had been organised for the night I was due to arrive.

I got there as quickly as possible but still 20 minutes after kick-off and walked along the running track to the dugout – to be greeted by cold shoulders from everyone.

'You should have been here a week ago,' Terry Venables said. 'Sit down and I'll speak to you later.'

In all good faith, I didn't think I'd done anything wrong. If they were coming back to train a week earlier, someone should have told me.

The next day I went out to train with the lads. We had a run through a forest that morning but I couldn't manage anything more than a jog. Out of nowhere, the pain in my ankle was too much.

After the final I hadn't had an operation. They put me in a plaster boot for a while but that came off and my rehabilitation was basically just a long spell of rest.

I'd been fine walking around on holiday and going for a swim but suddenly the realisation dawned on me: I was still injured.

I limped back into the changing room to see the physio. He told me to rest and it wrecked my pre-season.

After being fined a week's wages for a late return – something I contested in vain – my ankle took about three months to feel right again, meaning I watched the start of our Second Division campaign from the stands.

The run to the 1982 Cup Final had given us belief we could compete with the best sides and everybody around the club felt promotion was a real possibility.

Ironically enough, the opening day of the season felt like another final as we went to Newcastle for Kevin Keegan's first game for the club. He had pushed for a move from First Division Southampton earlier that summer and his desire to drop down a league for Newcastle sent the already fanatical Geordie support into overdrive.

The week's build-up focused inevitably on Kevin. But it wasn't lost on us that various people in the game, including prominent figures like Jack Charlton and David Pleat, were predicting we would be promoted.

In fact, the general consensus was we were favourites to go up. But Terry played it down, pointing out the strengths of various sides including Wolverhampton Wanderers, Leeds United, Chelsea and Leicester City.

The game itself was an incredible occasion given the backdrop of deafening jubilation courtesy of 36,185 fans crammed into St James' Park, all desperate to see their new idol.

Injuries throughout the squad made it an even harder test for us – Tony Currie, Glenn Roeder, Mike Flanagan and Steve Wicks were all next to me on the sidelines.

Perhaps inevitably, Kevin scored the only goal as Newcastle won 1-0. Despite the result and the depleted line-up, we played well and looked the better team for long periods. It was just one of those days where we were destined to be a footnote in Kevin's fairytale.

We got off to winning ways against Cambridge United three days later and followed that up with a home victory against Derby. But it wouldn't be until the beginning of October that I would return to the first team, scoring the equaliser as we came from 2-0 down to beat Burnley 3-2 at Loftus Road. I felt rusty on my return and missed a few chances but getting a key goal in a comeback like that felt good.

We'd been jeered by a few fans at half-time after falling behind but on the whole things were progressing well. A week later I scored the only goal in a win over Barnsley and after ten games we were second in the table behind early pace-setters Wolves.

We went top of the table in November by beating Cambridge again in the reverse game. I scored twice with two good finishes that made me feel like I'd finally rediscovered my sharpness.

Our positive form continued in to the New Year and by early February, I had ten goals to my name and was the team's top scorer. We were still behind Wolves in the table but our promotion push had got people talking to the extent First Division sides were already concerned about having to play on our artificial 'Omniturf' surface.

So much so, in fact, that Southampton boss Lawrie McMenemy rang Terry Venables to organise a friendly on it. Some of their players criticised the bounce of the ball but they beat us 5-2 and afterwards McMenemy described it as an 'innovation' which created an environment for forwards to thrive.

Terry was still regularly having to defend our use of it in press conferences but it was certainly helping me. Two goals in a 3-0 win at Palace at the end of January took me to double figures in 20 games – bang on one-in-two. We were unable to get another FA Cup run going, losing 3-2 at West Brom in the third round, but it was probably a blessing in disguise anyway, helping us concentrate on the main aim of promotion.

Not that it stopped Terry's superstitious streak. A party of 20 players and coaches went to Brighton at the end of February for a four-day break. We trained at Sussex University but also played golf and squash; beyond just freshening up our routine, Terry wanted to continue a version of the trip which had served us well on the way to the 1982 FA Cup Final.

We remained on track in the Second Division although it wasn't until 5 March that I got on the scoresheet again – a hat-trick in a 6-1 thrashing of Middlesbrough.

Now we were just two points behind Wolves. More importantly, we were able to play with a degree of comfort because automatic promotion was looking highly likely; the top three went up to the First Division and by this stage we had a 13-point lead over fourth-placed Leicester, with Fulham immediately below us.

Big wins over Rotherham and Charlton followed and a 1-0 victory against Leeds United on 23 April secured our return to the top flight after a four-year wait.

It was nothing more than we deserved. We hadn't been out of the top two since November and had only lost one in 14 games to secure promotion. The television cameras came into our dressing room afterwards as champagne flowed and the lads celebrated.

But as the party was getting into full swing, a few people noticed Terry had disappeared. A short while later, a sudden announcement came from upstairs.

QPR chairman Jim Gregory appeared on television.

'I have been here now 18 years,' he began. 'With a lot of regret and a lot of emotion, the time has come... the club is in a very good position... I will be standing down as chairman at the end of the season.

'I've come to an arrangement with Terry that if he can get a consortium together, he will be taking over the football club. The stadium basically would create too many problems for the football [side of the operation] and that will be left as a business entirely on its own.

'There will be a 20-year lease for the football [operations] and all the players will go into the new company. I shall do everything in my power that it happens for Terry.'

The players had no clue any of this was even in the pipeline. Terry, sitting alongside him, responded.

'It is one where Jim is very determined to do what he is going to do. We've spoken about it many times and I've tried everything I can to make him change his mind.

'Therefore if someone else is going to take over the football side, I think it might just as well be me. He is a very wise man – I've learned a lot in two-and-a-half years - and my ambition is to be 50 percent as good as he is. I'd be thrilled if that was the case.'

It was a huge blow to everyone connected with QPR. Jim was so central to the club's growth and development plus he was a good, honest man to boot.

The situation made everyone determined to win the Second Division title – something the club had never done before – and we did just that.

Victory over Wolves at Loftus Road sealed top spot by 10 points, a further five ahead of the third-placed side, Leicester.

People were quick to claim the pitch had helped us massively and while it was a factor, we also had a very impressive record away from home, winning 10 games – more than anyone else – and drawing four.

Terry also used just 21 players during the whole season – we were a close-knit group who believed we belonged in the First Division.

Terry reflected that feeling in the summer by making just one signing: midfielder Mike Fillery from Chelsea.

It was a busy time for him, eventually organising a consortium to take control as managing director, but that didn't mean Jim walked away as planned. Hundreds of fans sent letters asking Jim to continue and he agreed to stay on as Chairman but with non-executive duties.

Several new board members were appointed while the club also signed a major new shirt sponsorship agreement with Guinness.

I hadn't played as much as I would have liked in the final weeks of the 1982/83 campaign but the prospect of a proper crack at the First Division with a club that felt like it was going places was very exciting.

The opening day of the season threw us straight in at the deep end – Manchester United away. And for all our pre-season optimism, they overwhelmed us at the start, racing into a 2-0 lead as we chased shadows.

I scored to halve the deficit but we ended up losing 3-1 and although there was an improvement in our performance as it went on, United gave us a harsh reminder of what First Division football was all about.

Ahead of our first home game, the 'Omniturf' pitch was continuing to cause a stir. Aston Villa's visit to Loftus Road would be the first top flight game in England played on a synthetic surface.

The Football League's decision to grant Luton Town their wish of using an artificial surface from 1985 helped deflect the complaints but there was still as much focus on the pitch as there was on our football.

We beat Villa 2-1 to record our maiden victory of the league campaign before signing off in September with two big wins, over Sunderland and Wolves.

I got three goals in those two games before 26,293 people saw us beat Arsenal 2-0 back at Loftus Road. The press made a big deal of me facing the Gunners but, as I told them in interviews beforehand, I wasn't there long enough to hold a grudge against the Arsenal players. In truth, I wasn't really there long enough to do anything but it was nice to get the upper hand against Terry Neill.

That match drew record gate receipts of £88,000 as supporters warmed to signs we were capable of competing against the top sides, leaving that opening weekend naivety at Old Trafford firmly behind us.

In fact, our results were getting so good that we pushed the big boys at the top of the table.

We were in third place going into a home game against Liverpool in mid-October having won five-in-a-row in all competitions, including an 8-1 hammering of Crewe in the Milk Cup second round, first leg.

Liverpool edged a tight game 1-0 but the setback didn't affect us too much. My own form, however, began to dip. Over the next month, I went six games without a goal and found myself dropped for a 1-0 defeat at Coventry.

'Clive's lost a bit of confidence,' Terry told the newspapers. He told me to play a reserve game to find my touch again but instead I picked up a minor knee injury. I wasn't angry that Terry had gone public like that; it was a device he used to motivate me and I understood where he was coming from.

And just as I returned to full training, I damaged my Achilles and was ruled out until early March.

It was a hugely frustrating period in which I felt my future might be threatened. Jeremy Charles arrived at the club as a utility player, stepping in and doing very well.

I obviously wanted the team to succeed but watching him score in wins over Everton and Stoke made me question whether I would have put those chances away myself. Simon Stainrod and John Gregory were also chipping in with goals and it took an unusual mid-season break to force my way back in.

Teams we were due to play in the league had advanced in the FA Cup which meant we had a gap in the fixture list.

Terry took the opportunity to introduce another getaway, except this time we traded Brighton for the Middle East and two games against the Oman national team.

We won the first 3-1, drew the second 2-2 and I scored in both games. It was the first time I got back into the team and Terry felt I'd shown enough because I retained my place when we returned to England, keeping me in for a defeat at Sunderland.

I scored the winner against Coventry three days later, a goal which marked the start of a really strong end to the season for both QPR and me.

By the time we faced Ipswich Town on 7 April, we were in sixth place and on course for an unbelievable first season back in the top flight. League leaders Liverpool were 12 points ahead of us on 66 with Manchester United just two adrift of them, third-placed Nottingham Forest were on 57, two clear of West Ham and Southampton on 55. We had 54 before beating Ipswich 1-0, a victory which sparked a run of six consecutive wins and meant not only were we in the hunt for European qualification, but there was talk we could even win the title. I was desperate to get us as close as possible. A hat-trick in the last of those matches – a 3-0 win at Notts County – kept us within touching distance of the leaders, and took me to 15 goals for the season (14 in the league), ten of which had come since my return from injury in March.

We were one point adrift of Manchester United and three behind Liverpool in early May but the top two had a game in hand.

We needed to keep winning and hope the others made mistakes, but a draw against West Brom and defeat at Everton in our final two matches meant we finished in fifth place, seven points behind champions Liverpool and then also below Southampton, Nottingham Forest and United.

Qualifying for the UEFA Cup was a massive achievement but in some ways it felt like a disappointment given we had been on the fringes of the title race for several months.

My form had led to speculation over a move to Italy. Scouts from a couple of Italian clubs had been spotted at Loftus Road and although I hadn't heard anything concrete, it set my mind racing as to what was possible.

Part of me had started to feel like I wanted a new challenge, although playing abroad didn't particularly appeal to me at this stage. Italy had obvious attractions then as the best league in the world but I wanted to make it in England first. The money wasn't a driving force either. It never was.

Terry had created something special at QPR, though, and it was a great place to be. I was torn.

The decisive factor came when Terry left that summer to manage Barcelona. There had been regular media reports that he could replace Keith Burkinshaw at Tottenham and so his departure was not the biggest surprise but it felt like the end of a journey at QPR.

Now I knew I needed to move on. I told Terry's successor as manager, Alan Mullery, I wanted out. The phrase I think I used at the time was to 'broaden my outlook'. I didn't want to disrespect QPR – they are a great club and remain so to this day. I felt I'd served them well with 83 goals in 158 games over two spells but I was ready for a step up.

I left the training ground after speaking to Alan with the club now willing to consider selling me. After travelling on the Underground across London, I got home and within an hour, the phone rang. It was new Spurs boss Peter Shreeves.

They had agreed a fee and he wanted to ask how I felt about a move to White Hart Lane. Deep down, I always believed it would one day be my destiny to follow in my Dad's footsteps and play for Tottenham. Now that time was here.

The Allen connection with Spurs was deep-rooted and Peter knew it.

'I think you know where the ground is, I'll see you in the morning,' he said.

CHAPTER SEVEN

Tottenham – It Was Meant To Be

'AT QUEENS PARK RANGERS YOU CAN TURN IN AN OUTSTANDING performance maybe one game in four – that isn't good enough at Tottenham.'

On my first day at Spurs, manager Peter Shreeves left me under no illusions about the step up I was making.

'The pressure is greater here. That kind of exceptional performance is expected every game. They demand more than you have been used to and you can't appreciate it until you have lived through it. They demand the best here from the manager and the players.'

This time, I felt ready. Arsenal passed me by in a blur, a whirlwind where my feet barely touched the ground, but now I was older, more established, had plenty of senior football under my belt and my ankle wasn't causing any problems.

Tottenham had underlined their pedigree by winning the 1984 UEFA Cup – beating Anderlecht on penalties in the final – but I didn't need to be convinced of that.

The club was in my blood. I turned them down as a 15-year-old but always maintain that was the right decision because I had chances to play at Loftus Road much earlier than I would have done at White Hart Lane.

Peter gave me assurances over my role in the team. The plan was to partner me with Mark Falco in attack and I couldn't wait to get started.

I played against Mark when I was at Hackney and he was at Havering and then later together for London Schools. After that, he was at Spurs while I was at QPR but all the way along we had respect for each other.

He was a different type of forward to me: big, very strong, good in the air. As an old-fashioned pairing, I always felt comfortable playing with him. To this day we are good friends.

Peter felt we could knit together and so did I. On the opening day of the season, we beat Everton 4-1 at Goodison Park and I scored twice. A draw against Leicester preceded a 3-1 win over Norwich and things looked promising.

But then Sunderland took the first step to becoming my jinx club of the season. We lost 1-0 at Roker Park in early September, a game in which both Graham Roberts and I were sent off. He was dismissed for retaliation while I chased down a ball and collided with the Sunderland goalkeeper. The crowd went mad and the referee showed the red card. I thought I was unfortunate and so did Peter.

After that hiccup we continued ticking along nicely in the league – I had 12 goals in 24 games, precisely the one-in-two ratio I was always after – when we played Sunderland again, this time at home, in a Milk Cup replay.

What followed was the beginning of an 18-month nightmare during which I feared my career was over.

It started in the simplest way. A few minutes into the game, I crossed the ball with my left foot. As I began to watch it travel in the air, I felt a sharp pain and collapsed in a heap on the ground.

I carried on for a short while but quickly knew I couldn't make a meaningful contribution and had to come off. The doctor told me I had a nasty groin strain which further tests suggested would sideline me for two or three weeks.

I could cope with that. A fortnight out was irritating but not debilitating. After 14 days, I tried to return to training but the pain continued. It was the same the next day. And the day after that. Days turned into weeks and with no sign of improvement, Spurs sent me to see a specialist.

He said I'd torn a muscle and it would only heal with rest. I've never been great at sitting around and doing nothing but the frustration was multiplied by Spurs doing well in the league and the fact that mine and Mark's partnership had been put on hold after such a promising start.

Lisa and I moved house that winter but I was unable to lift a finger because of my injury. Maybe it wasn't all bad. Rest was the only solution on offer but I had a hunch there was a problem which required more definitive action.

On New Year's Day 1985, I made a three-minute substitute appearance at

Highbury against Arsenal. We won 2-1 and although I had little to do with the result, it felt good to be part of things again.

Twenty-four hours later, I played in a specially-arranged friendly at Tottenham's Cheshunt training ground to help build up my fitness. But after I twisted for the ball, my groin went again. When I got back to the treatment room, I passed out with the pain.

That original two-to-three-week period had now become eight. I was infuriated. Inactivity drives me crazy.

I couldn't train but Spurs physio Mike Varney still kept telling me everything would be fine. I started having cortisone injections, which only provided short-term relief.

Eventually, I was sent to see a Harley Street specialist by the name of Jerry Gilmour. The joke among players was if you went to see Jerry, it was inevitable you had a hernia operation.

Within a few days, that's exactly what happened to me. That meant another six weeks out in the wilderness.

I was guilty of trying to rush it. I sought Lisa's advice and more often than not she would concur with the doctors. But I wouldn't listen. A quick aborted run here, maybe an attempted gym session there. Whatever I did, I always ended it in pain.

On 23 February, I tried another return to action in a friendly but early on I went to challenge for the ball and the pain shot through me like a lightning bolt.

My whole stomach area was sore but once again I was told rest was the only cure. Hearing that over and over again sent me into a mental tailspin.

Lisa was working at Basildon hospital and, trying everything to get fit, I went to the hydropool there. She tested the strength in my legs with a simple exercise, kicking off while standing on one leg. I could almost knock her over with my right leg in the water. With my left planted, she could put a finger on my toe and I could not move her hand. There was nothing there, I had no power. I went home and cried my eyes out, lying on our bed.

'I'm done,' I said. 'My career is finished.'

By now, people were starting to question my character. The club doctor told me it was all psychosomatic, which I took as a huge insult. Did they really think

I was faking it? That I didn't want to make a success of myself at Spurs?

I prided myself on professionalism – Dad taught me that above all else – yet here I was having to listen to informed opinion suggesting I was mentally fragile.

I was sent to see a surgeon for the British Olympic team, one of the best in the business. He recommended yet another cortisone injection.

Lisa knew about cortisone and the possible problems it could cause down the line. I'd had enough of all that anyway and Mike Varney and I nearly came to blows outside his office.

'I'm not having any more,' I said.

'He's the top man in the country!' insisted the physio.

'Mike, I've had eight injections, I don't want any more. They've not helped me.'

'Well, what do you want to do?'

'I need another opinion.'

I'd lost confidence that anyone could get to the root of the problem by the time I was sent to see Alan Lettin – a specialist consultant orthopaedic surgeon in London.

He told me that every player he'd ever examined had wear and tear in the groin area because of the strains the game placed on the body.

I was sent for an X-ray. It came back clear and I was ordered to rest for another two weeks before returning to see him.

We went round in circles again. I told him I still felt something was wrong and it was threatening to wreck my career. Every time I tried any form of moderate exercise, the pain was overwhelming. Lettin was reluctant to operate given he only really had my word to take for it.

We were now in April – six months after I was told two-to-three weeks – and I was at my wits' end.

Peter Shreeves remained supportive. He sent Lisa and I on a week's holiday to Malta but I spent most of it worrying about what would happen.

I met with Lettin again once we were back. Finally, after another conversation bordering on begging, he agreed to an explorative operation in June.

'You know that you have to play on if they don't find anything,' Lisa told me the day before I went into hospital.

I knew that but deep down I believed they would find something. This was make-or-break.

I was still groggy when I came around in my bed, located inside the Hospital for the Clergy off Euston Road. But I felt fantastic.

It might sound odd but I sensed something had been cured. Lettin came in to see me and explained what he'd found.

'I'm 99.9 percent sure I've found the cause,' he began. Essentially, I'd ruptured the adductor brevis muscle from the bone. It had rolled up and attached itself to the adductor longus. The adductor brevis is more of a stabiliser than anything to do with strength. And every time I did anything, it was pulling and tearing the adductor longus. He opened me up, saw the issue and took the brevis away.

Relief overwhelmed me. I had been proved right. Peter Shreeves called me the next morning.

'I wasn't imagining it then, it wasn't in my mind,' I told him.

'I never doubted you,' Peter quickly explained. I knew *he* hadn't.

'But there were a few people who did and a few more who didn't believe me.'

'Well, that might have been the case...'

'Then they don't know me and they don't know what football means to me. Football is everything to me, it is my life. I'm a professional and no way would I want to be injured and mark time sitting out the season. I hope this proves what kind of person I am.'

I hadn't been given the benefit of the doubt by some people.

'It's all in your head son, there's nothing wrong with you,' I kept hearing. The only way I knew to respond was to work harder but I was being told not to work at all, to cure the problem with rest. How do you show people you want to knuckle down when you can't lift a finger?

Now it was a case of getting fit. I knew it would be a long road back – much more difficult than after the hernia operation – and although I tried to join in during pre-season, I was well short of the required fitness.

There was a real incentive to get back involved. We ended the 1984/85 season in third place after our title challenge fell away following a 2-1 defeat to Everton on 3 April. I felt some frustration over not being able to play any part but honestly my main concern was just how badly the injury was threatening my entire career.

That summer, the club added Chris Waddle and my cousin Paul to the team.

There was a lot of speculation that Paul would go to Liverpool and so him joining me at Spurs was something I was really looking forward to. In our earlier days, we'd always played against each other, aside from England youth teams, so the idea of linking up at club level only made me want to get back even quicker.

Chris and I had played together for England and I knew what a great talent he was. He was the best I ever played with from a standing position. He'd have the ball between his feet and would rock, a defender would react and he'd drag the ball with either foot in the opposite direction. He was deceptively quick so that one moment of skill was all he needed to get away.

I was desperate to start playing with him but it wasn't until November 1985 that I was involved at the highest level. I had played in a Screen Sport Super Cup game – an unpopular domestic competition which was supposed to replace European football for English clubs banned after the Heysel tragedy – against Southampton a month earlier but was sluggish and, in truth, miles off the pace.

I needed more time to rediscover my sharpness and a spell in the reserves followed. But at the end of November, almost exactly a year after I first picked up the injury against Sunderland, Peter Shreeves suddenly threw me back into the first team at Aston Villa. I had no idea I was playing until the team meeting a few hours before the game.

'He has been out a long time,' he told my teammates, 'so let's help him through.'

Mark Falco scored the goals as we won 2-1. I did okay but, more importantly, came through unscathed. It turned out to be a difficult time to come back, however, as inconsistency was undermining our season and Peter was under pressure as a result.

A good FA Cup run was important and after starting the third-round game away at Oxford United, I was taken off for John Chiedozie when we were losing and dropped for the replay.

I went to see Peter about it.

'You are on the bench so you are still involved,' he said. 'So, if I need a goal from you tonight, you can go on and get me one, can't you!'

I was disappointed. The team was struggling for goals and if he really felt I could solve the problem, why not play me from the start?

As it turned out, I came off the bench and got the winner in a 2-1 win but I still wasn't happy.

White Hart Lane went crazy and I remember Glenn Hoddle stopping me as I ran back to the centre-circle.

'What's the matter? You have scored the winner!' he said.

'Leave me alone,' I said. 'I've scored. That's all.'

I knew I needed to do much more to reassert myself after such a long time out. We were knocked out in the fifth round by Everton and the season was over in terms of trophies.

In the league, we drifted along in mid-table, finishing in tenth place. It may have been the case that we had little to play for collectively in the last third of the season but I had a point to prove.

I scored eight goals in our last 12 matches as we recorded wins against Arsenal, Leicester, Birmingham, QPR, Aston Villa and Southampton to sign off the campaign.

It wasn't enough to keep Peter in his job, however. Chris and Paul had needed time to settle in after their transfers and injuries prevented him from picking the same team consistently.

But more than that, Peter probably wasn't cut out to be a number one at Spurs. He'd come through the White Hart Lane coaching ranks and found that transition from coach to boss very difficult. The job was arguably too big for him.

I had my differences with Peter but I still owed him a lot. He signed me for Spurs and stood by me when a lot of people didn't. Only Lisa gave me more support during what was undoubtedly the worst period of my career.

But that was all behind me now. All I wanted was to make up for lost time.

CHAPTER EIGHT

1986/87
He Only Scores Goals

DAVID PLEAT RANG ME IN THE SUMMER OF 1986 SHORTLY AFTER succeeding Peter Shreeves as Tottenham manager.

'What's your plan for the time off?'

'I'm going to train every day,' I replied.

'Don't do that,' he said. 'It is a long break – ten weeks because of the World Cup. Pre-season will be hard. If you want to sharpen up before then, fine, but don't do too much.

'Start no more than three weeks before we officially come back.'

He was right that I needed a break but I decided to start working four weeks beforehand on my own: sprints, gym sessions, long runs – everything that would build my strength and stamina.

I trained every day with the intention of reporting for pre-season in the best shape of my career. I'm glad I did.

'This is going to be a year when I assess the players,' said David on the first day we were all together. 'I am going to sort out the people I want and the people I don't.'

I flew through pre-season, feeling better than I had done for 18 months. I'd seen how David's Luton team played and felt it would be a good fit for my strengths. He was football mad and still is today. There was a connection between us in that respect which has endured over the years. He is quick at accurately assessing each player's specific abilities and tailoring a system accordingly.

I was also excited about the squad David was assembling.

Richard Gough and Mitchell Thomas looked like shrewd signings from Dundee United and Luton Town respectively. David said our aim for the season was to go for everything in all competitions.

By the opening game at Aston Villa, I'd trained for eight full weeks – something you wouldn't recommend as a rule, but I'd had a year off and nothing was going to hold me back. I ran out at Villa Park with a clear sense of purpose. I'd heard the whispers about whether I would ever come back to full fitness. Did I still have the hunger and ability to play at the top level? Everyone was about to find out.

I scored a hat-trick in a 3-0 win. The team performance was superb – solid defensively, dominant in midfield and incisive up front.

Everything I had done in preparation worked perfectly, so much so that I replicated my pre-match routine before every game of the 1986/87 season.

There wasn't a team warm-up as such. Some players would go out on the pitch but I wouldn't, home or away. I didn't want to kick the ball in the net in the warm-up. It was just something I got in my head so I stayed in the dressing room.

About 45 minutes to an hour before kick-off, I'd go through a routine of step-ups on the bench. Then, I'd go into the bathroom and play the ball against whatever surfaces there were – at White Hart Lane it was a two-foot tall wall – and after off the sides, left and right, to get a feel and touch for the ball.

It was quite lively in there at the Lane because the ball would ping off brick walls. I'd come back out, stretch and then strap myself up. I did the whole thing on my own, including sorting my own boots out, changing my studs rather than relying on the kit man.

I put new studs in each game. I'd had routines before but this particular one – starting it at the beginning of the season with a hat-trick as I did – felt like it was working.

I'm not sure why I stopped shooting at goal in the warm-up. You wouldn't advise it to players now. Even defenders often want to shoot at goal in the warm-up to get their eye in. I guess it was a superstition – I wanted the first time I hit the back of the net to be in the game and not sully it beforehand, like waiting to run out into untouched snow drifts. It might have been illogical but it was effective.

I scored again in our second game – a 1-1 draw at Newcastle – before Graham Roberts struck the winner in a 1-0 win over Manchester City. Disappointing defeats against Southampton and Chelsea followed but just at the point I might have tipped into an obsessive spiral at the prospect of things going wrong, Lisa gave birth to our first child Oliver on 7 September. The first time he was allowed home came a few hours after we'd lost to Chelsea.

Oliver brought a new dimension to my life from that moment onwards. At the time, I probably didn't fully appreciate it but I needed a release, another avenue down which to channel my thoughts and focus my mind.

I was so intent on proving people wrong who had doubted my character and whether I could make it at a big club like Tottenham. But you go home and your baby doesn't care about any of that. You change nappies, you give them all the love you can and they become your world.

The timing had a big impact on my career. The public often don't know what is going on in a player's personal life that can have an effect on their football. Some strikers, for example, have long goal droughts and might not be playing well but the root cause could easily lie in off-field issues. Similarly, top form can often come when all aspects of your life are in sync.

And the latter was how I felt. Next time out I scored both goals in a 2-1 win at Leicester, but, despite the result, it was the first time David lost it with us as a group.

He accused us of lacking professionalism because we failed to kill the game off at 2-0 and almost allowed Leicester to snatch a point. It was a 90-minute example of our inconsistency: great in spells, errant and wasteful at other times.

He looked at everyone and analysed what he wanted from them. That's where I thought he was very clever – different players needed different messaging and this was a chance to make his point about various weaknesses.

In my case it was working harder to close down defenders and putting more of a shift in without the ball. My argument was I tried to take up dangerous positions so that when we did win it back, we could threaten. We had the attitude that 'if you score two, we'll score three', but he demanded greater discipline. Why not win 2-0 rather than 3-2?

We did just that in our next game against Everton, who had been First Division runners-up the year before and were unbeaten in the league until facing us.

I scored them both. Paul crossed the first, I headed in at the near post. The second, Ray Clemence cleared it long downfield, I rolled off the centre-half and volleyed past Bobby Mimms. They were a top team but we never gave them a sniff. That's what we could do.

David wasn't done in the transfer market though. Mark Falco was sold to Watford for £300,000. A sign of how times have changed can be found in the circumstances of his departure.

Mark felt David would sell him if the right offer came in, but one day he arrived for training and said to me: 'I'm on my way.'

I asked where.

'I haven't a clue!' he replied. 'All I know is that the manager has agreed a fee but he won't say with who.'

Imagine that happening nowadays. That's where there has been a massive shift in football with the rise of agents and, of course, the Bosman rule. Players have a lot more control now than we ever did.

Nico Claesen was Mark's replacement, signed from Standard Liège. It was very difficult for foreign players to come into English football back then. Nico was part of the Belgium side which reached the World Cup semi-finals earlier that summer but had struggled to integrate during a spell in Germany with Stuttgart in the 1984/85 season.

The boys took him out for dinner a few times and he quickly understood the psyche and the banter of an English dressing room. The other foreign player we had at the time, Ossie Ardiles, loves it to this day. That cultural interaction is one of the reasons Ossie still lives in England but a lot of overseas players struggle with those dressing room dynamics, even in today's game.

By the beginning of October, I'd scored ten goals in nine games. Losing Mark was a blow but my form was attracting media attention.

I went on *Saint and Greavsie* – a weekly ITV football show hosted by Ian St John and Jimmy Greaves – for an interview about Tottenham's start to the season.

Out of the blue, Jimmy said 'you could break my record'. I honestly didn't know what he was talking about.

In 1962/63, Jimmy scored 44 goals in a single season, including two in the Charity Shield. I wasn't aware of that tally but he was someone I looked up to from a young age. My Dad had played with Jimmy and I even met him a few times as a child.

Jimmy lived in Upminster, not far from where I went to school, and I knew his son, Danny. We'd played junior football against each other and although we weren't close, we'd bump into each other from time to time as my Dad and

Jimmy remained friends.

Dad said he was the best goalscorer he'd ever seen. I only saw clips but Jimmy had a calmness in front of goal which I tried to emulate.

Jimmy wasn't all about power or pace – even if he glided across the ground and was exceptionally quick – he just always seemed to have the ball where he wanted and took plenty of touches to give himself a chance to shoot. Dad always said: 'Look at Jimmy, look how he passes it into the goal.' It was calm, clinical and smooth. So to have him discuss me as a possible record-breaker was quite surreal but I honestly didn't pay it any attention.

I was just desperate to play. David left me on the bench for a Littlewoods Cup game against Barnsley. We were leading 3-2 from the first leg and I had a slightly tight hamstring.

David told me he wanted to rest me but I didn't want to miss anything.

It brought back memories from a couple of years earlier when I was suspended, Garth Crooks came in, scored a hat-trick and kept his place in the team as my injury problems began to take hold.

I had a fear it would happen again. Sean Close made his debut that night but even just a youngster coming in like that, it made me think 'How can he leave him out if he scores a hat-trick?'

It is less likely nowadays but back then I felt it was a genuine concern. Shaun started well enough, scoring our first goal inside the opening 15 minutes – a moment that evoked one of those strange mixed reactions where you are happy collectively but concerned individually. I shifted uncomfortably on the bench, itching to get on. It felt very satisfying to play the final few minutes and score the fifth in a 5-3 win.

In hindsight, David made the right decision. I could easily have torn my hamstring and have been out for a couple of months. Getting that goal still felt like a good way of keeping me uppermost in his thoughts for the weeks ahead. Little did I know, David had a bigger challenge for me just around the corner.

Pretty much everybody in England played 4-4-2 or 4-2-4 in the 1980s. A 4-4-2 system was certainly working for us but every now and again we might try some alternative shape work in training, just as we did on the Friday before playing Oxford United in mid-November, experimenting with a 4-5-1 formation.

We just thought it was something different to freshen up the session, but in the team meeting afterwards, David Pleat dropped a bombshell: 'We are going to play like this in tomorrow's match and I will take responsibility, win, lose or draw. This is going to work for us. Any objections?'

Ray Clemence put his hand up. 'Yeah, we tried it at Liverpool. It didn't work. It is a system that isn't right for us.'

'Don't worry about it, it'll work.'

Glenn Hoddle also had his say – as did one or two others – but David was adamant. A tactical change like this is commonplace nowadays but it is no exaggeration to say this was revolutionary at the time.

Glenn was designated to play in an advanced midfield role – a little like a modern-day number ten – behind me as a lone striker. The extra man in the middle of the pitch was designed to help us play through sides and create more chances while giving us greater solidity without the ball.

Saturday came and the players were still sceptical in the wake of David telling us all just to go and enjoy it.

'It is okay saying that boss,' said one player, 'but what happens on Monday morning if we have been beaten 5-0? Are you going to say don't worry about it then?'

Initially, it seemed as though we were going to find out. After 20 minutes, Oxford were 2-0 up.

But we stuck at it and began to dominate possession. I found a lot of room, more than I expected, and Oxford's players started to show signs of confusion as to who to mark.

Both Chris Waddle and I scored twice as we stormed back to win 4-2. Some of the football we played was magnificent: short, sharp passing and with the extra body in midfield, Oxford couldn't cope. Glenn was in his element.

People said I was on my own in attack but that wasn't true. I was never isolated. Glenn linked the play between midfield and me superbly. And he was free to roam. It made us so unpredictable.

I became less of a target man and really more of a penalty box player. I had to get myself in there at the right times and find space no matter how packed it was.

Part of me – a big part – didn't want to change given my goal record to that point. But I knew that playing with this group of players in any system would give me chances to score.

And it did. I scored my 20th and 21st goals of the season against Nottingham Forest at the end of November.

There were still a few teething problems. Chris Waddle had to stay wide and hated it. He went to see David and said he wanted to play centrally but got short shrift in response.

I suffered a broken nose when scoring during a 3-3 draw at Manchester United – there's a picture of me holding Olly with panda eyes a few days after it happened, courtesy of a kick to the face from Gordon Strachan – but generally my fitness was good and we got to the middle of December still in the Littlewoods Cup and not too far away from the leaders in what looked an open First Division title race.

Yet two pieces of news threatened to check our momentum. Firstly, Glenn Hoddle told us during a short break to Bermuda that he would be leaving at the end of the season. He wanted a new challenge and felt the time was right to go abroad and test his skills in Europe.

Then David sold Graham Roberts to Glasgow Rangers. He has since alleged that Graham was tapped up by Rangers boss Graeme Souness but whatever the truth, it was a surprise because he gave us a really good balance.

Steve Hodge, a £750,000 signing from Aston Villa to replace him, was a completely different player. Steve gave us energy and pace going forward, making us more dynamic, but it was definitely a mistake to let Graham go. We had a tendency to be flaky in matches and Graham was usually our best chance of stopping that. With his departure, while we gained another attacking dimension in Steve, we lost a bit of steel which changed the balance of the team. A resounding victory over West Ham – an emotional day for Paul and I, given he played there earlier in his career and a lot of our family were Hammers fans – preceded a 4-3 defeat at Coventry and a 2-0 win at Charlton on New Year's Day.

Another FA Cup campaign began with wins over Scunthorpe and Crystal Palace, while in the league we had lost to Arsenal but still felt there was a chance of staying in touch with them, Everton and Liverpool at the top of the table. There was everything to play for.

Perhaps the knowledge of Glenn's impending departure made me appreciate what we had even more. My injury nightmare certainly did. I'd joined up with the

England senior squad for the first time in a couple of years just beforehand, which felt like another small step in re-establishing myself over the course of the season.

And here were Tottenham, going for trophies on three fronts and playing matches with increasing frequency.

We needed a replay to beat West Ham in the Littlewoods Cup quarter-final and our fixture list was starting to pile up. Of the 11 matches we played between 10 January and 4 March, eight of them were in the domestic cup competitions.

And to compound the intensity, three of those came against our bitter north London rivals.

After winning the first leg of the Littlewoods Cup semi-final 1-0 – I scored the only goal – we played Arsenal in the return game at the beginning of March.

It was a tense occasion. White Hart Lane was rocking and with a goal advantage, confidence was high – even more so when I put us 1-0 up on the night.

At half-time, the Tottenham supporters were told over the PA system how to book tickets for the final.

We were within touching distance of Wembley. But Arsenal fought back as Viv Anderson and then Niall Quinn scored and suddenly we were left hanging on for a replay. That fragility David had tried to address was coming back to haunt us.

Back then, there was no penalty shoot-out and instead a third game was required. The two managers tossed a coin to determine the venue. David won and so the Lane would host another derby just three days later – a period that began with having to deal with the fall-out from the night before, as several newspapers blamed me for Spurs failing to reach the final.

I'd missed a few chances yet scored in both legs and felt the criticism was unfair. I suppose it was a consequence of increased expectations resulting from the season I was having and precisely what Peter told me about on arrival. But being singled out like that still surprised me.

It was a test of my mindset. Forgetting the chances you miss is key to being a consistent goalscorer. Your mind cannot linger on what goes wrong, either in games or afterwards. I've had many absolute stinkers but when a chance presented itself and I took it despite playing badly, that was very satisfying. It is the mentality you need to have. This is also where having Olly helped. He didn't care what anyone else had said about me, he just wanted my focus and attention.

I was helped by another big occasion coming so soon. No time to dwell. Glenn was ruled out of the third Arsenal game through injury but we had Gary Stevens fit again after a shoulder problem to deputise. Gary was a defender by trade but had played in midfield for Tottenham and also at international level with England. He obviously didn't possess Glenn's attacking flair and we missed his skill but Gary gave our five-man midfield solidity, while we still had Chris Waddle and Nico Claesen to help create chances.

The first half was tense, tight and goalless. In the second, my moment came. Richard Gough headed down a free-kick and I swept the ball past John Lukic for my 12th goal in the competition which, I later found out, was a record.

We held onto that lead entering the final ten minutes. For the third game in succession against Arsenal, we were 1-0 up and I'd got the breakthrough. Charlie Nicholas, the Gunners' talisman, had to go off injured and was replaced by Ian Allinson, a winger, who rarely played for the Gunners. Losing Charlie was a big blow to them which only accelerated the momentum in our direction. Or so I thought.

Allinson went to chase a long ball upfield and our defender Danny Thomas tried to close him down. I swear Allinson was just crossing it but, regardless, the ball struck the bottom of Danny's foot and squirmed past Ray Clemence into our net.

We were shellshocked and Arsenal knew it. Suddenly we were under siege. They capitalised on the moment and in the last minute, David Rocastle scored from the edge of the box.

I was in tears afterwards. They gave me an award for breaking the League Cup scoring record but it meant nothing.

Several other players were crying and David Pleat went around the dressing room consoling each one. Everyone was so flat. But as the disappointment slowly subsided, we tried to pick ourselves up in the knowledge we still had the league to fight for and the FA Cup was about to get serious.

A low-key third round win over Scunthorpe preceded a comfortable 4-0 win over Crystal Palace, which set up a fifth round tie with Newcastle ten days before the second leg of our clash with Arsenal. For me it meant a reunion with Glenn Roeder, my old roommate at Queens Park Rangers.

I scored the only goal of the game after a fiercely contested penalty award. We rode our luck during the 90 minutes and afterwards Glenn said to me:

'You'll win it now.'

I'd obviously gone close five years earlier and I'd say the experience helps second-time around but in a way, you also know the older you are, the fewer chances you are going to have.

With that Spurs team, I thought we had a great opportunity right from the start of the competition, especially given how the season was going. We could win one-off games against anyone.

But the quarter-final pitched us against Wimbledon away. They had exceeded all expectations during their first season in the top flight. Tipped as relegation certainties, they were hardly ever out of the top half of the table. They were even the leaders at one stage.

They beat us 2-1 in the league when each team had one man sent off and booked their place in the last eight by beating Everton 3-1 after being 1-0 down. The game was televised and, as usual, everybody wanted the underdog to win.

Eleven days earlier, we'd lost the Littlewoods Cup semi-final to Arsenal and that only heightened the importance of the occasion in our minds. We'd come so close in one competition, surely we weren't going to be knocked out of the other by Wimbledon?

They always tried all the tricks. Before the league game in November, someone disconnected all the sockets in their dressing room so they claimed the only place they could play their pre-match music was in the tunnel at White Hart Lane. They beat us and had it blaring out again at full-time. 'We'll see you back at our place,' one shouted as they danced about in celebration.

This time, the intimidation tactics started days before kick-off in the papers. Every day we would read what they were going to do to Chris Waddle, Glenn Hoddle and Ossie Ardiles.

Mentally you have to stay focused. You know it's coming but it is very difficult to keep your emotions in check. They goad you all the time: verbally, physically, collectively, individually.

They had no fear. They were good players, too, proving it by winning the 1988 FA Cup with that famous 1-0 win over Liverpool. A lot of them went onto bigger clubs and had good careers.

But that day we stood up for ourselves against a barrage of long-throws, free-kicks, rough-tackling and crowd hostility. We won 2-0 and it felt particularly nice to do it with two classy goals, one each from Chris and Glenn.

And afterwards we couldn't resist: our music was turned right up to maximum volume in the tiny Plough Lane dressing room, everyone singing loudly in unison so they could hear us through the walls.

That was the first time when I started to think winning the FA Cup was a genuine possibility. I fancied our chances all along but now it felt real.

Drawing Watford in the semi-final enhanced that feeling. There was media interest in me beforehand because a few days earlier I had scored the only goal in a league game at Sheffield Wednesday to reach 44 for the season and equal Jimmy Greaves's Tottenham record.

Everybody mentioned the possibility of me breaking it during the semi-final which wasn't exactly the ideal mental preparation, but the omens were with me and the team.

Watford had to put part-timer Gary Plumley in goal because they had injuries to Tony Coton and his back-up Steve Sherwood. Plumley was a former Newport County goalkeeper, but had dropped out of the professional game several years earlier and at the time made his living as the manager of a wine bar in Wales.

Goalkeeper is the one position on the pitch you can't hide a weakness like that. We were strong favourites and the match itself was a completely different occasion to the fraught game I'd played with QPR against West Brom at the same stage in 1982.

Watford tried to negate the gulf in quality by man-marking our best players but that just suited the fluidity of our midfield. We were 3-0 up at half-time. Plumley had made a mistake for the opening goal, scored by Steve Hodge, before I found the net along with my cousin Paul. It finished 4-1 and everything went right. Another FA Cup Final beckoned.

Progressing in both cup competitions stretched the squad to its limit. We didn't train. It was just play, recover, play. It was brilliant. Players always prefer matches than training sessions and we were going from game to game with a real momentum to the season. It helped with my rhythm and focus. Play, recover, repeat.

However, there's only so long you can go on like that. We didn't have the squad like teams do now. You had to be patched up and go again and again.

Every team was in the same boat, of course, because that's what it was like back then, but we had played a lot of games – effectively a full League Cup programme as well as a run to the FA Cup Final.

We played eight matches in April and our chances of winning the league suffered a huge blow against West Ham, losing 2-1 at Upton Park as the old fear about Spurs underperforming there rang true once more.

A draw at Wimbledon meant we lost more ground but Glenn Hoddle scored a magical goal to beat Oxford, worthy of being his last at White Hart Lane. He ran from the halfway line, ghosting left and right past opposition players before waltzing around the goalkeeper to score.

But either side of a thumping 4-0 win over Manchester United – a result which included my 48th goal of the season and caused new United boss Alex Ferguson to publicly call out his players – we were beaten at Nottingham Forest and Watford, ending the league campaign with four defeats from seven games. We finished in third place, 15 points behind Everton. Only the FA Cup could avoid such a promising campaign ending without a trophy.

You might think there was more pressure on me going into the 1987 FA Cup Final compared with five years earlier but in fact the opposite was true.

I was back in the England squad and enjoying a prolific season with Tottenham, but we were all in Glenn Hoddle's shadow. Glenn's final game for the club would be a Wembley final and rightly so, therefore he got all the attention.

Glenn and Ray Clemence knew how to handle the build-up and the rest of us were in their slipstream. We all made personal appearances and recorded a cup final single – 'Hot Shot Tottenham', written by Chas & Dave.

The perks pool was professional and very organised. It included Danny Thomas despite him getting injured just before the sixth-round match at Wimbledon and I thought it was a nice touch – a sign of how united we were as a team and particularly poignant because we were facing Coventry, his former club.

Everybody had us down as favourites even though they gave us problems in the league games: we beat them 1-0 at White Hart Lane but lost 4-3 at Coventry. Nevertheless, we finished seven places higher in the table and had a greater pedigree, which pointed to success in many people's eyes.

Nothing distracted us from our preparations, though, and I was determined to stop the few hours before kick-off becoming a blur as had happened in 1982.

This time, I took in all the sights down Wembley Way. I saw my parents up in the stand with Lisa and waved. Then I went back to the dressing room to concentrate 100 percent on the challenge ahead.

I said to David Pleat at the Football Writers' Association dinner on the Thursday before the final that I didn't want my season to finish like Gary Lineker's at Everton the year before. Like him, I'd scored a lot of goals and had competed on mutilple fronts but he ended up with nothing. Liverpool beat them to both the league and cup. I went out with the intent of writing a different ending.

Two minutes into the 1982 FA Cup Final, I got injured. This time, five years on, I scored. Chris Waddle crossed from the right and I planted a header past Steve Ogrizovic. It doesn't get any better than that feeling. A goal to put your team ahead in a cup final.

But it made Coventry – clear underdogs on the day – come out and attack us. They'd proved they could cause us problems in the league and it didn't take them long to get going here either.

Dave Bennett equalised before I missed a difficult chance at 1-1. Watching the video back in researching this book brought it back but I had no memory of it beforehand.

I wonder whether that is a by-product of the mentality I tried to develop over the years of taking each chance on its merits, not allowing the past to influence the present.

Ogrizovic had got himself into trouble and I picked up the loose ball with a chance to shoot at an unguarded goal from a tight angle, but could only hit the sidenetting.

Gary Mabbutt spared my blushes a few minutes later as he bundled home Glenn's free-kick to put us back in front.

We were 45 minutes from the trophy. But we lost the lead just after the hour mark when Keith Houchen's diving header hauled Coventry level and as the game went into extra-time, Gary scored the most unfortunate own goal, deflecting Lloyd McGrath's cross past Ray Clemence.

I don't know if you ever get over losing a big final, and it feels different the second time around. I did start to think it might never happen for me. You don't get many chances to play in a cup final and given we fell short in all competitions that year, I wondered if I'd ever win a trophy.

But over the course of a couple of weeks in the summer, you get away, change

CLIVE ALLEN

the scenery and begin to get some perspective. I eventually became philosophical about the result, that it was written in the stars that Coventry would win. That's how I coped – I convinced myself there was in fact nothing we could have done to change the outcome.

What's strange is that until about two years ago, I believed that Houchen's header was the winning goal. I don't know why. I even had an on-air disagreement with Richard Keys and Andy Gray about it while doing some television work.

'Mabbutt's own goal was the winner,' said Keys.

'Keysy, I played in that game,' I said, incredulously. 'It wasn't. Houchen's header was the winning goal.

'No, it wasn't,' he replied, chuckling to himself.

We then watched a couple of highlights and of course, Keysy was right. I'd deleted it from my memory.

I remember watching Gary's own goal from the other end of the pitch. But the memory is out of order in my mind – I'd swear I had it right for years.

So, we ended up with nothing. People say to David Pleat now that, apart from the 1960/61 side, the Terry Venables team of 1990/91 and the current side under Mauricio Pochettino, that his 1986/87 team was as good as Spurs have had in the last 60 years. That makes me very proud.

But we had nothing to show for it. That final is remembered as one of the most entertaining in history – and also for a sponsor controversy as only some of the Tottenham shirts carried the Holsten logo.

There are a number of theories but from what I remember, I walked into the Wembley dressing room to prepare for the first warm-up and each player's pile of kit was stacked like this: a tracksuit top, a shirt with Holsten embroidered on the front, a plain Spurs shirt, a t-shirt, socks and shorts.

Some took the tracksuit top and put a t-shirt on underneath to warm-up, some pulled a shirt out without Holsten on it, others took the Holsten shirt which should have been the match shirt for everyone.

I'm not saying it was done wrong but the match shirt should have been hanging on the peg to distinguish it from the rest, which was normally the case in a run-of-the-mill league game, or it would be the top shirt on the kit. Invariably, it was in the same position in the home dressing room each week or if you were away, they would be laid out in ascending numerical order and you'd go to your number to identify your kit.

I put on a t-shirt, a tracksuit top, shorts and socks for the warm-up. You have to bear in mind there is a lot going on – the manager is talking, some players are finishing off their preparations, others might be having a little bit of treatment – and therefore nobody is really co-ordinating what happens next.

I threw my t-shirt into the washing skip – as per usual – and so in my position was the Holsten embroidered shirt and a plain shirt underneath it. As we prepared to go out, the lads were putting on whichever shirt they didn't warm up in. But nobody picked up there were different shirts being used because everyone immediately put on a tracksuit top to cover it up. So, by the time we went into the tunnel, nobody could see it.

We walked out to the deafening Wembley roar, went through the pre-match formalities and broke away to loosen up before kick-off. All 22 players spread out across the pitch and gradually began to take off their training kit.

We were just about to kick-off when I noticed Glenn Hoddle wearing a blank shirt.

'What about your Holsten?' I said to him.

'Clive, I've got a game to play,' he shot back. 'I don't think I should have a drink just now!'

It wasn't the players' responsibility to address the situation and nobody even mentioned it at half-time. During the interval in a cup final, you tend to be a bit preoccupied. We were leading and focused on encouraging each other to make sure we were in the right frame of mind for the second half.

To this day, I'm not sure why the situation wasn't properly managed but whatever the truth, senior kit-man Johnny Wallis paid the price in the fall-out by being relegated to working with the reserves as Roy Reyland took his position. Club secretary Peter Day lost his job altogether. Holsten could have been furious but they actually got some good publicity out of it, so much so we are still talking about it now.

The final is also remembered as one of the most entertaining ever but that is no consolation.

I set a new goalscoring record, scoring 49 goals in all compeititons, but I would have traded all 49 of them just to win something, even if from an individual point of view I didn't finish empty-handed.

✳

Midway through the season of my life, my relationship with Mum and Dad began to deteriorate, initially over something completely innocuous.

Each player at Tottenham received two season tickets and two more complimentary tickets to be distributed among family and friends. After we got married, I gave Lisa the season tickets because that was where all the wives sat with their parents or children.

I gave Dad the two complimentary seats. There wasn't that much of a difference – in fact, the seats weren't even very far apart inside the ground.

But we had a row about that. I don't think he was generally sensitive about things like this, he just believed in this instance that he was entitled to the better seats. He told me he felt the season tickets should have been his but I argued that during his playing days, he would have given them to his wife, just as I was now.

The littlest things sometimes have the biggest consequences. My stalemate with them should have ended around the time my goalscoring form put me in the mix for the Players' Player of the Year award, voted for by the Professional Footballers' Association.

But the situation had grown into something of a stand-off, made inadvertently worse by my uncle Brian – my Mum's sister's husband – speaking to the papers later that season. He claimed Dad wasn't getting tickets from me at all but that just wasn't true. I was annoyed and disappointed because Brian hadn't spoken to me about it before going public yet they had obviously consulted each other. I've never known whether my Dad knew what Brian was thinking because we've never discussed it.

I had no thought of ever winning individual awards. We played Norwich at home the day before the PFA awards evening in early April. I had the most dreadful game you can imagine.

Three of the ex-Spurs youngsters were at Norwich – Ian Culverhouse, Mark Bowen and Ian Crook. I had about three proper touches on the day but scored a hat-trick. After I knocked in the third, I walked back to the halfway line and Crooky turned to me. 'You're a lucky bastard,' he said. 'And you are going to win the PFA award tomorrow.' That was the first moment I even considered it.

'What do you mean?'

'All our lads have voted for you and you'll win it hands-down.'

Chris Waddle, Glenn Hoddle and a couple of Liverpool players were in the frame. I voted for Ian Rush.

The night itself was surreal. I'd been to the dinner as an 18-year-old, finishing third in the voting for Young Player of the Year. I was a little lost in reflecting how far I'd come when they read my name out as the winner of the main award.

I honestly don't think you appreciate the magnitude of it at the time. I didn't. It is only when I reflect back now that I realise how special it was to be voted the best player by your peers. They know what it takes more than anyone else.

I like to think I scored all different types of goals – with power, subtlety, dinked finishes – and I tried to be effective in all types of situations by being dedicated and focused.

I ended with 49 goals from 54 appearances. There were only two other Tottenham players who got into double figures that season: Chris Waddle and Nico Claesen, who both got 11. Glenn got eight, Steve Hodge had six to his name. But I never felt pressure to score. There were top players around me who could chip in. And I knew all along that chances would come my way.

Fifty had become a target to some extent because people started talking about it when I got close. I fell short but the record still stands today and I'm proud of that.

Harry Kane wasn't a million miles away in 2017/18, reaching 24 by Boxing Day of that season. If you are in the mid-20s by then, you have a chance. He finished with 41 but if anyone does it in the next few years, it'll be Harry. And if he manages to do so, he'll deserve it.

To win the Football Writers' Association award a few weeks later as well was amazing. That prize is judged by different criteria and so to win both meant I'd had a complete season in many ways.

The FWA judge you, in part, on the example you set as a professional and that means an awful lot because I always prided myself on that.

It was everything to be recognised in my own right for what I'd achieved. I was no longer just the 'Son of Les'.

But my Dad wasn't there on either night. These were probably the biggest moments of my professional life. It is difficult to talk about because you can't go back and relive it. He should have been there.

I didn't think about reaching out because we just weren't communicating during that period, as stupid as that was.

And yet, the biggest thing for me would have been some recognition from him. 'Well done.' That's all I wanted.

I went on holiday to reflect on a bittersweet season. Both trophies took pride of place in my study at home along with the golden boot. They are, to this day, my three prized possessions in professional terms.

But I would have traded everything to win the league. I wished I'd experienced winning the First Division title or a domestic cup.

Dad won the league, the FA Cup and the League Cup. I didn't. But he never won the PFA Player of the Year or the Football Writers' Award.

Fewer people have won what I have but that doesn't mean I wouldn't swap. Dad played in the best Tottenham team ever and I had to live with that. How could I emulate it? I didn't, because we didn't win anything, but then I won individual honours. Does that make me a 'never-was'?

Despite a great individual year, it triggered a familiar inner fear. Can I do it again? Would I ever be a winner? Is two FA Cup Finals in five years as good as it gets?

I didn't feel like a high-class goalscorer in my own right. I was still trying to prove myself. In what way, I don't know. I still didn't feel like I'd reached the next level.

Maybe that was to my detriment and I should have relaxed a bit more. It might have given me a bit more freedom.

However, whatever insecurities I had, I never thought the 1987/88 season would be my last at Tottenham.

CHAPTER NINE

England
– Taking Your Chances

IT WASN'T EXACTLY HOW I PICTURED ONE OF THE MOST SEMINAL moments of my life. I'd just meandered through a Queens Park Rangers reserve team match against Swansea in 1984.

The pitch was a bog. The game was an end-of-season irrelevance. I trudged off, covered head-to-toe in mud to be greeted by reserve team coach Theo Foley.

'Arnie Warren [the club's chief scout] rang during the game to say you and Simon Stainrod could be in the next England squad,' he said.

My eyes widened. I wiped a fleck of mud off my forehead.

'There have been a few withdrawals, a couple of injuries, and there is a chance you could be going.'

I couldn't believe what I was hearing. Playing for your country is the biggest accolade you can achieve as a footballer. I'd earned caps through the ranks – schoolboy, Under-18s, three appearances for the Under-21s – but now here was a shot at the big time.

Shortly after I got home, my inclusion was confirmed with a follow-up phone call and I was asked to report to Bisham Abbey where the senior squad were training.

My head was spinning. No matter how your career progresses – and I'd had three good years at QPR – you still always wonder if playing for England is something that will ever happen.

But here I was, invited on merit to train with the country's finest just days after thinking my season would end in the mud-bath of Swansea's old Vetch Field stadium.

I was very conscious of the company I would suddenly be keeping. The games were friendlies but prestigious nevertheless: an end of season trip to South America, comprising matches against Brazil, Uruguay and Chile.

It was an experimental squad with manager Bobby Robson looking to assess his options ahead of World Cup qualifiers beginning later in the year but there were still several senior figures including Peter Shilton, Bryan Robson and Ray Wilkins.

I was 23 years old and about to join up with the best group of players I'd ever seen assembled first-hand. I had to trust in my own ability and give it everything I had.

At the end of the first session, there was extra shooting practice. This was an opportunity to showcase why I'd been included.

And I have to say, what followed was probably the best session I've ever had in my life. Wherever I planned to put the ball, it followed that trajectory like I'd fired it out of a cannon. Chris Woods was in goal and he started goading me to find one corner or the other on command. And I did, time after time. Bobby was watching on and at the end he simply said: 'Quality finishing, son.'

I'd heard Bobby was always sparing with his words of praise so to receive that after my first proper test meant a lot.

It was one of those days you can only dream of in terms of trying to make an impression. Playing like that helped the group to accept me. Ray was brilliant in helping me settle. I don't know why but I had a rapport with him, dating back to a day when I came on against Chelsea for QPR at Loftus Road and Ray, who was a young captain at the time, tapped me on the back and wished me good luck. He was great at involving everyone on the trip.

Nobody gave us a chance in South America. England had failed to qualify for the 1984 European Championships and Bobby was facing fierce criticism. During a 2-0 defeat against the Soviet Union at Wembley on 2 June – just a few days before we were due to depart for Brazil – home fans abused and spat at him. We were painted in the press as lambs to the slaughter but I think that helped bind us together.

I didn't care. I was so excited to earn my first cap. People always ask me which game it was and what happened. My answer is always the same: 'John Barnes.'

Everyone remembers John's goal in the Maracanã against Brazil; it was a match staged to celebrate 75 years of the Brazilian FA but for all the flair and skill they had given world in that time, it was a Kingston-born, London-raised Englishman who produced a stunning moment befitting of the occasion.

I had one of the best seats in the house on the substitutes' bench. Just before half-time, he picked the ball up midway inside Brazil's half on our left. And he just started running. And running. And running. He jinked through the heart of Brazil's defence and rolled the ball past goalkeeper Roberto Costa into the net. It was a work of art.

As the game ticked into the final quarter, Bobby gave me the nod. Mark Hateley had added a second not long before so we were 2-0 up, well on the way to the most improbable, unforeseen result. I was so pumped up. This was what I had been waiting for and the nervous energy almost overwhelmed me on the touchline. I kept looking around and thinking: 'What a place to win your first cap.'

After 76 minutes, I came on for Tony Woodcock. Brazil were probing for a way back into the game but suddenly we broke at pace. England captain Bryan Robson found himself clean through, one-on-one with the goalkeeper. I sprinted to catch him up. I was unmarked and still hadn't touched the ball. A thought raced through my mind: not only could I score the third goal in one of the most famous England victories for years, but it could happen with my first touch. How many players have scored with their very first touch for England? *Against Brazil.*

This would be a tap-in. I couldn't miss. I shouted for the ball. The skipper decided to shoot and hit the side-netting.

'Unlucky, skip,' I shouted over as we ran back up the pitch. It remains a vivid memory to this day. Things could have been so different if I'd scored then. Some goals set players on very different paths and that could have helped establish my reputation at international level. If my first touch is 3-0 against Brazil, who knows what might have happened?

The collective experience was still a privilege to be a part of, however. The Maracanã is always an iconic arena, even in its dilapidated state back then. The stands were almost falling down and the pitch was one of the worst I'd ever played on but it still retained an aura given the history that had been written there.

The dressing rooms were in the bowel of the stadium, more like dungeons.

Bobby addressed us all at full-time, making a Churchillean speech about the impact this result would have on the country. We were the first England team to beat Brazil in their own backyard. Productivity would be up in the offices and factories back home. The magnitude of what we had done really resonated with the group. I could only imagine how that feeling intensified during a tournament.

The whole experience was something I struggle to put into words, even now. In playing for England, I'd achieved something very few people had done. Nobody in my family had ever managed it.

I don't remember speaking to Dad after my call-up or my debut. I'm sure he was happy, he just had difficulty expressing it. This was the essence of the relationship we had. He gave me the drive and determination but achievements like this were not considered moments to savour. They were stepping stones on a never-ending climb.

It was a massive moment in terms of becoming my own man. Playing for England validates the journey you've taken to that point, a chance to look back down the mountain at the uphill struggle and the obstacles you had to overcome.

But in the whirlwind of three games in eight days, there wasn't much time to dwell. I started the second match against Uruguay. It was very tough. The surface wasn't the best once again and I was absolutely desperate to impress. Mark Hateley played up front alongside me and we had never been paired together before. It was difficult to strike up an immediate understanding in that environment.

Luis Acosta's seventh-minute penalty put us on the back foot early on and they doubled their advantage when Wilmar Cabrera scored with 69 minutes played. I was taken off six minutes later. I had a couple of half chances and did okay without having a great game.

The step up in class in both games was obvious in terms of the defenders I faced. Physically, the challenge was a lot harder and their technical ability was impressive throughout the starting line-ups.

I realised movements and runs that might have been effective for me at QPR were not going to be enough at this level. Space was harder to find, chances in shorter supply. It became clear I wasn't as good as I thought I was. I had to take the performances I had produced in earning this opportunity up higher once again.

Our third and final game of the tour against Chile was in doubt virtually until kick-off. The team was under pressure to boycott the fixture on the basis it was due to take place at the Estádio Nacional in Santiago, the site of terrible atrocities in 1973.

For almost two months after the military coup that overthrew Chile's democratically elected president, the stadium was used as a makeshift prison camp. Nobody knows exactly how many people died there but official records state 41 lives were taken while estimates claim as many as 20,000 people were tortured in the stadium by a military junta led by General Augusto Pinochet.

The stadium had become a symbol of Pinochet's brutal regime and as a result players were receiving letters telling them not to take part in the game. Talks were held on a political level about the pros and cons of fulfilling the fixture.

Chile stuck me as a beautiful country but one on permanent edge as a result of military rule. I have to confess I didn't really have any moral qualms about playing in the game, chiefly because I didn't really understand it all at the time. That was naivety on my part. I just saw it as a chance to play for my country. I was young, focused on my football and relishing the challenge of representing England. It was wrong but I didn't think at the time it was my place to pass judgement on the games England should or should not play. I'm sure if I had been more experienced at that level and a bit older, I would have reacted differently but I'd only been in the squad for a few days. There wasn't a discussion about it within the squad either from what I can remember.

Despite widespread concerns, the game went ahead. I played the full 90 minutes. It was a strange occasion. The stadium was eerie, haunted by that distressing past not of its own making. There were a few rows of wooden seats behind one goal reserved in perpetuity for those who died.

The game finished 0-0, very little happened and the less said about it, the better. I came back from that tour immensely proud at breaking through into international football but also knowing I hadn't done myself justice. It was early days, though.

That summer I moved from QPR to Tottenham. Breaking through with England only opened my eyes to the next level I wanted to reach in club football. I started the season well at Spurs and expected a call-up – if not necessarily to play – but missed out on the squad which beat East Germany 1-0 in September 1984.

That rejection was compounded by not being selected for the 5-0 win over Finland a month later and then my injury problems began at Spurs. It would be almost three years before I played for England again.

The 1986 World Cup came and went. Things conspired against me having a consistent run of opportunities to play, not least Gary Lineker winning the Golden Boot at that tournament with six goals in five games and establishing himself as one of the best strikers around.

Gary and Peter Beardsley had become Bobby's clear first-choice pairing. With Mark Hateley also in the mix, I felt there was no chance of dislodging either of them permanently unless they got injured or a new of manager saw things differently.

At the back of my mind throughout the 1986/87 campaign was an England recall. It helped drive my mentality of scoring in every game. If I kept delivering, how could Bobby Robson leave me out?

And yet England played Sweden in September, Northern Ireland in October and Yugoslavia in November but the phone never rang.

Finally, in February 1987, I'd done enough to earn a recall. A hat-trick against West Ham at the beginning of the month had taken my Tottenham tally to 33 for the season and Bobby brought me back into the fold for a friendly against Spain in the Bernabéu Stadium. He never explained why I'd been left out but that was in the past now anyway – here was a chance to stake a claim.

The pitch was dreadful following prolonged rain – something which affected the attendance as only around 35,000 turned out to watch. I didn't care though – it could have been against anyone in front of any amount of people as far as I was concerned. I was itching to get a chance.

Bobby named me on the substitutes bench as he favoured a very strong team including Terry Butcher, Viv Anderson, Bryan Robson, Glenn Hoddle and Chris Waddle, with Beardsley and Lineker in attack.

Things started badly. Spain right-back Chendo broke forward and pulled a cross back from the byline for Emilio Butragueño, who fired a shot low past Peter Shilton to put the home side in front after 14 minutes.

But what followed was one of the most remarkable displays of finishing you could ever wish to see. The catalyst came with 23 minutes on the clock. Robson hit the post, Hoddle had a shot saved by Spain goalkeeper Andoni Zubizarreta but turned the rebound into a looping cross to the far post. Lineker nodded England level.

Four minutes later, he put us in front. Anderson won a header in the box and found Gary, who drilled a low shot first-time past Spain's number one. Almost immediately after half-time, he was at it again, converting from inside the six-yard box after Zubizarreta could only push Beardsley's shot high into the air.

It got even better and his fourth was the best of the lot, collecting Beardsley's pass into the box before shooting low, left-footed with unerring accuracy. Spain got a late consolation goal but it didn't matter. Gary's four-goal blitz in 34 minutes had done the business.

He took his overall tally to 18 goals in his first 21 internationals, a rate matched only by Jimmy Greaves and Nat Lofthouse.

I sat on the bench watching this incredible feat – desperate to impress after spending forever in the wilderness – but was left thinking: 'I'm never going to get the opportunity now'.

I'm not knocking Gary for that. He took his chances throughout his career and never looked back, which is precisely what you have to do.

But I knew in that moment, sat in the rain and in the form of my life, that the England career I wanted would never happen. I had a bucket-load of goals for Tottenham but was still sat on the bench watching Gary score four against Spain. In Spain. How was I ever going to get in front of him? That thought didn't depress me, though. That's football. That's life. And it wasn't going to deter my from trying.

My Tottenham form kept me in the picture, however, and I earned a fourth cap in April 1987 against Turkey at the Atatürk Stadium in Izmir, a Euro 1988 qualifier. Beardsley was not in the squad and I started with Gary in attack.

We were on top from the start but couldn't find a way through. A big chance came my way. I chested the ball down in the box and volleyed towards goal. It arrowed into the bottom corner. I thought I finally had my first England goal but as I turned to celebrate, I saw the linesman's flag go up. Guess who was offside? Gary Lineker. He was adjudged to be fractionally ahead of play as my shot travelled past him.

I couldn't believe it. Not long afterwards, with 17 minutes left, I was substituted and as I came off, I gestured furiously to Bobby, protesting that it was a goal. He consoled me and I didn't think anything more of it until the press interpreted it differently.

They claimed I was arguing with Bobby about being substituted. The journalists in attendance tried to destroy me that day.

I attempted to defuse the situation by speaking to reporters after the game but they ran with the story anyway.

Bobby was fine about it – which was the most important thing – but it taught me a harsh lesson about the spotlight on an England player. Everything is magnified and often taken out of context or misinterpreted altogether.

The bigger issue was that Turkey were whipping boys in Europe at the time yet we had failed to win and dropped two important points in qualification.

It would be 10 months before I played for England again. My fifth cap came in February 1988 against Israel when Gary was unavailable. I played alongside Peter, captain for the day, and lasted 68 minutes. The game finished 0-0 and if I'm honest, it was another poor performance from me. Another chance I missed.

It proved to be the last time I played for England. I was 26. If I had one regret, it was that I never went to a World Cup. The timing of those tournaments worked against me in terms of the peaks and troughs of my career. England had missed out on the 1984 European Championships, when I was in the picture for Bobby Robson. When they went to the 1986 World Cup I was still coming back from a bad injury. By the 1990 finals, I was struggling to get a regular starting place at Manchester City.

I never played for England at Wembley either. I was on the bench against Brazil once but didn't get on. It was a catalogue of events that had they transpired differently, my England career could have been much more fulfilling. I was also unlucky in many ways, not just in the timing of my career set against England's tournament appearances, but in coming up against Gary Lineker at a time when he was on his way to becoming England's second highest ever goalscorer.

Gary did brilliantly in his career with the ability he had. He was an amazing goalscorer who made the most of his talent. Unfortunately for me, we came along at the same time. We were both Number 9s but different types. I didn't have his pace, but I believe I had more variety in the type of goals I scored. Yet Gary hit the heights. He won a World Cup Golden Boot and went on to become England's second all-time top goalscorer behind Sir Bobby Charlton until Wayne Rooney surpassed them both in 2015.

I never formally retired from international football but by the time I joined Manchester City, commentators were describing me as 'former England striker Clive Allen'.

I respect what he did. I know how hard it is to seize the moment and deliver consistently, and playing two Number 9's together wasn't really ever a possibility. That was highlighted by Gary's partnership with Peter Beardsley, who was a deeper-lying, more creative forward.

Harry Kane is an example of someone doing it more recently. Whatever level you get to, you have to take your opportunity. And if you don't manage it, you don't take that step up. Every time Harry gets an opportunity, he takes it. He gets into Tottenham's Premier League team, he scores. They go into the Champions League, he scores. He makes his England debut, he scores.

I didn't do it with England, for whatever reason. I never scored a goal for England and felt I was better than five caps. I regret not taking the opportunity. Gary Lineker might have replaced me at Tottenham and kept me out of the England team for several years but I don't blame him at all.

People often said throughout my career that I had a good first touch. I only wish my first touch for England had been a goal in the Maracanã.

CHAPTER TEN

Bordeaux – Les Girondins De Bordeaux

HOW DO YOU REPRODUCE THE SEASON OF YOUR LIFE? THIS WAS THE question that plagued me all through the summer of 1987. In my heart of hearts, I knew I couldn't possibly do as well again.

The wider circumstances didn't help. Glenn Hoddle departed for Monaco after more than a decade running Tottenham's midfield. Early into the season, Ray Clemence had to retire after failing to recover from a damaged Achilles tendon and joined the coaching staff.

We actually started reasonably well, occupying second place in mid-September after five wins from our opening eight games, but manager David Pleat left the club a month later following non-football related newspaper allegations and three police cautions for kerb-crawling.

Things were changing fast. Trevor Hartley and Doug Livermore were put in temporary charge. They did the best they could but a permanent appointment dragged on for a month and the club felt like a rudderless ship.

Results suffered badly. Between 4 October and 19 December, we didn't win a single league game, losing seven in nine. I didn't score once during that period amid deeper concerns about where my future lay.

I'd been double Player of the Year in the previous season and had one of the most prolific campaigns any striker could wish for. Yet nobody spoke to me about a fresh contract offer despite entering the final 12 months of my existing four-year deal.

The silence was deafening. Any striker – almost no matter what the situation – would have been offered a new contract after the kind of season I'd had but for whatever reason, Spurs just didn't want to have the conversation. I never took it upon myself to demand a new deal. Maybe this was an instance where I would have benefitted from an agent to help achieve greater clarity.

My hopes were briefly raised when Terry Venables was eventually appointed as manager towards the end of November. I was excited about his arrival – someone who knew my game so well could help reignite my season and play to my strengths.

I scored in a 2-1 win at Derby just before Christmas to help end our dismal form and again on New Year's Day 1988 as we beat Watford by the same score, but still there was no indication the club wanted me to stay.

Belatedly, Terry called me in for a meeting early in 1988.

'What are you going to do?' he asked.

'Well, there's been no sign of a new deal here yet and so I think I want to play abroad.'

'In all honesty, I can't sit here and say "Don't do it, it is a waste of time." I have just come back from managing Barcelona and it was the most incredible experience. I would love to have done it as a player.'

'That's why I feel like I should go now,' I said. 'I don't want to regret it – I'll be 28 in May and this will probably be my last chance.'

'Okay, I understand,' said Terry. 'But we'd like to make you an offer to stay here.'

'I'm definitely willing to talk to you about it.'

My existing contract was way below the going rate at the time and to add insult to injury, after months of waiting, they finally offered me a deal which represented an increase of just £10,000-a-year. Tottenham chairman Irving Scholar dictated the terms but never even presented them to me directly. Terry looked embarrassed to make the offer on his behalf, not least because he said it was completely non-negotiable.

'Is that really as far as the club will go?' I asked.

'Yes,' came the curt reply.

'Okay, well in that case I want to explore what options are open to me.'

In hindsight, I believe that the club had wanted Terry to bring Gary Lineker with him and the wheels were in motion on that deal a long time before he eventually joined Spurs in 1989.

Terry had taken Gary to Barcelona from Everton in 1986 and was always keen on bringing him back to England. There were also possible financial reasons.

Newcastle midfielder Paul Gascoigne was emerging as one of the brightest talents in English football and Spurs were competing with Manchester United for his signature, a race they would win in the summer of 1988.

Spurs spent a total of £3.5m on Gascoigne and Paul Stewart from Manchester City. At the same time, work was being undertaken on renovating the South Stand at White Hart Lane – a stadium modification that ended up over-running into the start of the 1988/89 season – and as it turned out, six players left the club that summer, with my £700,000 fee being the highest.

Perhaps they also thought I wasn't capable of repeating the feat, that my 49-goal season was an outlier and not a sign I had become a better player. Maybe they felt I'd peaked.

Whatever the truth, I started looking elsewhere and the idea of playing abroad appealed to me.

I realised I needed help to explore those options and employed Dennis Roach, a prominent agent who represented Glenn Hoddle among a host of others, to speak to various clubs. My first choice was Italy. There was some speculation about Roma and also Bayer Leverkusen in Germany. But Italian football was in its pomp then and I would have loved the challenge of trying to score goals against the best defences in Europe.

I felt I had to play in continental competition to improve as a player and to give me the best chance of furthering my international career.

Dennis was scouring the market to raise interest but when Bordeaux entered the picture, they quickly became my preferred option.

Bordeaux's enthusiasm to sign me was in stark contrast to Spurs's attitude. They could have waited until I became a free agent in the summer but chose to move for me in the spring.

Although Spurs would have been due compensation via tribunal at the end of the season, the final figure would almost certainly have been lower than the £700,000 Bordeaux actually paid in a transfer fee.

Moreover, they offered me five times what Spurs had put on the table in wages. There was no negotiating but I did speak to a few people first. A journalist who had significant experience covering French football sold Bordeaux to me as the 'Liverpool of France' run by Claude Bez, an eccentric, outgoing man who had made his money running an accounting firm and bought the club in the late 1970s.

One of his first acts was to appoint Aimé Jacquet as manager. A highly-decorated player with Saint-Étienne, Jacquet transformed Bordeaux into a very successful team throughout the 1980s, winning three Ligue 1 titles and two French cups before I arrived. They had also competed in European competition every year since 1981, reaching the semi-finals of the European Cup in 1985 and the Cup Winners' Cup two years later.

Bez was able to secure low-interest loans and subsidies from the Mayor of Bordeaux, Jacques Chaban-Delmas, and investment from rich backers on top of negotiating unprecedented sponsorship deals and maximising television income. All of which made Bordeaux a powerhouse of French football, only really rivalled by Marseille.

Lisa and I were at a stage of our life where if we were ever going to take the plunge and go abroad, it had to be now.

Olly was 18 months old and we wanted to have more children. It wasn't going to be as easy to do later in life. We talked it over for a long time and came to the conclusion that if we didn't take it there was a chance we could sit together in years to come and wonder what the whole experience would have been like. That was the overriding factor. I wanted the challenge. New country, new experience, the whole thing.

We agreed the deal in March to give us as much time to prepare. I really wanted to start the 1988/89 season well. We moved into a house and I tried to pick up enough of the language to get by but Lisa was virtually fluent after three months. I had dressing room French, which basically meant I could swear a bit.

In later years when I was coaching at Spurs, the French boys – Younès Kaboul, Benoît Assou-Ekotto and Sébastien Bassong among them – would be in on the treatment tables chatting away in their own language while I was in the room. I could sort of understand what they were saying and eventually they realised I was getting the gist of it. Over time, their tone changed and I got a little bit more respect as a result. They became aware that I'd played out there and retained some French, which helped keep them onside.

Sometimes when I didn't understand what they were saying, I'd just smile and nod and they'd think I knew what they were on about. Things were very different in France. The players had to be in every day, there were often two or three sessions a day, warm downs after games – all things that we never really did in England at that time.

A typical week would involve a Saturday match, warm down on Sunday, two sessions on a Monday – one in the morning and the other in the afternoon. Tuesday, the same. Further sessions on Wednesday morning, Thursday morning. Friday, we would prepare for the game and then if we were at home on the Saturday, we would have a loosener in the morning and always head to a hotel before the game.

Back then in France there was more of an understanding in terms of the physiology of what you were capable of over one or two sessions. The biggest thing I found over there was the amount of running we did. You'd think it would be all technical. There were sessions purely like that, but a lot of it was what they called 'footing', or jogging. It wasn't explosive running but plodding, designed to increase stamina. I had the same playing weight – 12 stone – for ten years in England but quickly became a stone lighter at Bordeaux. Conditioning, blood tests, climate, diet and lifestyle – all of it was radically different in France.

I felt I was adjusting to the challenge pretty well. My teammates included Enzo Scifo – one of the most promising young Belgian players around, but had joined Bordeaux to revive his career after disappointing at Inter Milan – as well as Jean Tigana, the midfield general of the side, and Dominique Thomas, who signed around the same time as me from Lille. Our families quickly become friends.

Jean and Enzo didn't see eye-to-eye. Jean was the ultimate professional and a driving force in the dressing room. He would call players out if they weren't doing things right and Enzo was often on the receiving end. Enzo was much younger and very talented but Jean used to say 'he needs his own ball in matches'.

He just didn't play for the team. I'm not sure he even really wanted to be at Bordeaux and although he had plenty of ability, Enzo was much more difficult to play with than Glenn Hoddle, for example.

By contrast, Jean was fiercely competitive, playing a very simple but effective game and a natural leader.

Lisa was acclimatising well, her mood buoyed dramatically by falling pregnant with our second child. It was, all things told, a promising start.

Six weeks in, I walked into the dressing room at the end of a training session and Jacquet said: 'Clive, you must go to the president's house today at 5 o'clock.'

'Okay, fine, no problem.'

I turned to Tigana, our captain, who I sat next to in the dressing room.

'Jean, what's that about?'

He looked at me and laughed before saying just two words even I could understand.

'Au revoir.'

It took a few moments for that conclusion to sink in. I was one of the top-scorers at the beginning of the season having scored something like five in six games.

'What do you mean, Jean? This is crazy.'

'Au revoir,' he repeated, with a little more stoicism than before.

I met the president in his study. It was a beautiful, richly decorated room with a stunning, high-backed chair at one end where he sat, looming over me imposingly as my seat, no doubt deliberately, rested at a lower level. The subservience was inevitable.

'Clive, you are a great player,' he said.

'Thank you, Mr President.' I responded. This is going well.

'But you must go away.'

Oh. 'Sorry?'

'You must go away. Find yourself a new team.'

'I've only been here six weeks.'

'I know but it is not working. Find a new team – England, anywhere. It doesn't matter.'

'Mr President, I'm not going anywhere.'

I called my agent, Dennis, and he spoke with the club. They wanted to move me on but Dennis stalled for time. I was baffled but I reacted in the only way I could: knuckling down and dedicating myself to the club.

Illness complicated the situation. The night before a UEFA Cup away game against Újpest FC in Hungary, I felt terrible all through the night. I thought I had food poisoning and went to see the doctor. He stuck needles everywhere – and I mean everywhere – trying to find out what was wrong with me.

There was no firm diagnosis but I missed the game regardless. I felt awful.

I managed to get on the flight home and after further tests, I went back to London to have my appendix removed at the Princess Grace hospital in Marylebone, where I knew the surgeon.

Tottenham chairman Irving Scholar was visiting one of their players who was also in for surgery and he came to my room to say hello. It was the first time he'd seen me a stone lighter than when I was playing for Spurs in the previous season.

'My God, are you ill?' he asked. I didn't look great after having my appendix out but he couldn't believe how much I'd changed.

Things calmed down a little over the next few days once I returned to France. A couple of slightly edgy weeks passed while I recovered and then the rumours about Jesper Olsen started.

Jesper was a top player but it didn't quite work out for him at Manchester United. However, Claude saw Jesper as someone who could play to my strengths, mirroring my understanding with Chris Waddle at Tottenham.

'Chris regularly crossed the ball from the left for you to score,' he said to me. 'He can do that here for you.'

The logic really was that simple and Jesper duly joined the club. The fact Claude was seemingly shaping his transfer policy around me made me feel wanted again, yet in early 1989, I was told once again I had to go and see the president.

'Clive, it is all going well, but you must go away,' he said again. I told him I was staying put and, as before, he turned his attentions elsewhere. The turnover of players was unusually high but another deal was struck before the end of the season which suggested I was back in the good books.

Eric Cantona signed for Bordeaux. He was an 'enfant terrible', in disgrace with French football. He had started to develop a pretty hefty rap sheet, including an incident in which he punched his own goalkeeper at Auxerre in 1987, and in the following year he entered into an unbelievable row with France coach Henri Michel. Michel handed Eric his debut but after dropping him from the squad, he responded in what was rapidly becoming his own inimitable style.

Eric went on national television and called Michel a 'bag of shit'. He was banned from international football for a year and only returned to the France setup when Michel Platini took over as manager.

So, he was a strong personality even at a young age. He played just behind me in a number 10 role and I enjoyed it. You could see, even amid all the histrionics, that he had great talent. The president's basic football logic that apparently led him to sign Jesper – the thought that a creative player operating just behind me would help increase my effectiveness – also applied to Eric.

'He is like Glenn Hoddle – he can make a pass,' said Claude. 'He makes passes for you, you score.' It sounded simple enough.

Eric was only on a six-month loan from Marseille and it is fair to say he wasn't really focused on cutting out the controversy.

We were beaten in the Coupe de France by AS Beauvais – a second division team – and Eric missed in the most ridiculous circumstances during a penalty shoot-out. He chipped the ball, Panenka-style, towards goal but it didn't reach the line and the goalkeeper, who had dived the wrong way, had time to get up, shuffle back across and keep it out. He didn't play much after that.

I NEVER FELT COMFORTABLE THROUGHOUT THAT WHOLE SEASON. I did my best to focus but how could I be sure Claude wasn't about to try and ship me out again?

I sought comfort in family life. Lisa was now seven months pregnant. There had been a few early problems in the pregnancy which meant she had regular monthly scans in France but we had no major concerns.

However, at 37-and-a-half weeks, Lisa became alarmed that the baby hadn't moved for over 24 hours and so we went to see her consultant.

Various medical staff tried to identify the problem with a series of tests. The longer it went on, the more we started to fear it was something serious.

Eventually, after what seemed like an endless wait, the doctor entered the room with a pained expression on his face. He told us the baby had died. Lisa still had to go through the unimaginable horror of giving birth in such circumstances and they wouldn't allow me to be at her side.

Her strength in that moment was incredible. I did all I could to keep it together but she had to do that and more.

Lisa gave birth on Wednesday 3 May 1989. I can't describe the sense of loss and I'm not sure anyone ever completely gets over something like that. Lisa's bravery in going through that awful experience was remarkable. Her strength remains an example to all of us.

As we took the very first steps in that process, the way Bordeaux treated us was scandalous. I thought they were showing some compassion as the manager's wife, Madame Couecou, and another club official arrived to see Lisa in hospital and express their condolences.

Except what they actually did was quickly move on to asking Lisa to talk me into training on Friday and then playing a Ligue 1 game on Saturday. Imagine that. It was all they really cared about.

Lisa and Madame Couecou had become close acquaintances during our time in France but they came in on that pretence before cynically turning the conversation to their own ends.

Lisa said I had to make up my own mind if I felt able to. She never compromised my career in any way and felt there was enough of a support network around her to cope as both of our mothers had flown out to France to support us and help with Olly.

At that time, we were arranging to come home, to bring the baby back for his funeral but, with Lisa's blessing, I decided to go in. It wasn't easy but, at the same, to me it was the professional thing to do.

I trained on the Friday, going through the motions mentally but trying to push on. The club were fully aware of the plan for Lisa's mother, my mother, Lisa, Olly and the baby to fly back on Saturday at midday.

We had another discussion about the weekend and they wanted to know my availability for the match. There was a training session on Saturday morning before the game in the evening. Playing would mean flying back separately from Lisa.

I said: 'I'll train and play but I'd like to return to England late on Saturday night or Sunday because the funeral takes place very soon.'

The club agreed. Saturday morning came and my family went to catch their flight as I headed off to training. At the end of the session, Didier Couécou called me over for a word.

'You are not playing tonight,' he said.

I couldn't believe it. I checked my watch. The family had just taken off. I hadn't even seen them to the airport.

'What? That's why I'm here. I could have gone home.'

'Well, we just don't think you are in the right frame of mind.'

I lost it. I was furious they'd left me in this position. What was the point in staying to sit on the bench?

I walked out and got a plane back to London at 5 o'clock in the afternoon. I decided that was it, I was never going back. Lisa certainly didn't want to. She wanted to stay with her mother and in any case, the city was now linked with awful, raw memories.

I stayed in England with Lisa at her parents' house for four days. Dennis spoke to the club and then rang me.

'You've got to go back because if you don't, it'll be a breach of contract.'

I was trapped. I had to go back to France to move forward with our lives. Lisa stayed in London and I returned on my own. The time apart didn't help either of us but at least Lisa had her parents close at hand.

I spent nights alone grappling with losing the baby and how the club had treated me in the aftermath. I'd made it perfectly clear that I could play. They never questioned it at any point until deciding I wasn't ready. That's what really got to me.

Even with hindsight, I don't think they made the right call. They knew Lisa was gone and then they wanted to do that to me. I think they planned it. I can't prove it but when the president tries to sell you at least twice, why else would they keep me there in that horrible situation to then leave me out of the team? It was the final straw. They were forcing me out and that was it. I was done. But I had to go on my own terms.

The 1988/89 season ended and I gradually packed up our things to move back to England. We only had a two-week summer break before returning for pre-season, the start of what would have been my second year for the club.

We all arrived in the car park and the kit was laid out for us to get to work. There were 20 sets of training gear for 29 players. Couécou addressed the group.

'I'm going to read a list of names. Those selected, take your bags and go down into the dressing room.'

I was one of the nine left without any kit.

'Didier, what are we doing?'

'You see the hut on the other side of the training camp? You go there. You go away.'

'What about our kit?'

'Use last year's.'

'Okay, what do we do? What do you want us to work on?'

'Do what you want. We don't want you anymore.'

Some players got on with it and pushed themselves, others were quickly worn down.

I kept coming in for a few days, training in this diminishing, unwanted, uncontrolled group until there were three of us left. Players had gradually begun to sort themselves out with moves and Manchester City made contact for me. I met the club's representatives but, even though I just wanted to get out of there, we couldn't agree terms. I still had to make the right move. Ossie Ardiles was manager of Newcastle and was interested in taking me there. There were one or two other English clubs who were yet to reveal their hand so I opted to wait a little longer.

I went to see the president, this time in his office at the stunning Chateau which doubled as Bordeaux's training base.

'Why are you here? I thought you were going to Manchester,' he said. He hadn't become any friendlier.

'I can't agree a deal so I'm going to stay here.' I didn't mean it but I wanted him to see he couldn't just hound me out.

'Okay, Clive, come to the window. You see the driveway?'

'Yes.'

'And the gate at the end?'

'Yes.'

'There are *gendarmes* stationed the other side.' These were two armed guards responsible for the club's security.

'Yes.'

'If you drive out of the gate today, they will arrest you.'

'Why?'

'Because you are driving a club-owned car that is no longer yours. So, what are you going to do?'

I reached into my pocket, pulled out the car keys and placed them in his hand.

'There you go Mr President. I'll call my wife and she will pick me up.'

He paused and replied: 'Very clever, very clever.'

Dominique Thomas took me home. When they wanted you, nothing was too much trouble. When you were surplus to requirements, they made you feel worthless. The contrast was unbelievable.

City made a more amenable offer and I accepted. Looking back on it now, I regret not staying abroad but it was extremely difficult in the circumstances.

I don't think you ever fully cope with it. You just exist, adjust and try to come out the other side a stronger person, a stronger family. I don't know how we did it. I was of no use to the club and they didn't want to help. That was the ruthless side of the game to me. I felt totally helpless.

But I have a lot of fond memories from my time in Bordeaux as well. We both enjoyed the culture and lifestyle before suffering as we did.

The life experience was incredible, purely from a football point of view. I had a three-year contract but it turned out Bez's approach wasn't about getting the best players or creating a winning team. He was using the club for his own gain.

It wasn't until much later I found out he was syphoning money out of Bordeaux through their financial dealings. About six months after I left, an investigation team came over from Paris with information on all the transfers Bordeaux had conducted – my deal to Manchester City, Jesper's from Manchester United and numerous others.

And when the success of the 1980s completely dried up, culminating in the club's relegation from Ligue 1, the truth gradually emerged. Bordeaux initially admitted debts of FF10million in unpaid tax.

When Bez was forced to step down in 1991, the books revealed a debt of over FF240m. Bez was sentenced to three years in prison for fraud in 1995 having been involved in illegal payments made to members of his family after the club's headquarters underwent construction work during the 1980s.

It is not hard to believe he wanted to make me part of a list of players that were allegedly also bought and sold for personal financial gain. Maybe I was in the wrong place in the wrong time but how could the players know what was happening in the boardroom?

I don't feel any anger towards him, even now in hindsight. I still got a chance to play abroad. I don't regret going there.

Of course, I had no idea at the time but things never felt quite right at Bordeaux. You get that feeling very quickly whether it is going to work out or not – the way you feel around the group of players, the type of footballer you are and whether that is a good fit for the club's style.

I ended my only full season with 13 goals from 19 league games but the team finished in mid-table. That was in no small part due to Jacquet's strange philosophy. He prioritised keeping clean sheets in order to win matches. That defensive mentality – which went into overdrive away from home – didn't suit many of the players we had.

A lot of opposing teams also employed man-to-man marking and that was very frustrating for me. In that situation, the key is moving the ball with a fast tempo and giving players on the ball multiple options.

Often I played up front on my own, which of course I did in my best season at Tottenham, but Bordeaux didn't have the same individual quality that Spurs did.

We got the ball forward quickly at Spurs but Bordeaux played a possession-based game which was very slow at times. And given Jacquet's approach was to avoid over-committing players in attack, it was tough as a striker to always be effective. That change was a real education.

More players should go abroad – and the youngsters like Reiss Nelson and Jadon Sancho who have recently gone to the Bundesliga will benefit from the experience – but the financial rewards on offer in England now make it so much more attractive to stay in the Premier League.

For the top players, the best option is England unless Barcelona or Real Madrid come in for you. That's why there are so many foreign players here. If you are a top player of any nationality, you want to be in England.

The experience I had abroad was incomplete. I could have taken my money at Bordeaux and sat in the stands but it wasn't me. And the family situation made returning home the right move at the time.

We all needed a period of stability. Olly would soon be starting school and Manchester City was a big club offering a fresh challenge. I was hopeful things would settle down for a while. They didn't.

CHAPTER ELEVEN

Manchester City – Heading North

MY ONLY PREVIOUS EXPERIENCE OF MANCHESTER LIFE PRIOR TO 1989 wasn't a happy one. Aged just 14, I had gone back to my hotel after finishing a trial at Maine Road when I bumped into goalkeeper Iain Hesford.

We decided to go out for some fish and chips but as soon as the local lads heard my London accent in the shop, they chased us both all the way back to the hotel.

I had no desire to go back for a long time. In fact, that incident influenced my thinking when City offered me terms to sign two years later. I rejected them, Tottenham and Ipswich to join Queen's Park Rangers.

The fact I'd had experience of City as a kid, though, meant I had some idea of the club I was walking into up there.

City had paid £700,000 but I didn't feel like I had a point to prove. I had scored goals at Bordeaux and the way that period of my life unravelled was not a reflection on my ability or attitude.

A little bit like when starting out at QPR, I felt at home straight away. They had several staff who had been there for a number of years which created a friendly environment – chief scout Ken Barnes, who spotted me years earlier for that trial was still around, as was the physio Roy Bailey. The atmosphere, the welcome – everything about it was good.

On the day I signed, I was in the Maine Road car park about to leave when

I bumped into Colin Hendry, who had also joined the club at the same time from Blackburn Rovers.

Colin was walking across with his agent Paul Stretford, who later became best known for representing Wayne Rooney.

'Hi Colin,' I said, shaking his hand. 'I just wanted to say I'm looking forward to playing with you.'

Colin thanked me and returned the sentiment before Stretford piped up. His first words to me were: 'You'll be one of mine next.'

I'll never forget that. Colin introduced me to him and we had a chat. I never had any dealings with him but his confidence struck me at the time as reflective of how agents were beginning to grow in influence, even back then. It also showed my reputation hadn't suffered from a mixed year abroad.

Although I didn't experience everything I wanted to in France, I was quite comfortable with the fact I had at least tried it for a year with the good and bad I'd been through. The lads and staff at City asked a lot of questions about the lifestyle and training methods. I'd go into detail about the different demands they placed on players.

'Oh, that's interesting,' the coaches would say, without ever really thinking about implementing any of it. 'That's the way they do it there but this is the way we do it here.'

It was a far more traditional pre-season at City and I put a stone back on before a ball was kicked in August. It wasn't a conscious decision but just a consequence of the routine we were in at home and City's training plan.

The manager was Mel Machin. City were back in the top flight after earning promotion from the Second Division, two years on from relegation in 1987. They had done it on a shoestring budget – surviving a wobble in their final few games to go up with a draw at Bradford City on the final day – but had several talented young players coming through including Andy Hinchcliffe, David White, Paul Lake, Steve Redmond and Ian Brightwell.

Mel thought my experience as an older head coming into the group would help them along. Colin and Gary Megson, who helped City gain promotion, were also there in the same capacity.

We trained at Platt Lane – very close to Maine Road – and shortly afterwards at the university grounds. Both had basic facilities. We had a lot of pitches available and changing rooms but not much else. There was no canteen, no food, no gymnasium either. You'd do the session, shower and leave. Some of the lads went and got fast food. I went home. Although it was quite a change from the chateau and facilities at Bordeaux, this was typical of English clubs at the time. It was alarmingly basic by modern standards but City was no better or worse than QPR, Tottenham or anywhere else I'd played domestically back then.

Everything was monitored in France. We'd all eat together and it would be a controlled diet. There were hydro-pools for use after training, physios and masseurs always on hand.

We were staying at Mottram Hall Hotel near Prestbury to start with. Lisa was obviously there and Olly was less than three years old so I always went home. Although my salary was considerably lower than in France, we were out of the hotel within ten weeks as we wanted our own home which we found in Wilmslow. So my routine was always to go in, do the work and go home. It was pretty primitive. City were way off the pace back then.

A lot of the lads were more than ten years younger than me and a close-knit group. They had come through the academy together and went off afterwards to do their own thing, not in an unfriendly way – it was just a generational divide as much as anything else.

On the pitch, the first few months were difficult. We were under pressure almost straight away because we started the season poorly. I had a few minor injury problems and wasn't playing all that regularly.

The team was struggling to find its identity in the harsher environment of top level football.

Yet out of nowhere came one of the magical matches they still talk about in the blue half of Manchester to this day: 23 September 1989 – Manchester City 5-1 Manchester United.

Alex Ferguson brought an expensively assembled squad – including Gary Pallister, Britain's most expensive player at the time costing £2.3million – to Maine Road as favourites but left in complete embarrassment. Fergie later said he went straight to bed once he got home and described it as the worst defeat of his career.

City hadn't won a derby since 1981. There was an inferiority complex, the by-product of City's recent relegation and United's lavish spending under Ferguson.

I was injured that day and Mel allowed me to go to my sister-in-law's wedding. One of the other guests had a radio and told me at full-time what happened. It was quite unbelievable that City won in the way they did, racing into a 3-0 lead at half-time before Mark Hughes scored for United shortly after the restart.

Any suggestion of a comeback was flattened as David Oldfield and Hinchcliffe scored to ensure United got a battering. It was an astonishing scoreline, all the more impressive given there were six young local lads populating the team.

United were so powerful at the time with City firmly in their shadow and for a lot of the younger players, it gave them self-belief that they could become established stars. Redmond, Brightwell, White, Hinchcliffe – they had a lot to offer.

Paul in particular would have had an outstanding career had he not suffered a knee injury against Aston Villa which would hamper him for years. My son Olly was City's mascot that night and I remember how innocuous the incident was: he just jumped for the ball and collapsed in a heap.

It was a savagely cruel moment for him. The group were comparable to Crystal Palace's 'team of the Eighties' in the sense of they had a similar level of ability and came through en masse together, something which is quite rare in football.

They probably didn't take City to the level everybody hoped. What I found at Palace was as soon as there was a little bit of adversity, sometimes a homegrown group can struggle to deal with it, especially if everything has been on an upward curve to that point. Addressing those problems and moving forward is very difficult to do and City fell short in that regard.

Results like that one against United usually give managers time but if anything it raised expectations that we already weren't reaching. Ferguson came under pressure from fans and media alike but Mel was feeling the heat too.

I scored three goals in as many games across the end of October and the beginning of November but it wasn't enough to steer us away from a relegation fight. Two league wins in two months left us bottom of the table and chairman Peter Swales couldn't wait any longer. Mel was sacked on 26 November.

The man who had brought me back to England had departed within four months. Some people found Mel to be aloof but I struck up a good relationship with him pretty quickly. He valued my experience and as a result we talked a lot about how I saw the game.

Uncertainty had quickly returned. Lisa was enjoying Manchester and our new home and Olly had started at a local preparatory, The Ryleys School in Alderley Edge. Life was better as we put the worst of what happened in Bordeaux behind us, but a new manager can change everything.

It could have made my head spin if I'd had a more sheltered career, but by then I knew this was just football. You have to concentrate on what you are doing.

Rumours persisted that Joe Royle would replace Mel but he decided to stay at Oldham and within a few days Howard Kendall came in, boasting a fantastic reputation. By the age of 40 Howard had managed Everton to two league titles, an FA Cup and a European Cup Winners' Cup. Even today he remains the most successful English manager of the last 35 years. He had left Goodison to manage Athletic Bilbao in 1987 and his return to England with City was considered a coup.

Howard addressed the players briefly for an away game at Southampton – a match for which Tony Book took charge of the team – and I didn't meet him properly until his first training session at the beginning of the following week. The strange thing was he joined in, which he subsequently did most days. You could see he had been a player. He had a love for the game, wanted to be involved and one of his great strengths was creating a positive atmosphere among the group.

It didn't take him long to completely reshape the squad. His first day was in early December but before the end of 1989, seven players left the club including Gary Fleming, Oldfield, Hinchcliffe, Trevor Morley and Ian Bishop.

In came five players who Howard had managed at Everton: Peter Reid from Queens Park Rangers, Adrian Heath from Aston Villa, Wayne Clarke from Leicester, Mark Ward from West Ham and Alan Harper from Sheffield Wednesday. The dynamics of the group changed almost overnight. The Everton lads all had a way of working together and quickly became the nucleus of the team because of their understanding with Howard. It was difficult for the ones who'd been there a long time.

There was a drinking culture at the club which primarily centred around the Everton lads. They were all very close. We'd have lunch every Wednesday, which would descend into a bit of drinking session. I always felt Howard was looking at the players to see how we handled the drink, how we interacted with each other and that was difficult for me. He wouldn't allow players to leave at 3pm to pick the kids up from school or go back and see their families. That wasn't a problem for many of the younger players but I wanted to get away. Invariably, I'd get stick. 'Oh, the missus says you've got to go,' the players would say, cracking a fake whip.

Howard practically encouraged that kind of banter.

I never stayed and got drunk with them. It just didn't interest me. I didn't have a problem with it at all but I had other things to do. Whether that alienated me from the group, I don't know. At the time, I didn't feel like it did. The whole situation was probably harder for the kids trying to ingratiate themselves. I was older and more experienced and it didn't bother me to leave early.

But one incident definitely soured my relationship with Howard. He had settled on a partnership of Adrian and Wayne in attack, which restricted my time on the pitch.

I was frustrated. Trevor and Ian left to join West Ham in the same week and I saw that as an opportunity to see Howard. After all, I went to City to play every week and it quickly seemed as though part of his transfer strategy was to bring in players to replace or marginalise me.

'Look, if I'm not part of your plans and there is a chance of me being involved in a deal to go to West Ham, I would go,' I said.

He didn't like that. He interpreted it as me not wanting to be there but that wasn't the case. Coming back to London had its appeal, but while I was at City I wanted to play. We were happy in Manchester and had built a life there. To this day, we still have a lot of friends in that part of the country.

I feared the worst when Niall Quinn arrived for £800,000 from Arsenal in March 1990, shortly before the transfer deadline. Niall was, however, very complimentary about me when he came in.

'I think Clive is one of the best finishers in the last ten years in British football,' he said in a television interview just after signing. 'Usually, I look in envy from the other team and watch him score against us but it is nice to play with him.'

The feeling was mutual. 'To play with a big man like that who occupies defenders because he is a threat in the air is good for me because I feel I can exploit the spaces he creates,' I told the same programme. And I meant it.

Injury robbed me of the chance to play regularly with him but I still scored ten goals that season as we recovered to finish fourteenth in the table.

It only became clear to me that Howard had essentially black-marked me once he left to go back to Everton in November 1990. Reidy became player-manager and that was when things properly turned sour.

I knew very quickly that the boys he primarily trusted were those he'd played with before. I wouldn't say there was favouritism there but at that point in his career, he was a very inexperienced manager, still a player-manager, and he wanted people around him he knew well.

I was completely ostracised. A few weeks into Reidy's reign, an opportunity arose for me to go to Luton. I spoke to their manager David Pleat, someone I still had the utmost respect for and had got the best out of me in 1986/87, but I didn't feel the club was big enough for me at the time and wanted to wait for a better opportunity. David completely understood where I was coming from.

The next day, I went into training at City. Reidy called me over.

'What are you doing here?' he said, bluntly.

'I'm not going to Luton so I am here to train,' I replied.

'Well, you are not training with us. You can go and train with the kids.'

I was shocked but I didn't protest. And I did it right.

Lisa and I spoke about it and obviously I wasn't happy but there was no point crying or moaning. I had to make sure if I got an opportunity – be it with City or to move elsewhere – I would be in the physical shape necessary to capitalise on it.

Some people talk about a bullying culture in football. There were tough lessons to be learned but it was the making or breaking of you to deal with the way it was. I never felt I was bullied and the sort of experiences I encountered were not unique to me.

Initially, I took the challenge head on. But a week became two and soon a month had passed by. Then six weeks.

Motivating myself every day was tough but my upbringing came into play. Work hard and you win back the opportunity to make it right. That's what I kept telling myself.

Moreover, I had an insight into the way football clubs work from my Dad. We were on speaking terms now. Losing the baby in Bordeaux had, to some extent, brought us together again as a family, although infrequent squabbles persisted.

He would say to me: 'Look, the chairman won't be happy paying the transfer fee and the salary they are. They will be asking Reidy for answers.'

Reidy may well have been asking to bring another player in but the board would demand to know why I was there – not injured, but nowhere near the first-team. They may well have told him he had to ship one out before bringing a new player in – that is often the way it goes.

Yet nothing happened. Eight weeks. Then ten. I never saw Reidy or spoke to him once. For ten weeks. It just became a stand-off.

Fans would approach me in Manchester and ask why I wasn't playing. I never lied to them. I guess nowadays, a striker of my experience being left out for so long would be back-page news. I'm not comparing myself to Carlos Tevez but he was a City player who spent months out of the team in the 2011/12 season – albeit in his case going on strike – and it was one of the biggest stories in the Premier League.

There were bits and pieces on local radio and in the *Manchester Evening News*. I'd score in a reserve game and they might speculate on me coming back, but nothing major.

It got to the point where I didn't really think it would end.

Out of the blue, I got a call on a Friday night from Sam Ellis, Reidy's assistant.

'You need to be at Maine Road tomorrow morning for first-team training,' he said. 'We've got Notts County away on Sunday and you are involved.'

There was a flu epidemic in the squad – I don't know if, in addition, something had been said in the boardroom about why I was training with the reserves, on full pay, for so long – and suddenly I was brought in from the wilderness.

I turned up and ran out to a chorus of good-mannered abuse from the senior lads. Reidy emerged last, as he would in his player-manager role, to join us and the banter started.

'Who's this new signing, gaffer?' said one pointing in my direction. Gary Megson came up to me and introduced himself as if we'd never met before.

It was all a bit near the mark given the whole situation had been a real test of my character. This was the beginning of October 1991 and I hadn't actually played a first-team game since March. I'd had a few injuries at the end of the previous season which only made being frozen out under Reidy all the more difficult.

Sunday came and I was named on the bench at Meadow Lane. During the game, I went to warm up several times and deliberately ran towards the City supporters tucked away at one end of Meadow Lane. The fans were all going mad, shouting and waving, singing my name.

It wasn't something I'd ever done before but by now I really felt I did have a point to make. I'd become something of a forgotten man, an answer to a tough quiz question about yesterday's footballers.

The game was a typical, hard-fought affair. Dean Thomas put Notts County in front before Mike Sheron equalised. Thomas handled in the box to give City a penalty but goalkeeper Steve Cherry saved David White's spot-kick and we were locked at 1-1.

I came on with 20 minutes to go. With pretty much my first touch, Mike had set me up for a tap in but as I turned the ball goalwards, Thomas stopped it with his arm. While the referee was digging out his cards to send him off, I grabbed the ball.

As I turned around, Steve Redmond was walking up to take it. I put my hand up and said: 'It's alright, I'm taking this.'

This was it – a huge chance to make a positive impact again. I was so focused and I knew I'd score, but not everyone agreed. I felt eyes burning into the back of my neck. Sure enough, Reidy was stood right behind me, hands on hips giving me the deathliest stare you can imagine. I ignored him, ran up and sidefooted it to the goalkeeper's left. He went the right way but the ball had enough pace on it to find the corner.

I celebrated in front of the supporters. Reidy, in fairness, shook my hand and put an arm around me. I ran back to the touchline. There was more work to do.

A few minutes later, Craig Short made a mistake and gifted possession to David White by the corner flag. He ran infield and crossed towards me at the back post. I rocked back and hit a first-time volley with my right foot into the net. I immediately celebrated with the City supporters at that end of the ground, kissed the badge and did a reverse somersault, or as close to that as I could manage. Half a dozen players came to celebrate with me again. Reidy ruffled my hair and ran off.

'There's only one Clive Allen,' the City fans sang at full-time.

I went back into the dressing room and the lads congratulated me. Reidy never said a word. I knew at that moment he didn't want me at the club at all, regardless of my recall. I had put him in a difficult position because I'd scored twice to turn the game.

After a quick television interview, I went and spoke to the newspaper boys and, of course, the questions as to where I'd been started straight away.

'Have you been injured?'

'No.'

'Where you've been then?'

'I think you'd better ask the manager that. I've been training with the kids for the last ten weeks.'

I could have gone to the press during those ten weeks with the youth team. I didn't think that was the right thing to do but scoring twice on my comeback after so long out gave me the prerogative to speak my mind.

The press pack then got Reidy as he came out and put what I'd said to him. I was expecting a call that night but heard nothing.

The papers had a field day. Headlines ranged from 'Allen slams boss', to 'Reid and Sam Ellis are trying to ruin my career, blasts Clive Allen' to 'Reid v Allen: the bitter feud that is splitting a club'. One of them blew up a quote from Reidy in large print. It read: 'Clive is talking nonsense but I want to keep this just between us'.

At 8am on Monday morning, Reidy rang me and said: 'Get your arse to the ground, I want to see you now.'

I walked into his office and he had all the newspapers fanned out across his desk. 'What the fuck is this?' he said.

'It's the truth,' I replied. I turned to walk out and he came after me.

'Where are you going?'

'I'm going back to train with the kids at the other training ground.'

'No, you're not. Get yourself ready to train at Platt Lane because you are playing on Tuesday night.'

Tuesday came around and as I was warming up against Chester for the second leg of a League Cup tie, Reidy gave an interview to Granada's *Soccer Night* programme.

'We sorted a few things out and I think that's the best way to do it,' said Reidy. 'Anything that I say to any of my players is kept private between us. He's out on the pitch and hopefully he'll do the same job as he did on Sunday.

'Is it a truce or a stand-off? It is a football club. You have disagreements but you go out, you work your hardest for the club. I'm doing that and Clive's doing that.'

The reporter asked him: 'Does he have a part in your plans?'

'Certainly tonight and if he keeps scoring goals, who can keep him out?'

I did score with a right-foot volley as we won 3-0 on the night, 6-1 on aggregate. I was named man of the match and the City fans sang: 'Are you watching Peter Reid?'

'I've always wanted to stay at the club,' I told *Soccer Night* after the game. 'I want to play. I've played professional football now for many years and it is something I want to continue to do. There's no problems. That's history. I'd just like to get on and play football.'

Incidentally, that was the first time I met *Soccer Night* producer Mark Schofield, who was then working at Granada Television and very supportive of me. He would have a profound influence on my post-football career.

We were playing Tottenham on the following Saturday. I thought I was going to play after having a good week. But during a shooting session I always did at the end of training, I took a shot and felt a sharp pain which turned out to be a partial rupture of my Achilles, ruling me out for about six weeks. In that time, the club came to a decision that I couldn't stay. It had all got too much for them despite my promising comeback.

Reidy wanted me out and Chelsea showed an interest. The deal was agreed and I knew I was going back to London, which gave me a target to regain my fitness as soon as possible. We've had many conversations about it since – some of which came while researching this book – laughing and disagreeing as we looked back. Because of the type of careers we had, we see so much of the game in the same way. I like the way he calls things. He is a passionate football man and that has always come across when I've worked with him in media. But I didn't speak to him properly for years.

That's football. It is what happens. Reidy had to make decisions. I didn't agree with them but I understood the job he had to do.

He has said to me that in hindsight, had he been a more experienced manager, he might have handled it in a different way, which I suppose gives me a sense of closure, but nobody can give me back those ten weeks during the peak of my career.

Moving clubs again wasn't ideal but throughout my career I would go anywhere just to play. If I ever had the feeling I wasn't going to be a central part of the team, changing clubs felt like the right thing to do and it held no fear for me whatsoever. I didn't feel a sense of entitlement after having scored 49 goals at Tottenham or performed well in Bordeaux despite difficult circumstances. The drive to play and prove myself was always there and if I was denied that opportunity, it just wasn't the right club for me.

There was personal joy during my time at City, however. Our second child Ed was born on 26 May 1991. After our heartache in Bordeaux, now we had another beautiful baby boy to add to our happiness.

Once I was back in full training and the day before I was due to sign for Chelsea, we played Middlesbrough away in the FA Cup. Out of nowhere, he put me on the bench.

I was sitting there during the game thinking 'He knows I'm going to Chelsea tomorrow, there is no way he is going to use me.' There was quite a lot of talk about my move at the time. A few of the lads knew it was happening and they had no idea why I was in the squad either.

And then, suddenly, he put me on at 2-0 down. 'Go on and get me a goal,' he said. I ran on but couldn't understand it. I remember my first touch: I had a shot from the edge of the box – a half chance really – which hit the base of the post. I think to this day he thought I missed it on purpose. I could never be that precise if I tried.

The following morning, 5 January 1992, I signed for Chelsea. Within a month, I'd be facing Manchester City.

CHAPTER TWELVE

Chelsea – Capital Return

PRICE TAGS WERE NEVER A CONCERN OF MINE AFTER WHAT happened at Arsenal but Chelsea got me cheap at £250,000. I was the first £1million teenager and with all the press attention that brought, it drilled into me at a young age that I was a commodity.

My value was set by the people who were buying me. The same thinking meant I never felt uneasy about going to Chelsea, despite having spent four years at Tottenham.

My Dad played there before he went to Spurs and I always felt I'd do my job and be accepted for what I do. Besides, the opportunity to come back to London was hugely appealing and this felt like a massive chance to rejuvenate my career.

It justified everything I had done in terms of my approach to training with the kids at Manchester City. I knew I'd put the work in and was desperate to play.

Perhaps I was also a beneficiary of Chelsea's need to watch the purse strings – a far cry from the Roman Abramovich era that followed years later.

Ken Bates had bought Chelsea for £1 in 1982 but inherited debts of more than £2m. He was embroiled in a seemingly endless battle to own the Stamford Bridge freehold, which stayed in the hands of holding company SB Holdings after his takeover.

Bates had fought off various challenges to keep Chelsea afloat – racking up millions in legal fees along the way – and not owning their ground really held

Chelsea back from growing as a club.

They finished eleventh in the season before I joined in addition to reaching the semi-finals of the League Cup.

There was all sorts of speculation about Ken and his ownership but it didn't bother me because I was so keen to get back on the pitch. There were big personalities in that dressing room: Andy Townsend, Vinnie Jones, Paul Elliott, Dave Beasant, Steve Clarke, Dennis Wise, Kerry Dixon – a mainstay striker for so many years. It was a completely different dynamic to the one I'd faced at City.

I felt there was a respect from that group of players because of the career I'd had to that point. And, as I've been fortunate to experience before, I felt at home walking into Stamford Bridge.

It is possible that was because my Dad started his career there but whatever the reason, it felt right. I was being given another chance. I was really confident from day one, back in London and with a chance to kickstart things.

There had been a degree of turnover in the squad with Gordon Durie joining Tottenham for £2.2m, Tony Dorigo moving to Leeds for £1.3m, while Paul Elliott came in from Celtic for £1.4m, Tommy Boyd arrived from Motherwell for £800,000 and Joe Allon left Hartlepool to join the Blues for £200,000.

Bobby Campbell had also departed as manager after Ken had tried to move him upstairs to become general manager. He left the club following a falling out and Ken appointed Ian Porterfield, who had been Campbell's first-team coach.

They'd had a mixed bag of results by the time I came in for my debut in early December, a 3-0 defeat at Sheffield Wednesday.

I was confident I could hit the ground running because of all the work I'd put in at City, but the build-up to my first home game against Manchester United gave me a snapshot of what I'd walked into.

The routine was to eat at the stadium before going down into the dressing rooms around an hour before kick-off to begin preparations. I was changing next to Kerry Dixon and roughly 45 minutes ahead of walking out to play, the dressing room door bowled open and in walked Ken with his huge fur coat billowing along behind him.

'Right lads...' he said, addressing the group before Wisey interrupted immediately.

'What the fucking hell have you got on?' he said. I had to remind myself this was the club captain talking to the chairman.

'You are just a little shit,' Ken replied before adding: 'And I could still knock you out.'

Wisey's eyes widened at that comment. 'Come on then, old man!'

And they went for each other. Wisey threw Ken on the floor in the middle of the dressing room. Water bottles went flying and as some of the lads were pushed back, a scrap ensued.

I turned to Kerry. 'What the fuck is going on here? Do we break it up?'

'Oh, no,' Kerry replied. 'Every time he comes into the dressing room they have a wrestle or a fight.'

The rest of the players were egging them on but eventually one of the backroom staff got involved to break it up.

Ken reorganised himself and caught his breath but remained transfixed on Wisey.

'You are still a little shit,' he said, before turning to leave. 'And the rest of you… you'd better fucking win today.'

I'd never seen anything like it before. Chairmen often come into dressing rooms and address players. That's commonplace. But a pre-match scrap? Yet Ken loved it. He felt Wisey was showing him respect in, well, let's say a unique way. Ken just loved the banter.

We lost 3-1. Denis Irwin opened the scoring with a long-range free-kick before Brian McClair doubled their lead from close range. Steve Bruce scored a penalty to make it 3-0 before I managed to mark my debut with a goal.

Graeme Le Saux crossed in and I steered a header from in front of the near post into the net. I went to grab the ball and as Peter Schmeichel decided to hold onto it too long, I gave him a bit of a shove before turning to run back to the halfway line. He was an absolute beast, one of the best goalkeepers I faced.

Six days later, we played Oldham at home. Wisey put us in front with a penalty before he turned provider, rolling the ball into my path so I could finish high, first-time into the net. Paul Elliott got in on the act with a towering header either side of two goals for Ian Marshall. Graham Stuart then broke through their offside trap and squared a pass to me for a tap-in which I celebrated in the knowledge we'd finally won the game.

I felt like I'd started well – striking up a good understanding with Kerry in the process – and I believe it was just reward for reacting in the right way to being frozen out at City.

Halfway through December there was a Christmas party at Stamford Bridge which Lisa attended with me and Ken welcomed us to the club in his own inimitable way.

As we walked in, Ken stood greeting everyone, just behind a couple of directors who made the initial contact.

'Hi Ken,' I said, shaking hands. 'This is my wife Lisa.'

Without saying hello or anything, he took her hand and said: 'So that's where the fucking signing-on fee went then.'

Lisa didn't react beyond a half-smile, walked on a couple of paces and said to me: 'Who's that horrible, obnoxious man?'

'Oh, that's Mr Bates, the chairman.'

'Christ.'

He knew how to rub people up the wrong way but I always liked him. You knew where you stood. He was in a difficult position at Chelsea and that combative style was how he navigated a way through it.

We finished the year with successive 2-0 defeats at Notts County and Luton Town before Manchester City visited west London on New Year's Day 1992.

There was a bit of friction with City given what had happened in the previous season. I was desperate to do well.

With the score at 0-0, Dennis angled a forward pass to me and I let it bounce before hitting it first time with my left foot from the edge of the box. It wasn't the sweetest strike but it had enough accuracy to beat City goalkeeper Andy Dibble.

I'd now scored four goals in five games but that one meant the most. Mike Sheron equalised with about five minutes to go to draw 1-1. I was very fortunate that when I played against my old teams, I nearly always scored.

I always celebrated a goal. That was my job. I did it for the supporters of the team I was playing for. In more recent times, players refuse to celebrate against their old clubs and I just can't understand that.

Denis Law famously did it when scoring for City against United to help relegate them but that was a pretty extreme set of circumstances and lately it seems more players do it against their old clubs as if it's somehow respectful. It isn't. Your first thought should be for your current club and fans.

For Chelsea at the time, blowing the chance to win like that could have had a negative effect on us, but it marked the start of an unbeaten run in the league that wouldn't end until 29 February.

Ten days after the City game, we played Spurs, who had packed their defence under Peter Shreeves. We still caused them problems and I broke the deadlock with a pleasing finish from a difficult angle in off the crossbar. I had plenty of chances to add to that strike but, in the end, had to settle for an assist as Wisey secured a 2-0 win.

I got another goal in an FA Cup fourth round win over Everton – a volley to beat Neville Southall for a 1-0 victory – as Tony Cottee missed a late penalty to ensure Howard Kendall's side were out of the competition for another year.

Although we were knocked out of the ZDS Cup in the Southern Section semi-final to Southampton, I was enjoying my football. I scored for the third game in a row as we beat Wimbledon at Plough Lane on 18 January 1992 which put us eighth in the table but some way off the leaders, who at that time were Leeds United.

We beat Graeme Souness's Liverpool at Anfield, ending their own 13-match unbeaten run – Vinnie Jones scored the opening goal in a 2-1 win, firing a long-range volley in off the crossbar – and securing Chelsea's first win in the league there for 57 years with a 2-1 victory.

Yet I came crashing back to earth shortly afterwards. Ian Porterfield was looking for a big man up front and brought in Tony Cascarino in a straight swap deal for Tommy Boyd, worth £1m.

That deal came out of the blue. Andy Townsend was a big pal of Tony's, given they played for the Republic of Ireland together. To this day, I don't know if he'd spoken to the manager about him but it obviously made things more difficult for me.

I never felt like Chelsea would be a short-term option. I'd signed a three-year deal and was really thriving. I thought I'd be there for the duration of that contract given how well things had started.

I stayed in the team for Tony's debut against Crystal Palace where he made an immediate impact, scoring an equaliser three minutes from full-time in a 1-1 draw. But within two months I'd be gone.

We played Second Division Sunderland in the FA Cup quarter-final on 9 March. I opened the scoring with a close-range effort but we were unable to hang on as Sunderland struck late to force a replay.

The key falling out happened ahead of that second game. Ian left me out of the team, opting for Tony and Kerry in attack. He didn't tell us the line-up until an hour before kick-off, which wasn't the way he usually worked – we always knew the day before.

After falling 1-0 down, Dennis Wise looked like he'd got us into extra-time with a late goal but Gordon Armstrong produced a bullet header to cause an upset and trigger raucous scenes at Roker Park.

I was fuming, not just because we were out but because I'd been dropped. I sat there stewing on it for the five-hour coach journey back to Harlington and asked to speak to him when we arrived back at 3am.

'I'll see you here at 8am in my office if you want to talk to me,' he said. I got a few hours' kip and met him on time the following morning.

'Why did you leave me out?' I asked. 'I've been playing well, scoring regularly and felt I could contribute.'

'It was windy so I went with two big strikers.'

'What?'

'It was windy.' That was the explanation. I'd never been left out because of weather before. He may well have been thinking about defending set-pieces as much as attacking but whatever the rationale, it was a real body blow.

'You must be joking,' I said. He wasn't. We left on speaking terms but I couldn't fathom what he was on about. My cousin Martin had been in touch with me around the same time to say Billy Bonds was asking after me about a move to West Ham.

I called him the next day after my conversation with Ian.

'That's ridiculous,' said Martin. 'I'll have a word with Bill.'

It unravelled quite quickly at Chelsea. We lost 2-1 at home to Sheffield United and the club acted by agreeing a deal to sell me to West Ham for £250,000.

One disagreement with a manager doesn't have to lead to a transfer but the rumour at the time was that I was one of three deals – Jason Cundy to Tottenham on loan and Kevin Wilson to Notts County for £225,000 being the other two – that were supposedly key to Chelsea's future.

Bates had bought the club in 1982 but spent ten years trying to secure the Stamford Bridge freehold. He eventually bought the lease from the Royal Bank of Scotland with a 20-year option to purchase it in December 1992 but I was told that somewhere in the build-up to this, the money from my transfer was used to help secure Chelsea's financial situation – although that may just have been a rumour which became apocryphal over time.

As dramatic as it sounds, my transfer may have played a small part in the club surviving and if that's the case I'm glad some good came out of it for Chelsea.

I had no fear about moving again but I was genuinely devastated to be changing clubs in circumstances beyond my control.

Only now when I look back on it does it seem so crazy. But the early part of my career had taught me where players sat in football's food chain during the 1980s and early 1990s.

And this time, I don't think I would have been sold had Chelsea not been in significant financial trouble, even if Tony coming in had increased competition for places.

In any case, I chose to focus on the positives. I was happy to go to West Ham because I felt I was coming full circle.

Once Martin had alerted them to what was happening, West Ham agreed a fee and asked me if I wanted to speak to Billy Bonds. He was as honest as I could have hoped for. I wasn't bothered about going from a team chasing the top six to one fighting relegation. I've said it a thousand times before but it was still true: I just wanted to play.

Playing was my primary motivation over winning trophies. That was a product of having such a high turnover of clubs after leaving Tottenham.

I don't know if I could cope with the rotation policy in place at most big clubs these days. I needed the momentum and regularity of playing every week to be my most effective. Strikers need that more than any other position on the pitch because goalscoring is linked so closely with confidence. The support and security of a manager trusting a player – even if you have a lean spell – often yields a good goal return. The flip side is you start snatching at chances because there is too much riding on it for the team and you as an individual.

Martin being at West Ham was also an obvious pull. He gave me an insight into what was happening so there were no real surprises going in.

And it only helped give me a sense that in travelling from west London to east, I was going back to my roots.

CHAPTER THIRTEEN

West Ham – Into The Premier League

HARRY REDKNAPP, THE WEST HAM ASSISTANT MANAGER, CALLED me over for a quick word during my first training session as a West Ham player.

'How can you possibly be related to this guy?' he said, nodding in the direction of my cousin, Martin. 'He's fucking crazy. I've never seen two more different people in my life.'

Martin had earned the nickname 'Mad Dog' from Hammers midfielder Ian Bishop. During games, Martin's face would become so intense in his desire to win that he would froth at the mouth. Ian noticed it one match and told him to wipe his face.

'No, it's staying,' said Martin.

'You look like a mad dog,' said Ian. Martin smiled. And that was that. The name just stuck.

Martin was a combative player, an excellent professional and a good guy. It had been several years since I'd had the chance to play football alongside a family member, when Paul and I were at Spurs, and it softened the blow of leaving Chelsea.

I'd played with Martin very briefly at Queens Park Rangers when he came into the first-team squad, right at the beginning of his career as a 17-year-old.

We flew out to Jakarta to take on Feyenoord in a friendly and Martin had to mark Johan Cruyff, who was playing one of the final games of his career.

I remember one or two of the lads telling Martin to kick him, but he couldn't get close enough even to do that. Cruyff was on a [...]

inside and out. He was phenomenal, even with a [...]

towards the end of his playing days.

Martin and I used to call each other 'cuz' on the [...]

played against each other, I like to think he had my bac[...]

Before a game in 1987 between my Spurs team an[...]

Hart Lane, we were waiting in the tunnel to walk out. I[...]

line-up with Martin at the back. It didn't stop him shou...ng over a sea of bodies in my direction.

I didn't want to engage with him that close to kick-off to be honest but he kept at it. Eventually I turned around. He pointed to Gavin Maguire and said: 'This guy's fucking mad.'

I didn't reply and turned back around to walk out. During the game, Maguire launched into a tackle on Spurs defender Danny Thomas that caused him a knee injury so severe it ended his career. He was later taken to court and ended up paying £130,000 in a settlement.

I don't know to this day whether Martin was trying to intimidate me. But maybe, in his own way, he was trying to warn me. I like to think so.

Regardless, I particularly valued being around Martin at West Ham because my relationship with Mum and Dad was still fractious.

I believed to some extent I had become my own man and joining West Ham added to that feeling because it meant I was no longer at a club where Dad had played.

He'd had trials at West Ham when he was 15 but wasn't taken on. The same thing happened to me at the time my cousin Paul was coming through the youth ranks. A lot my family are lifelong supporters too but for whatever reason, that call never came in my youth. But I was ready to answer it now.

They were, however, at risk of going down. I had to wait for my debut because of a two-game suspension carried over from Chelsea.

Ironically, that meant my first appearance came against the Blues at Stamford Bridge and I scored – having got a good reception from the home fans – but we lost the game 2-1. Within 16 days, we'd been beaten three more times and relegation was confirmed.

But contrary to what you might think, the whole atmosphere at the club changed for the better.

turned towards going back up next season and so all the immediate was off. It showed in the results. In the very next game, we beat ∪hester United 1-0 at Upton Park in a huge blow to their title hopes. Sir Alex ∫erguson moaned about what he called the 'obscene' effort of our players but what he saw wasn't work-rate, it was liberation. Kenny Brown scored the only goal as United ended up four points behind champions Leeds with a loss to Liverpool on the final day.

We ended our season by beating Nottingham Forest 3-0 thanks to a Frank McAvennie hat-trick.

Frank left for Aston Villa that summer. Ahead of my first full season at West Ham, all Martin said to me was: 'You'll need your running shoes for pre-season. We'll be running endlessly at Hainault Forest, doing the same pre-season they've done at West Ham for 25 years.

'Ronnie Boyce has his book. It's all mapped out. It'll never, ever change.'

It was tradition – and very basic – but I have to say I loved it. Good, old-fashioned graft.

We watched from the outside as the first season of the Premier League kicked into gear. It was pretty clear nothing had changed – it was the same football, the same players, the same First Division, just with a new name.

Nobody could have foreseen how a simple rebranding – as effective and innovative as it was – could ever transform English football in the way it did.

This was the first time I played in a country's second tier for ten years. I wouldn't say it was any easier back then, but the gap between English football's top two divisions was nowhere near as big as it is now.

Mike Small also left which meant I played up front with Trevor Morley. I'd played with bigger centre-forwards but Trevor was still a good target man and we'd struck up an understanding in training which was promising for the campaign ahead.

We were one of the favourites for the title along with Newcastle United and Portsmouth, despite losing Stuart Slater to Celtic for £1.5m, replacing him with Mark Robson on a free transfer.

No matter the objective, there was still a determination to play good football – the West Ham way – and it brought us the right result more often than not.

I scored the only goal in our opening game of the season – a 1-0 win at Barnsley

– and although we lost the next two games, we won six and drew two of the following eight including big victories over Bristol City (5-1), Sunderland (6-0) and Bristol Rovers (4-0).

Robson was being hailed by some sections of the press as the signing of the season as we started well, ending September in fourth place behind Newcastle, Charlton and Wolves. Nobody could match Newcastle, however, who won their first eight games and had established themselves as the team to catch.

By November, we'd risen to third but Newcastle's lead at the top over Tranmere had extended to 12 points.

Attendances had dropped off somewhat compared to the previous season because of the club's decision to pursue a bond scheme which caused plenty of unrest among supporters. Combined with disciplinary issues involving Martin and Julian Dicks, we weren't without criticism, but the team was playing pretty well and I always felt we'd win people over if we continued to play the right way.

In fairness, the fans were more upset at the club than the players themselves; they'd been asked to buy bonds in three price bands – £500, £750 and £950 – with ownership giving them the right to buy a matchday ticket or season ticket for a designated seat for up to 150 years. It was reported that only 808 fans eventually took it up before the club reversed the decision – meaning purchasing a bond was no longer required to buy a season ticket – in the wake of a series of protests.

Trevor and I had 12 goals each by early December. Our partnership was flourishing and I was enjoying life at the club, with the Anglo-Italian Cup – a competition that second tier English and Italian teams played in that replaced the Full Members' Cup – providing a great opportunity to play in Europe.

It was good to play any form of European football. The Italian sides gave us healthy competition and because English clubs had missed out on European ties in the second half of the 1980s due to Heysel, there was a real appetite to travel and play these games.

That said, the game against Cosenza on 9 December should never have gone ahead. The pitch was a lake. Many of the players – myself included – voiced their concerns and Bill was happy to fly home and let the Italians have the points but they insisted on playing it.

And, ironically, I scored my best goal by a million miles for West Ham that night.

You had to keep the ball off the floor due to the farcical conditions and that was probably what made me take a shot on the volley which flew into the net from 25 yards. It was the only goal of the game and one of the most bizarre matches I've ever played in.

Things were going well individually and collectively but after scoring in an early January FA Cup third-round win at Ossie Ardiles's West Brom, who were also in the Second Division at the time, I picked up a double calf injury that ruled me out for almost four months.

It was a devastating blow and – as I now realise – the beginning of the end.

They call it the 'old age injury' because you never recover to the same level. I hadn't experienced a calf tear before and in many ways I became my own worst enemy, trying to get back as quick as possible only to break down again.

It had all been so trivial. I was just running during the game and felt it pop. I'd never had any calf problems before.

My groin injury at Spurs was the worst I'd suffered to that point because it took so long to recover from but this calf issue was pain like I'd never previously felt from a muscle tear or hamstring strain.

The physios initially said I would be absent for four-to-six weeks but it took longer than that because I kept pushing it.

The team kept moving forward in my absence but everybody stopped in their tracks on 24 February 1993 when news broke that Bobby Moore had died. It had only been a week since Bobby told the world he had cancer and suddenly he was gone.

Bobby had been pictured at Wembley looking worryingly gaunt while working as a radio pundit for a World Cup qualifier between England and San Marino but nobody thought the end would come so soon. He was only 51 years old.

Upton Park became a shrine to Bobby, adorned with scarves, flowers, notes of condolence and replica shirts.

Everyone sat around one afternoon at the club telling their own personal stories about him. It was something cathartic people felt they needed to do to aid the grieving process.

We played Sunderland at Roker Park on 27 February – a day of that became one of national mourning. A lot of the lads didn't really want to be out there. It finished 0-0.

The first home game after Bobby's passing was against Wolves on 6 March. It was a sell-out crowd and an eerie occasion. Geoff Hurst and Martin Peters carried out a large wreath in the shape of Bobby's No 6 shirt and displayed it in the centre-circle.

Ian Bishop wore number twelve as the number six was temporarily retired (it was later removed for good in 2008). The feeling of loss in the stadium that day was overwhelming. I don't know how we won 3-1.

Once the shock was absorbed, it made everyone push that bit harder for promotion to honour Bobby's memory. Billy and Harry brought in David Speedie on loan from Southampton and his experience helped us kick on in the run-in.

It wasn't until the penultimate game of the season when I was able to return to action and the promotion chase had reached a critical point.

Portsmouth had knocked Newcastle off the top of the table for the first time all season at the end of April but they then lost 4-1 at Sunderland so our destiny was back in our own hands.

We needed to win by two goals at Swindon to put us back in the automatic promotion places. I'd played one reserve game prior to being named on the bench. Deep down, I'm not sure if I truly believed I was fit but I'd been out for so long and wanted to play a part in getting the team over the line.

Trevor burst through the Swindon defence to put us 1-0 up early on with his 22nd goal of the season but it remained really tense. Billy gave me the nod in the second half and Julian Dicks made one of his powerful forward runs before playing me in. I took two touches and finished low, left-footed across Swindon goalkeeper Fraser Digby. I slid on my knees in joy.

It was a massive moment for the club and also a personal release after the long spell I'd had out.

'Those old predatory instincts are there as good as ever,' said commentator Brian Moore in covering the game. That summed up how I felt.

Swindon cut the deficit but Kenny Brown struck after more good work from Julian to restore the two-goal advantage we needed.

Back then, placings were determined by goals scored if two teams were level on points. Goal difference didn't matter. We'd scored one more goal than Portsmouth – 79 to 78 – and if we kept that advantage on the final day, assuming we both won our matches, West Ham would be promoted to the Premier League at the first time of asking.

We were confident of doing the job but everything – the entire season – had come down to 90 minutes against a Cambridge United side desperately fighting relegation.

The home support – our largest crowd of the season at 27,399 – was deafening from the first minute. I started on the bench and looked around the crowd to see hundreds of people with portable radios glued to their ears, desperate to know what was happening at Portsmouth, who were playing Grimsby – a top ten team but with nothing to play for.

We were struggling to play our typical flowing football. The boys were going long, desperate to apply pressure on Cambridge and subconsciously knowing goals were the order of the day.

Help was welcome and it duly arrived. News filtered through that Grimsby had taken the lead after 32 minutes. We went in 0-0 at half-time. The dressing room was very tense. Anxiety was etched on several players' faces.

Billy and Harry did their best to instil confidence in us by telling everyone to relax and the goals would come.

They were right. It took two minutes after the restart to make the breakthrough. David Speedie hooked the ball high into the net and the crowd went crazy.

Chances came and went after that to kill it. The tension increased as Portsmouth equalised. They still had over half an hour in their game to turn it around and ramp up the pressure even further. I was sat next to Harry in the dugout. He could barely watch.

Fans were biting their nails, wearing pained expressions. I could see them as I ran along the touchline keeping myself sharp. Suddenly, Billy called on me. I'd scored at Swindon and so while my calf problem was still at the back of my mind, I'd proved I could be an impact player and that's what we needed.

With 28 minutes left, Mark Robson came off, I went on. Cambridge had an equaliser ruled out by a tight offside call.

Concern poured from every corner of the stadium. Somebody shouted: 'Portsmouth have scored!' Confirmation followed. They were 2-1 up. We were 1-0 up. They were going up. We weren't.

We continued to pour forward in search of a second goal. Julian was marauding all over the pitch, the embodiment of every fan willing the team on. And in stoppage time, my cousin Martin, on as a substitute just moments earlier, played a ball into the box which Julian did brilliantly to get to, wriggling free of a defender

Given my family's footballing background I found myself immersed in the game from a very young age. Here I am as a boy with Terry Venables, who would later manage me at Crystal Palace, QPR and Tottenham. [NOEL SAVA]

After two successful years at QPR I was signed by Arsenal in 1980, becoming only the fifth player in the history of British football to be signed for over £1 million. Here I am with manager Terry Neill and fellow new signing John Hollins. [GETTY]

Given my age and the money involved, the press had a field day, and all the attention led to one of the more bizarre photoshoots of my career with Page 3 girl Jilly Johnson. [JOHN PAUL, SCOPE FEATURES]

I was all smiles upon joining the Gunners, but it soon turned out to be a strange situation, and I was quickly sold to Crystal Palace in a swap deal with left-back Kenny Sansom having never played a competitive match for the club. I have not spoken to Neill about his sudden change of heart to this day. [GETTY]

At Selhurst Park I continued where I had left off at Loftus Road, and though we finished bottom of the top flight in the 1980/81 season, I finished as the club's leading goalscorer. [PETER JAY]

My form in a struggling side was enough for Terry Venables to take me back to QPR in 1981. Like everyone else I had to get used to the artificial surface that club chairman Jim Gregory had had installed at Loftus Road. [PA]

Celebrating victory after my goal gave us a 1-0 win in our 1982 FA Cup semi-final against West Brom. Unfortunately, we couldn't quite go all the way, losing to Tottenham in the final. [GETTY]

QPR finished fifth in the top flight in the 1983/84 season and I top scored in the league with 14 strikes, and my form led to me my making my England debut that summer on a tour of South America. In the first game I came off the bench against Brazil as John Barnes's iconic solo goal gave us a 2-0 victory in the iconic Maracanã. [GETTY]

I also came off the bench in the 2-0 defeat to Uruguay in Montevideo, and I started in the 0-0 draw to Chile that ended the tour. Though I was unable to get on the scoresheet, the tour was an unbelievable experience both on and off the field, with a visit to Christ the Redeemer another highlight. [GETTY]

At the start of the season it was time for a change, joining another club my dad had been so successful at, Tottenham, in a deal worth £700,000. I hit the ground running and found myself on the scoresheet against QPR in September in a 5-0 win. [PA]

In May 1986, during Ossie Ardiles's testimonial, I got to line up alongside the great Diego Maradona in a Spurs shirt. Just over six weeks later he was breaking English hearts at the World Cup in Mexico with both his gamesmanship and his genius. [OFFSIDE]

At home with Lisa and our first child, Olly, in February 1987. Spending time with my kids gave me perspective about the game of football – they didn't care what anyone in the press or the game were saying about me, they just wanted my attention as a father. [OFFSIDE]

Looking over some photos of us in action with my cousins Martin and Paul, who at this stage were playing for QPR and Spurs respectively. [OFFSIDE]

The 1986/87 campaign was my most prolific yet, and I was able to help Spurs the reach FA Cup final. Following our 4-1 win over Watford in the semi-final at Villa Park, a game in which I scored in, me and Chris Waddle are mobbed by supporters. [GETTY]

I was on hand to open the scoring in the final as well against Coventry, but unfortunately the Midlands side fought back to win the game 3-2, denying me an FA Cup triumph I badly craved. [GETTY]

Still, my staggering 49 goals in all competitions meant I received the PFA Players' Player of the Year and Football Writers' Player of the Year awards at the end of the season, a small consolation. [GETTY]

Introduced to Pelé by Bryan Robson at the 1987 Football League Centenary Match at Wembley. I was on the Football League XI, and we defeated the Rest of the World XI 3-0. [GETTY]

In January 1988 I travelled to Monte Carlo for the Adidas Golden Shoe Awards. Here I am with Brian McClair, the leading goalscorer from Scotland during the 1986/87 campaign, in front of the jet that took us to the ceremony. [GETTY]

Lining up with my England teammates in what would prove to be my last ever international against Israel in Tel Aviv in February 1987. Unfortunately, I never got on the scoresheet during my five caps. [GETTY]

In March 1988 I made my first move abroad, after being signed by Bordeaux. Here I encountered Eric Cantona before his fame in England, a strong personality despite his young age. He had recently referred to French manager Henri Michel as a 'bag of shit' on national television. [OFFSIDE]

I enjoyed my time in France and my goalscoring record was good – a record of more than a goal every other game – but my relationship with eccentric owner Claude Bez was a strange one, and he always seemed keen to chop and change the squad, which would mean I'd spend just one season abroad. [GETTY]

My departure from Bordeaux meant I was back on British shores, and in 1989 I signed for Manchester City. I didn't always enjoy the easiest of working relationships with Peter Reid, who took over as player-manager in 1990, but here we are in a slightly happier moment. [PA]

I was happier in the environment I found at Stamford Bridge, despite only being at Chelsea for three months. [GETTY]

My move to West Ham in March of 1992 meant I dropped down a division, but thankfully we were promoted back to the Premier League as runners-up in the 1992/93 campaign, with my goal on the final day against Cambridge United sealing the deal. Here are me and some of the other lads promoting the new kit at the start of that campaign. Julian Dicks is at the wheel. [MIRRORPIX]

After short spells with Millwall and Carlisle United, I hung up my footballing boots for good in 1995. I had scored 221 goals in 434 appearances, more than a goal every other game. [PERSONAL]

I found the initial period of retirement a tough one, especially the lack of routine and camaraderie. In 1997, due to my links with Sky, where I was working as a pundit, I was able to temporarily re-enter the sporting arena, representing the London Monarchs in NFL Europe for a season. I had followed the NFL in the 1980s on Channel 4 and though I had absolutely no experience of playing American football before this, my skills with my feet meant I was suitable to play as a specialist kicker. It was just what I needed at the time. [SEAN RYAN]

It wasn't long before I was back involved in the game I knew well, and after working with the England youth squads, I soon found myself coaching back at Spurs. Here I am with Chris Hughton offering advice to boss Jacques Santini in 2004. [OFFSIDE]

Following Santini's departure Martin Jol and Juande Ramos both had spells in charge of Spurs, and I was involved in working with both. But it was under Harry Redknapp that Spurs really started to push on. Our team consisted of Harry, Kevin Bond, Joe Jordan and me. [GETTY]

We went on a great journey with Spurs, enjoying some magical moments, including a trip to the Bernabéu to face José Mourinho's Real Madrid. [PA]

Of all the players I worked with Dimitar Berbatov was right up there in terms of ability, and he was also a consummate professional. He was a genius and I absolutely loved him. [GETTY]

Despite all the water that has passed under the bridge, me and dad were still able to enjoy a fitting send off to White Hart Lane together in 2017. [PA]

With my beautiful family: my sons Olly and Ed; my wife Lisa; my daughters Amelia and Lydia. [PERSONAL]

before playing a square ball to me for one of the simplest tap-ins of my career.

The supporters invaded the pitch. I was swamped. Pure euphoria. It was touch-and-go as to whether the stewards could get everyone back into the stands to finish the game but, after a short period of time, they receded long enough to play out the final few seconds before the ref blew for full-time.

I found Martin in the melee. We celebrated as family – one which ten days later welcomed a new addition on 18 May as our first daughter, Amelia, was born. We felt so blessed. Olly started at Brentwood school later than year. Life was back on track.

Had we not gone up automatically, I maintain to this day we would have failed in the play-offs. The devastation at missing out on the top two would have been too great to overcome.

Instead, we could start planning for next season. I spent most of the summer before the 1993/94 season trying to get fit because my calf still wasn't right.

Here we were, in the Premier League. I'd been sceptical about it from the outside but the first season had been a great success and it was hard not to get caught up in all the razzmatazz.

The summer brought considerable change. Dale Gordon was our most expensive new signing at £750,000 from Glasgow Rangers while Billy also brought in Simon Webster from Charlton for £500,000 as he felt we needed more strength in depth to take on the big boys.

Keith Rowland and Paul Mitchell also came in before a ball was kicked – both had played under Harry at Bournemouth – while the stadium was also undergoing renovation as a new south stand named after Bobby Moore was built. It meant there was a reduced capacity for the first half of the season and perhaps that didn't help us. We lost 2-0 to Wimbledon on the opening day, conceding two bad goals.

I was involved in the build-up to West Ham's first ever Premier League goal against Coventry City on 21 August 1993, playing the ball out to Tim Breacker whose low shot was saved by Jonathan Gould, with Dale bundling home the rebound. It was enough for us to earn our first point and our maiden win came four days later against Sheffield Wednesday.

The game was described as a 'personal triumph' for me by one commentator.

I scored both goals, the first turning it home from close range before finishing from a tight angle for a 2-0 win.

'You hear all these rumours that the club are going to struggle and we're going to have a tough time but that's just spurred the lads on to go well,' I said in a post-match interview at the time, precisely the sort of thing you are supposed to say, but we did find it tough initially.

QPR beat us 4-0 at home as we finished the month in the bottom six with four points from five games.

I did genuinely believe we had a lot of potential and it felt good to be scoring goals in the top flight again but I'd learned to never take things for granted and so it proved. We played Manchester United away at the beginning of September and I suffered medial knee ligament damage in a block tackle with Paul Ince.

Paul wasn't at fault. If anything, I blame myself because I was a little bit slow to the challenge and so my technique wasn't ideal – I'd opened up my body and because I was fractionally late, it cost me dearly.

It was clear straight away my injury was pretty serious and after starting the season with four defeats in seven games, the club felt they had to act.

Julian Dicks, a fans' favourite who had been at the centre of transfer speculation for some time, was finally sold to Liverpool in a £2million deal with David Burrows and Mike Marsh coming to Upton Park.

The one thing a lot of people missed about Julian was that he was a fantastic footballer. He was a left-back by trade but could have played on the left-wing or even as a centre-forward. He was a fierce competitor and had a great attitude towards the game. I enjoyed playing with him. The disciplinary and off-field problems he had diminished his reputation in some people's eyes and probably detracted from him getting the credit he deserved for just how good a player he was.

Lee Chapman signed on the same day – 17 September – from Portsmouth for £250,000.

Lee's arrival meant the club had an obvious replacement for me and that made me push hard to get back, but my body kept breaking down.

I tried everything, including training in a brace, just to get fit again but the knee was a nightmare.

The team responded well in my absence. The new trio made their debuts in a 2-0 win at Blackburn with Chapman and Trevor Morley both finding the net.

Billy had money left over from the Dicks deal and he signed another striker – Jeroen Boere from Go Ahead Eagles for £200,000.

That compounded the problem. The pressure was on and I could see the writing was on the wall. I wanted to scrub it out. I didn't deal with it well. I kept forcing myself, playing in several reserve games, joining in first-team training but always a little bit too soon. I was taking chances and it wasn't working. In that respect, I became my own worst enemy.

I was out for seven months in total. The road back to fitness had been difficult – it is tougher for everyone once you pass 30 – and that was probably why what came next was such a bitter blow.

I thought I was fit for our FA Cup quarter-final replay at Luton on 23 March 1994 but Bill didn't even put me on the bench. Sky asked me to work as a television pundit for the first time. I accepted – once the club approved – and thoroughly enjoyed it, even though we lost. It was life's way of telling me what was to come.

I couldn't criticise teammates, though. As a pundit, I've always tried to provide insight into a way of life I know rather than chase headlines criticising people.

Missing that Luton game was symbolic for me. Bill was honest: he felt my legs had gone. And as I struggled to get fit, Lee came in and scored a few goals. He was a different type of player to me but it didn't help the comparison that he was two years older yet available on a regular basis.

I couldn't do what Trevor and Lee were doing. I didn't like it but from a football point of view, I understood where Bill was coming from. And so it came back to the same thing, just as it did every time: I knew I wasn't going to be playing and my Premier League career was probably over. Six games, two goals. At the same time, Millwall showed an interest. And I didn't feel like I was done just yet.

CHAPTER FOURTEEN

Millwall – South Of The River

I WAS DRIVING BACK ACROSS LONDON ON THE DAY I SIGNED FOR Millwall when Tony Gale called me.

'What the fuck are you doing?' he said. 'You know they hate West Ham?'

'Galey, I'm alright. I'm not worried. I've played for numerous London clubs – it won't be a problem.'

And it wasn't. If there was some stick, I never felt it. It wouldn't have worried me if there was. I obviously wouldn't have liked it, but I wanted to play. The possibility of not being accepted never entered my thinking when I was deciding between clubs. This was my seventh London club and I'd been welcomed at all the others – many of whom were direct rivals – so why should this be any different?

Maybe people have a bit more love for goalscorers and I'd managed to be consistent in front of goal pretty much wherever I'd been.

But once I left West Ham, I knew my career was on the slide. That's no disrespect to Millwall but I was dropping down a division to play with a young group that were aiming to get promoted in hope more than expectation.

I saw a lot of similarities in going to Millwall with signing for Queens Park Rangers right at the start of my career: the size of the club, the new stadium and just the feel of the place. The manager, Mick McCarthy, believed I was a good pro to come into that environment and act as something of a role model.

There was a story in the newspapers at the time that Tottenham wanted me back as cover for Teddy Sheringham but that wasn't true. When he was Newcastle manager in 1991, Ossie Ardiles had reportedly been interested in taking me to St James' Park a couple of years after I returned from Bordeaux, but I never heard anything from either club when it became clear I was leaving West Ham.

My knee had fully recovered but my calf remained a private concern. It wasn't an issue in my medical, though. It was a muscle tear that had repaired so there was nothing obvious for a doctor to pick up on. I knew inside it was never as strong as before but that wasn't going to stop me.

In any case, Mick didn't see me as a number nine anymore. He wanted me to play in a slightly deeper role, effectively a modern-day number 10. I was open to it because it meant I could play regularly but it was difficult because I had no real experience in that position.

In spells, I could do it. But I couldn't score from deep. It wasn't until I couldn't do it that I realised how important that was to me. Scoring was like a drug and I couldn't get my fix from there.

If I'd been more influential in that position, it probably wouldn't have mattered but because I was struggling, not being able to offset a bad game with a scruffy goal made things worse.

I played 12 games for Millwall and didn't score. In hindsight, I was never fully fit and my calf always felt fragile. It made me play within myself.

We had a decent side and probably should have gone up but finished in third place on 74 points, nine adrift of Nottingham Forest in second and 16 behind title-winners Crystal Palace.

The play-offs pitched us against Derby County. After losing the first leg 2-0 away, we knew we were facing an uphill battle and it got worse when Marco Gabbiadini turned the ball home from close range after 17 minutes at The Den.

Six minutes later, Tommy Johnson fired in a second. Now, we were 4-0 down on aggregate and fans began congregating in the East Stand looking to start a ruck with police.

With 32 minutes on the clock, referee Brian Hill took all the players off the pitch as our supporters poured on to try and get the game called off.

Police came in on horseback as fighting broke out on the far side of the ground. One fan asked me for my shirt. During the first half.

Play eventually resumed but later on, it got worse. As the game entered the final 20 minutes, it happened again in ridiculous circumstances. Fans were running all over one end of the pitch but at the other, where we were attacking, Alex Rae went down in the box and the referee gave a penalty. Brian belatedly saw tens of people on the pitch and tried to get us all off but this time the fans had a headstart. Several Derby players were kicked and knocked over including goalkeeper Martin Taylor as they tried to get to the safety of the dressing rooms. Others said they were racially abused.

We finished the game – losing 3-1 on the night, 5-1 on aggregate – but not before delays totalling 33 minutes in all. Sometimes you just want to get as far away from the ground as possible after you lose – especially a game with the importance of a play-off semi-final – but we were all locked in the dressing room as trouble escalated outside. Reports later claimed about 1,000 fans went on the rampage in the stadium car park and surrounding streets causing indiscriminate damage and wreaking havoc wherever they went. Six police officers required medical treatment for injures as 17 people were arrested.

Nobody spoke in the dressing room. We had missed out on promotion and on top of that, you had no idea if your car was going to be in one piece when you did get away. It was like purgatory. Eventually, after what felt like an hour, but it could have been less, we were released. At least my car was alright.

I never got the chance to make a make amends in the 1994/95 season. During that campaign, I was playing a game of head tennis in the training ground gym having just got myself into a position where I was fit enough to play for the first team after six weeks out. The ball came over the net and as I stepped backwards and went to push off to return it, I turned towards a few of the young apprentices who were watching us and angrily said: 'What are you doing?'

I thought someone had thrown something or shot me with a catapult in the back of the calf. It was a brutal stabbing pain. I limped to the physio. He told me, just by loading weight on it in stepping backwards, I'd torn the muscle again.

In that moment, I knew I was finished. I drove home – which was a risk in itself as my right leg was throbbing and strapped up. I remember being in tears on the M25. I would turn 34 in May. I only had a couple of months left on my contract at Millwall. Everything was against me.

I still tried to get fit: over the next two months, I went through as much rehabilitation as my body could handle but Millwall didn't renew my contract and I understood why. I knew I wasn't fit enough.

It was a horrible period because my career was clearly coming to an end but I couldn't accept it. I was scared. What would I do without football?

Harry Redknapp was now in charge at West Ham and I called him to ask whether I could come in and do pre-season with them. I still wanted to play. Deep down, I knew I couldn't.

CHAPTER FIFTEEN

Carlisle – Final Stop

THE UNCERTAINTY OF WHAT CAME AFTER FOOTBALL TERRIFIED ME. My body was sending a clear message but the mind wasn't listening.

What would I do without competition? You can't turn off the desire to compete like a tap and I've always wanted to win everything, whether it is a game of table tennis with my kids or an FA Cup Final.

I went through pre-season at West Ham because it was all I knew. End the season, go on holiday, return for the start of next season. I was on autopilot. Except I had no destination.

But one of the benefits of being a goalscorer is clubs always want to take a chance on you. Strikers with a decent track record are worth their weight in goals.

Throughout July and August, I spoke to Carlisle chairman Michael Knighton and manager Micky Wadsworth. They wanted to sign me but I had to get fit first before I even considered it.

Micky kept calling me two or three times a week trying to persuade me to go up there. I knew my calf was fragile. An operation was pointless because it hadn't torn, it was just weak and I thought there was still a chance I could manage it. In the end, I succumbed. I wanted to show people I could still do it. Clive Allen from London going to Carlisle at his age? He can't go any further. I thought I could prove them wrong.

I was under no illusions: I wasn't going to get a contract at West Ham but I loved being around a good set of lads, without any pressure of playing.

I told Micky I had a young family in school and wouldn't move them up north at this stage of my career. I had five or six conversations with Michael. He was very persuasive.

'You can train at West Ham and just come up to play at weekends,' he said on one more than one occasion.

'Come up on a Thursday, train Friday, play Saturday and go back to London on Saturday night.'

It was a strange offer but one I thought could work. Lisa didn't like the idea of me being away regularly but it was only a couple of nights a week and she knew I wasn't ready to give up the game.

My heart ruled my head. I would try it for a month with a view to a more permanent, potentially season-long deal.

I travelled up on a Thursday and had my first training session the following morning as planned. We were playing at home on the Saturday and they called a press conference for the Friday afternoon.

I trained, showered and went into see Micky, who told me I had a meeting with Michael to sign the contract.

It was a bog standard one month deal: basic wage at the going rate, first-team bonus and nothing else. It was all very simple. Micky and his assistant Mervyn Day, who I'd known for years from West Ham, were sat there chuckling to each other while I waited for Michael to present me with the contract to sign.

'It won't be right, you know,' Micky said.

'What do you mean?'

'The contract. There will be something wrong with it.'

'How is that even possible? It is so straight forward.'

'It won't be right.'

I went in and Michael showed me the contract. It wasn't what we agreed. The wage was considerably lower.

'That's not right chairman,' I said, politely.

'Oh, what did we agree? Remind me.'

I told him and he apologised. He said it had to be retyped by the club secretary but we were running out of time because the paperwork had to be registered quickly with the Football League for me to be eligible to play that weekend. Plus, there was a press conference a couple of hours away.

I went back outside. Micky and Mervyn had upgraded to belly-laughs now.

'Told you,' Micky said in between. 'Oh, and when you go back in, it still won't be right.'

They were winding me up, surely. I had literally just refreshed Michael's memory about what we'd agreed, perfectly amicably, before. Half an hour later, I went back in. The contract had improved but the wage was still below the figure we'd shaken hands on.

'This still isn't right,' I said, more frustrated than before.

'What do you mean? This is what we discussed.'

'What's going on?'

'Nothing's going on.'

I said: 'Tell you what, there is a train back to London in an hour.'

'But there is a press conference before then.'

'Well, I'm not going to be there. Let's just call it quits here.'

'No, no, no – we'll sort it out. Please give me a few more minutes.'

I came back out. Micky and Merv said, almost in unison: 'It'll be alright now.'

And it was. I signed the deal and attended the press conference. There were questions about my motivation for being there but my answer, as you'll know by now, was simple: I just wanted to play.

I enjoyed being in competitive action again and despite my unusual circumstances, the lads were good with me. The senior players in particular understood what was happening.

But it wasn't long before the terms of our arrangement began to shift. Within a couple of weeks, Micky wanted me to come up on a Wednesday to train more often with team.

It wasn't an unreasonable request from his point of view given he chiefly wanted me to integrate with the squad but it wasn't something I had signed up for and he knew that. Things were altering too fast.

After one game up north, I needed to make the 5.10pm train back to London because the next one was several hours later and I would have struggled to get home.

I showered, changed and made it to the station in time but as I got to the platform, everyone was alighting.

'The bridge is down at Lancaster so you have to take the bus for three hours down the line and get on the train the other side of the collapsed bridge,' said the station attendant.

I took a seat right at the front of the rail replacement bus, at the back of which sat a big group of London-bound Celtic supporters. They'd been drinking all day but one of them spotted me and came lurching down the aisle to sit alongside me.

'Hey, are you Clive Allen?' he said, words hurtling towards me with a strong stench of lager.

'Yeah but please, I don't mind you giving me stick but there are loads of families on here and they don't need to hear any bad language.'

'Oh yeah, sure mate,' he said as he disappeared to the back before completing his return journey by proudly declaring to his mates: 'Yeah, that's him!'

What followed was three hours which felt like an eternity. I got a relentless torrent of abuse, a quite staggering array of songs and swear words in an almost impressive number of combinations, had it not been so offensive. It was wholly uncomfortable but there was nothing I could do. I just had to take it.

When we finally got to the train station, I jumped on board and hid in one of the carriages away from the Celtic supporters. Upon arriving in London, there was a tube strike which meant I had to get a taxi home. I got in at 3am, climbing into bed, weary and demoralised.

Lisa rolled over and said: 'You aren't doing that anymore, are you?'

'No.' And that was it. My last game. The following day I told Micky and Michael I'd had enough. We agreed to call it quits there and then. There was still another match but I couldn't face it.

There was a realisation that I wouldn't do anything to play anymore. It was an odd way to end.

There was no 'thank you and goodbye' at Tottenham, for whom I'd played the best football of my career, or QPR, where it had all began. I don't know what sort of finish you want.

I don't think there really is a good way to do it. You never want it to happen. Even if you score the winning goal in a cup final and plan to go out, that performance could easily convince you to give it one more year. But the reality was that I couldn't finish at the level I wanted to.

I had no desire to drop down even further. Once Carlisle hadn't worked out, I knew I was finished. I'd given it one final shot. But that didn't mean I knew how to handle what came next.

CHAPTER SIXTEEN

A Whole New Ball Game

I TRAINED EVERY DAY FOR 18 YEARS. EVEN ON A DAY OFF I WAS still focused on conditioning. Suddenly it was gone. There has never been enough support to help players deal with that transition.

Shortly after I finished playing, people talked to me about de-training: gradually winding down after so long in a daily rhythm.

One morning, I was supposedly starting that process and left the house to go for a run. I got 100 yards along the path, stopped and walked back to the house.

My wife was in the kitchen.

'I thought you were going for a run?'

'I can't do it anymore. What's the point?'

There wasn't the goal of a match at the end of the week. I wasn't getting fit in pre-season to play. I couldn't go through it.

I loved training. I was the world's worst when I was injured, complaining about not being able to get out there, but now the motivation had gone. I'll always remember that day as a result. It felt totally disorientating.

I didn't de-train at all. I committed to a few days here and there in the gym but couldn't follow a structure.

I put on weight. I lost my strength. I lost a sense of purpose. My family were there and of course I loved them dearly. Olly, Ed and Mimi made sure there was plenty going on at home. But professionally, it was like the end of the world.

Having had so much control for 17 years as a player, the discipline suddenly disappeared. Missing football is the main thing but being on your own is also a huge shift. The camaraderie is something I missed terribly and still do to this day.

Even with a wonderful family and friends, you feel lonely. A version of this probably exists for people in other walks of life when you work somewhere where you all have a common goal. But it is possible in many professions to change companies and find a similar version of what you enjoy.

When your career as a professional footballer ends, that's it. The dressing room door, as you know it, closes for good. There's nothing comparable to walk into. Coaching or management is the closest thing, but even the dynamic there is completely different.

Where else will there be 20-25 guys all of a broadly similar age, all dealing with the same pressures, all embarking on the same emotional journey? You define yourself to an extent by the people you are surrounded by and when they all disappear, there is a loss of identity in what feels like a new world.

Some of the corporate activity I now perform at Tottenham allows me to reunite with other ex-players and it is like walking back through the dressing room door. The chatty ones are still chatty. The jokers still joke. But there is no way of recreating that atmosphere in any other walk of life.

I started work at Sky Sports towards the end of the 1995/96 season, which helped in that regard, especially the new format Mark Schofield devised.

Mark was the producer I had worked for on Granada Television in Manchester when I was at City. I'd had no formal training but it gave me another medium through which to express my passion for football.

As a result of my upbringing, I didn't want to be there to criticise but to analyse the details and try to give people an insight from the players' perspective.

Sky Sports was then in its infancy and Mark came to me with the blueprint for a show called *Soccer Saturday*. It had six pilot shows at the end of the season as a test to see if it would work for the following year, the 1996/97 campaign.

Mark sold it to me as 'radio on TV'.

'You can watch the games live because we have the feeds coming into the studio but we can't show the public because of the Saturday afternoon broadcast blackout,' he said.

'So my idea is to put former players who come with a little authority in front of a screen to tell people what's going on in the match they are watching.'

It is a staple part of Saturdays for people up and down the country now but the show was a gamble at the time. They saw me as someone who had recently retired after a decent career with experience of the Premier League who could provide analysis on the matches.

I enjoyed it. However, whatever pleasure it gave me, it wasn't enough in isolation to fill the void created by retirement.

As a consequence of the stress of hanging up my boots and having no direction or purpose in life, my hair fell out. When the alopecia truly began to kick in, I found clumps of hair – in the shower, in the bed, the car, everywhere. I told Lisa she had to be honest with me because I was in full flow on *Soccer Saturday* and on air with Sky in some form three times a week. Could anyone see it? I wasn't bothered about my image too much but you always want to look right, especially on camera.

Lisa told me it never came across. One night, I did a phone-in evening show with Rob McCaffrey called *You're on Sky Sports* which finished really late. I returned home, got into bed and flicked on the television.

I never used to watch shows back but Lisa must have been watching some of it earlier on and left the television on the same channel. I watched a few minutes of the repeat. Rob and I were talking and then suddenly it cuts to an overhead shot of the studio. Nobody told me that camera existed. You could see a huge bald patch on the back of my head. I looked at Lisa.

'You said you'd tell me!'

'Honestly, I've never seen it before. I dozed off!'

I had to address it. I went to see a top skin specialist in London who had been recommended to me as a 'miracle-worker'. His luxurious London office contained a beautiful big oak table and we sat at it across from each other as he began his assessment.

'Have you had a bereavement, a divorce or a real fright in your life recently?'

'No,' I replied.

'Okay, tell me about yourself – what's happened in your life?'

'Well, I've just finished playing professional sport. I'd class it as since the age of six but technically from 17 to 34 – 17 years.'

'Okay, fine.' He got up and walked around the table in a slow, methodical circle passing around the back of me yet without leaning in for a proper examination before returning to his seat. A period of silence ensued before I broke it.

'Lotions, potions, tablets – what do I need to take?'

He didn't reply. Instead, he picked up a pen and began writing on a piece of paper. He signed it and pushed it across the table.

'This is my bill,' he said.

'What? I'm not paying that until you tell me what I need to do.'

'Do you really want to know?'

Slightly more incredulous, I said: 'Yes! That's why I'm here. Do you think I'm going to pay you for nothing?'

'Okay. Don't look in the mirror.'

'Are you kidding me?' By now I was furious.

'If you want my advice, that's it: don't look in the mirror. I'm 99.9 percent sure you have a classic case of alopecia. The hair follicles are still there and so within six to 18 months, it will grow back.'

'So what do I do in the meantime?'

'Don't look in the mirror.'

The following day I went to the barbers. I'd had basically the same haircut all my adult life but I knew I had to shave it right back, although the barber told me I had about twice as many bald patches as I thought.

It felt weird. I went home and sat in the bath, adjusting the mirror as I became accustomed to my new look: a grade one but with absent patches, albeit less pronounced than before. Mimi, who was just four years old at the time, came into the bathroom.

'Dad, it's alright. I still love you.' I could have cried.

Sky helped me no end. Two weeks before the season was due to start, I phoned Ian Condran, a producer at *Soccer Saturday* and told him about my new, enforced blotchy hairstyle. He told me to leave it with him for a couple of days, by which time I was due to come into the studio for a brief hit on Sky Sports News.

'We've got this idea,' Condran said. 'The make-up girls will fill in the patches and make it look like you have really cropped hair.'

They essentially coloured me in, experimenting with how long it would take in make-up for a short hit on Sky Sports News to see if it would be effective for *Soccer Saturday*, which is obviously a much longer programme.

It looked fine and the procedure was fairly straightforward so I went into *Soccer Saturday* as normal. On the first show with my hair made up, Jeff Stelling introduced us all along the line and – referencing the fact shaven-headed Italian striker Gianluca Vialli had just signed for Chelsea – he said: '... and on the end is our own Vialli, Clive Allen!'

That was the only mention of it. It was done and dusted. But I found out several months later that the Sky bosses wanted me to wear a wig. Instead, Condran came up with this idea to hide the patches with make-up and they allowed him to try it. Thankfully it worked.

I had to have make-up applied to my head each time I was on TV for about six months. Eventually the hair grew back a bit stronger each time and got to a point where I returned to a full head of hair.

That period coincided with my stint playing American Football for the London Monarchs, which only helped me get away with it because I kept hearing people say: 'Look at that idiot, he wants to look all tough in the NFL so he's shaved off all his hair.'

*

NFL Europe approached me while I was working for Sky in the early part of 1997. Oliver Luck, president of NFL Europe, called me at home one day out of the blue and asked me to play for the London Monarchs in the World League of American Football.

I was convinced it was a wind-up. Consequently, he spent the first part of a 20-minute phone call repeatedly telling me he really was Oliver Luck, a man I'd never met.

I don't know if someone at Sky had suggested him to me given they were covering the matches live, but once I got over the initial shock, it started to sound like an exciting, if leftfield idea.

I had followed the NFL as a fan when it was shown on Channel 4 in the 1980s. I watched the Washington Redskins, with their famous running back John Riggins, and remember thinking there weren't too many positions I could play. Everybody wants to be a quarterback but the kicker role was the obvious fit for me.

Each team in Europe had a national kicker. There were seven indigenous players included in each squad: seven English lads with the London Monarchs, seven Dutch boys with Amsterdam and so on. Although they were Dutch nationals, a lot of them were college boys being educated in America. The rest of the players were largely second-string from the NFL sent to Europe in the summer to give them game-time so scouts could assess them. They hadn't played much during the NFL season but thought they still had a chance of a career and therefore sent them over here.

Oliver kept trying to persuade me. The idea of being part of a team again and training for a purpose excited me but it was a step into the unknown.

'The major stipulation I have is that I need to at least try it first and practice,' I told him during one attempt at coercion. 'If I can't do it, I'm not going to set myself up to be a fool.'

'No, don't worry – we'll send you to a kicking coach in Miami. The guy's name is Doug Blevins. He's the Miami Dolphins kicking coach. We'll fly you out there, you'll spend a week with him, training, kicking, and see how you get on.'

That convinced me. Oliver made the arrangements and two days before I was due to leave, he called me.

'Doug will meet you at the arrivals hall in Miami Airport and don't be alarmed,' he said, before a long pause. 'He'll be the guy in the wheelchair.'

What? A kicking coach who isn't able to use his legs? Surely this can't be right? Oliver assured me it would be fine.

I got there and Doug arrived in his mobility vehicle. He introduced himself and spun off towards the exit. I walked behind him thinking: 'Are there cameras watching me? Am I being setup?'

As I prepared for our first session, I confess I didn't know how difficult it was going to be. At the end of the day, I was going out there to kick a ball and if I'd done one thing a million times in my life, it was that. Put a ball in front of me, I'll kick it. I mean, I had a few reservations about it – which is why I wanted to practice – but how hard could it really be?

Immediately, Doug put me right. He knew I'd played soccer but started me with different stepping and striking drills, barely kicking the ball initially, focusing primarily on technique and approach.

The analogy I was given – and I think it is a good one – is that because the ball was often not set correctly, it was like it was bouncing around in the 18-yard box in soccer. How often does it fall perfectly to strike?

It was true because so often the ball would come back to me in American football and the holder wouldn't have time to spot the ball – someone placing it on the ground and tilting it at the perfect angle with one finger on top to help you kick straight.

Ideally when there was sufficient time, he could place it with the laces facing away from you to avoid the ball deviating in the air, and you wouldn't have to kick through his hands to make contact.

But those opportunities were rare and so usually you had to deal with an imperfect situation, placing greater pressure on your technique. The NFL looked at it and they'd found that soccer players were better field goal kickers and point after touchdown (PAT) kickers than rugby players because the rugby lads were used to it always being perfectly still.

A few rugby players had kicked before me – Gavin Hastings won the 1996 World Bowl with the Scottish Claymores, making 23 out of 27 PATs – but the prevailing consensus was now leaning towards employing footballers.

Eventually, I started kicking but kept hooking the ball left because I was kicking it with a slightly bent knee.

Sat in his wheelchair, Doug suddenly exploded. 'Goddamn it, it's not a fucking soccer ball,' he screamed. 'It's a Goddamn American football!'

He'd been so placid to that point, I told him to calm down but that only made him more irate. He demanded I went back to technical work without the ball.

But he was right. From that first morning, it was clear he was a genius. I became aware of his back story – overcoming cerebral palsy from birth to become Miami Dolphins coach for six years. He would later earn an NFL Hall of Fame nomination.

The key to kicking is getting the ball up in the air as quickly as possible. It is not about distance. The ball is lighter than a rugby ball and it moves around in the air a lot more so striking it is very important. You have to hit through the bottom of the ball and that took me a while to fully appreciate.

This level of technical insight was not something I'd experienced in my playing career as a footballer. I worked hard to improve my technique but almost all of that was self-taught using simple trial-and-error.

I like to think Doug's approach influenced me when I moved into coaching; it gave me a different perception on relaying messages to youngsters about how to develop specific skills, concentrating on the process rather than the end product. Football today is moving even more towards that attention to detail given all the analytical tools the clubs have available to them now.

I got the message eventually and started to kick properly. After a week together at the Atlanta Falcons base, I'd made enough progress for both parties to think it was worth giving it a go so I signed up for a nine-game season with our home matches at Stamford Bridge, but not before the longest medical of my life.

Beforehand, everything was controlled, down to the number of balls I would kick in a day through to the ice baths I'd have afterwards. The medical was just as meticulously planned and executed.

Everybody had based themselves around Atlanta for pre-season and we all massed in a big hotel to go through two days of medicals. From the hair on my head – what there was of it – to my toenails, the whole of my body was checked and examined much more rigorously than it was in any of the transfers I went through in professional football.

So many guys who went there with slight injuries or problems from the NFL clubs didn't pass. I was a little worried I wouldn't pass given my recent history. My calf muscles were okay, though, as the one that had caused me most problems was my standing leg. My right calf was fine by this point so I got through it, finding out so much about myself in the process; they told me I had perfect vision, there were ear and nose tests which I'd never had before too. They knew me better than my own doctor.

Premier League medicals have caught up now. The value of players these days demands it – as do the insurance companies – but I had some of the most basic medicals imaginable during my playing career.

You'd go in, sit down, he'd check your knees to see if you had any damage. After Tottenham, they would assess my groin injury because everybody knew about it but I can't remember ever having scans or X-rays, which now is just commonplace no matter what the previous history. The whole thing would take an hour at the most – maybe just 30 minutes. I even had one medical that took ten minutes. You'd then walk through to the manager's or club secretary's office and sign the contract. It is unbelievable that was allowed to go on, really.

Some of these NFL guys had awful injuries. Because we were all in such close proximity, I got to know some of the other kickers. There was a Dutch lad who kicked for the Admirals who had played as a centre-half in Holland.

I must admit I was concerned about how badly you could get hit but I knew from watching it as a fan, that the kickers were always the most protected.

'You don't get hit in this game, do you?' I said.

'Are you really asking that?' the Dutch lad said, lifting up his right trouser leg. 'Look at this. After the quarterback, the kicker is the next prized scalp and one time they got me. I ruptured my anterior cruciate ligament. All you can hope is you have a good line in front of you otherwise they will take you down.'

Having a good relationship with the linemen was vital because these guys put themselves in harm's way to protect you.

Starting to build that relationship was complicated by the fact the American guys demanded to know immediately what I was earning.

It was a decent contract given we only played nine games. The fascinating thing was that because the American lads were second-string NFL players, they were on a set fee for the summer. The nationals were also on an appearance fee and the American players made it their mission to find out any disparity.

I was getting paid more than them but there was a publicity element to it – local lads and, in my case, footballer turned American footballer, which is how they justified it at the time.

We used to do a lot of promotion and media work in our respective countries prior to games, all of which was incorporated into our contracts.

But within a few days of being involved, one of the big American linemen approached me in training.

'You must have been quite good in your day,' he said, with a little condescension in his voice.

'Well, you know, I had a decent career.'

'No, no, I've looked you up. You work on the TV now, on that *Soccer Saturday* programme, you are a proper ex-player… I want to go to a soccer game.'

It sounded as much like an instruction as a request. 'Yeah, no problem,' I replied. 'I'll sort something out.'

Not long afterwards, I took a few of the lads to West Ham versus Middlesbrough on a Tuesday night. West Ham helped me out tremendously and showed them a good time. It was just before the start of the Monarchs' season so they were introduced on the pitch to the crowd before the game and given the best seats in the Directors' Box. They struggled to fit in them so Lord only knows what they'd have been like in a regular seat.

Typically, hoping for a thrilling game to showcase the best of British football, it finished 0-0. The final whistle confused them.

'So what now, overtime?' one of them asked.

'No, that's it. We go home.'

'No goals? No result?'

The concept of a draw was completely alien to them. As they shook their heads and shared a joke amongst themselves, I took them down to the dressing room to meet Harry Redknapp and the players. Harry was always great with in situations like that. The Monarchs boys absolutely loved it.

The next day, I went into training and about 10 more of them came up to me.

'Hey, I want to go to the soccer,' said one. 'The guys said last night you just walked in the front door at West Ham.'

'Yeah, well I played there and they are good people.'

I only ever did the one trip to Upton Park but it still helped me win them over. But, as in any sport, results on the field were the most important thing.

The NFL wasn't about stamina, it was more about leg strength. My calf muscles held up okay and I did the necessary work to maintain that. The demand was primarily mental rather than physical.

It was fascinating. For a very simple game – you get four chances to move the ball ten yards – I didn't realise how tactical it all was. It is warfare on a gridiron.

Conditioning was so specific to the positions you play in that very rarely would we all be put through the same exercises.

At the end of some sessions, there would be what they called a 'full kit run' including everyone from the linemen to the wide receivers, who are the real sprinters, alongside the special teams – me as a kicker or some of the punters – running with pads, helmet and full gear up and down the pitch. It was a breeze for me.

'Slow down, donkey,' they used to shout at me. I never found that sort of thing demanding. Everything in the NFL is explosive – short spells of extreme power.

We won our first game against Frankfurt Galaxy but lost the next three, two of them badly. I was six for six on my field goals but missed my first PAT, which are the easy ones, because our opponents successfully put me off.

I walked back to the bench, past all the linemen – massive, fearless guys.

'Sit down, donkey,' they said one after another. I wasn't going to argue.

Regardless, I was enjoying being part of a team again and it was also useful to see at close quarters the way another professional sports team trained and prepared.

Everything had a statistic behind it. Some players could convince themselves they'd had a good game because their numbers were okay. Every aspect of performance was measured and in that regard, English football has gradually caught up, just as with the medicals.

Back then, the NFL were years ahead in terms of collating, analysing and applying that type of information. They also filmed everything from training sessions to matches.

We used to go into a full team meeting on a Monday after a Saturday game. The coach would demand players spend hours in the video analysis room and deconstruct every element of their performance, right down to how they were standing in position.

During one match in which we lost a quarterback to injury, an English kid kept getting knocked over in the tackle. The coach showed him how he held himself with an unnecessarily high centre of gravity and by changing to a low, crouching position, he could drive up into a challenge rather than being knocked back.

The kid started crying. It looked like an odd response to what was some constructive, and insightful, coaching but everybody in the room except me seemed to know what was coming next.

I was sitting at the back and I turned to the guy next to me with a confused expression as the kid at the front wiped away his tears to a backdrop of stony silence.

'He's going to get cut,' he whispered.

'Really? You are joking aren't you? He's made a mistake but nothing THAT bad.' We were three games into the season at this point.

The coach paused as the crying stopped before he began laying into him like nothing I'd ever seen before. It probably only lasted two minutes but when you see someone getting torn to shreds like that, it feels like a lot longer.

Eventually, it reached a crescendo. 'I've fucking told you once, I've fucking told you twice – get out of here!'

There and then, he gave him a plane ticket home. And just like that, he was gone.

I quickly learned that happened in the NFL all the time. They hire and fire all over the place. For instance, I was told that five or six kickers would be brought into camp at the start of the season and they would be paid pro-rata for every day they were employed. Nobody could argue it because there was no contract. Each day you were on trial and at the end of it you could be cut without warning.

They couldn't fathom my old football contracts when I'd sign for three or four years with one club.

'What happens if you get injured?' somebody asked.

'If I'm playing in the first team, I'll get my bonuses for six weeks after I get injured and if I'm still out after that, it'll just be basic pay.'

'You get paid when you are injured? Once a few weeks pass here, you don't get paid at all. You are no good to them if you can't play. If it is a long injury, you are gone. That's why so many guys play in pain.'

And that was also why the medicals were so intensive. It was ruthless for players.

Yet, all along I never felt any resentment from anyone. Team unity was vital and I always felt the linemen had my back.

It helped that I kicked a couple of winning field goals, which I did at Murrayfield against the Claymores and the Olympic Stadium in Barcelona to beat the Barcelona Dragons.

There were a few hairy moments, made all the more frightening by seeing close up just how hard they hit each other. Some of them are happy to try and kill. I guess you have to be that committed.

In fairness, I only ever got into two proper scrimmages where the holder fumbled the ball. And I got off lightly – the holder got completely wiped out, suffering a snapped collarbone. We lost three quarterbacks that season and didn't have the strongest line but I got lucky.

After Barcelona, there was talk about me being drafted into the NFL in America, with the Monarchs still in with a shout of a play-off place.

It was all publicity drummed up by the NFL machine to get people talking about the European league – and I played along. I would genuinely have gone had I been asked but there were no formal offers and I'm not sure there was ever anything to it. I didn't pursue it, either.

We beat the Scottish Claymores at Murrayfield 10-9 but that was our only victory in the final four matches.

It was an unexpected bonus to my sporting career. Without necessarily realising it at the time, the Monarchs was just what I needed; after 18 months into retirement, my hair had finally grown back. I had adjusted to life after football.

CHAPTER SEVENTEEN

Talking Football

THERE IS NO CORRELATION BETWEEN PLAYING ABILITY AND coaching. Some of the game's best managers were average players while many top players have struggled to get their ideas across.

Coaching was something I had at the back of my mind for years but I was far from certain I could do it successfully.

I did my preliminary badge while at Manchester City and completed that qualification with Chelsea.

The next stage was to go to the 'A' licence. I was settled at Sky Sports – working on *Soccer Saturday* and at least one other show that week, with a further live midweek game usually involved – but it was hardly a full-time job.

I was happy being around to watch my kids grow up, do the school runs, attend sports days and the like but Howard Wilkinson came to me with a proposal that was too good to turn down.

He was appointed the Football Association's first ever technical director in 1997 and had been given what was basically a blank canvas to deliver a blueprint for English football.

Howard created what became known as the 'Charter for Quality', a strategic initiative which focused on the systemic development of young players and increasing the effectiveness of academies.

The National Football Centre project – which was eventually realised as St George's Park – was also formed on his watch, with the FA aware of various steps taken by other nations to centralise player development, France's national base at Clairefontaine notable among them.

As part of an attempt to help improve the sessions for young players, Howard wanted to give each age group a recently retired professional to act as a mentor alongside an FA coach. Each ex-professional would also have the chance to fast-track their 'A' licence.

It felt like a perfect step for me as the commitments were infrequent – during international breaks – and I was fortunate to work alongside Dick Bate, a really remarkable educator, and his assistant Kenny Swain.

Dick sadly died in April 2018. The level and depth of appreciation that greeted his passing from so many figures in the game only underlined how good he was.

He delivered coaching courses in 63 countries across the world and Howard said of him: 'He's worked on every continent except Antarctica and he'd have gone there to coach if he'd been asked.'

Dick was thoughtful, considered, eloquent and a real gentleman. When he spoke, kids listened and they got better because of him.

It was fascinating because there were things I didn't agree with in terms of the methods he employed but that was largely because I still had the mentality of a player.

I felt sometimes that was beneficial because you are on the same wavelength as the players. But other times, I was more of a teammate than a coach, which wasn't always the right dynamic. I wanted to be involved in every session, demonstrating and taking part in drills, but over time you learn to take a step back and observe.

Watching Dick structure training and apply a methodology taught me a lot I later employed as a coach.

We were assigned the Under-15s age group. Working with teenagers was new to me but Dick was really helpful on that score. I would approach it from a professional viewpoint but Dick would explain we couldn't coach them in the same way because while I knew the techniques at the level they aspired to, trying to coach kids in that mode assumed too much knowledge and in fact wasn't how to get them there.

Sometimes I was over-critical or too demanding but Dick knew how to judge his words better and I learned that. There was a good mix between us. I'd see things he wouldn't and vice versa.

I'd been an England schoolboy international and remember it fondly as the most amazing experience a youngster could have. I played against Wales and

France at Wembley, West Germany in the old Olympic Stadium in Berlin, and those memories stayed with me.

I was sent off once in a youth level qualifier against Italy in Rome – a dismissal everyone believed was unfair but a tough lesson at a young age in gamesmanship.

I'd also missed a penalty in the final moments of an England game at the 'Little World Cup' – a failure which meant we were knocked out. I knew a lot about the ups and downs of what they were going into.

Sky saw it as a good thing that I'd take a week out with the FA every so often because I was working with the up-and-coming talented youngsters, widening my knowledge of the stars of tomorrow.

David Bentley, who I would later coach at Tottenham, and Glen Johnson were two young players there who went on to do well.

Glen was the standout player for me at that time. He had physical attributes which obviously helped him in that age group but he also had a professional attitude far beyond his years.

Spells at Chelsea and Liverpool among other top clubs followed and it was no surprise – you can just see it in some people from a young age.

The second group I worked with included Jermaine Jenas and Dean Ashton, as part of the England squad for the 2002 Under-19s European Championships in Norway under manager Martin Hunter.

We went to a couple of different tournaments and those periods are quite intense. You obviously play several games close together and it was all about educating young players to handle tournament football, hoping one or two of them would go and play a World Cup with the seniors. Having that experience of being away, playing and recovering was an important step for them.

It is vital to tournament success at senior level. We used to say to them: 'You have to go to jail.'

For the period that you are there, you are in your room for long periods. You have to train, eat and recover exactly right because there are such short gaps between games. It takes time to understand that experience and thrive in it. Eventually, you learn to enjoy it.

Real competition at a young age is vital. Look at the success England had at youth level in 2017. We became Under-17 and Under-20 world champions because of the changes made several years ago to the development programme and approach in attitude to junior tournaments. For many of these kids, this is the most competitive football they have ever experienced because a lot of them are nowhere near the first teams of the clubs they are at.

Gareth Southgate did very well to harness that at the 2018 World Cup too but he also benefitted from Roy Hodgson taking such a young squad to Euro 2016.

Those players experiencing a second tournament – Harry Kane and Dele Alli among them – were a little wiser in Russia while the rest revelled in modest expectations and an atmosphere of expression.

Tournament football meant I was away in the summer, sometimes for a couple of weeks, but I had still got into a good work/life balance, being really active with football in coaching and media yet also in being able to watch my kids grow up. That said, it wasn't always easy viewing.

During the summer of 1996, Olly began to suffer from dizzy spells. Initially, we didn't think too much of it but they soon became more frequent.

In September, we took him to see an optician where tests revealed swelling on his optic nerve.

Olly was referred to an ophthalmologist, who saw him that week and ordered an MRI scan. A ten-day wait for the results only exacerbated the concerns that were already mounting.

Eventually, the call came. A shadow had shown up on the scan and we had to take Olly to Great Ormond Street hospital the next day.

The neurosurgeon told us he couldn't play any contact sport at all until we knew what we were dealing with. There was so much swelling on the optic nerve that an unfavourable blow could have made him go blind.

Further tests were required. We were both in shock but Olly, too young to appreciate the gravity of the situation having only turned 10, was furious with me and Lisa, as he had just become captain of his football team at Brentwood Preparatory School, the latest step in a promising youth career.

He was put on anabolic steroids but there was another agonising ten-day wait for the test results and this one was even worse given the possible outcomes. Neither of us slept. Olly couldn't really process what was happening.

Finally, the phone rang. It wasn't a tumour. It wasn't malignant. But they didn't know what it actually was.

To relieve the pressure he had a lumbar puncture, which helped temporarily.

We went through a lot of ups and downs after that. I can't convey how frightening that was.

His symptoms were bizarre and at times he was in a wheelchair. Every time they tried to reduce his medication, the pressure increased.

When he was poorly, he would be in bed or just sit in a chair all day to help cope with the pressure. Some days, people would come by to see him but he didn't have the energy to speak to them. He was in hospital a lot, sometimes for weeks on end.

You'd do anything for your kids but we were helpless and I hated it. Each time we'd take him to Great Ormond Street in agony, they would measure the pressure in his brain and it had increased.

As time wore on, they began to worry about the possibility of brain damage. I couldn't bear it. The effect on Olly was awful to see. The headaches would virtually paralyse him from the head down but then he would go in for a lumbar puncture and he would be relieved of the pain.

'It is like an elephant had been sitting on my head and he's just got off.'

That's how Olly described it. The pressure built over different periods each time – it could be a few weeks or a couple of months. But you could tell in his behavioural patterns when it was getting worse.

This went on for 22 months in total. He missed school for almost all that time. We tried everything but Lisa did not want to leave any stone unturned. We didn't ever stop at conventional medicine. We tried cranial osteopathy which helped a great deal to calm Olly and ease the discomfort he felt.

She read all sorts of medical journals in a bid to help aid a diagnosis. One such paper triggered the idea that if Olly underwent a dental procedure to widen his jaw, the roof of his mouth would drop and the fluid might flow better.

We discussed it with his neurologist and were given the option to try it. It was a throw of the dice.

Mercifully, the right number came up. Olly gradually recovered over a 22-month period as a combination of this dental bracing, cranial osteopathy, medication and a total of seven lumbar punctures brought him back to full health.

Lisa handled the whole experience brilliantly and thankfully, Olly is very bright and was able to make up the time lost in school. We are eternally grateful to the all the medical staff at Great Ormond Street, the dentists and Emma Bryant, the cranial osteopath for all their care and attention in addition to all our friends and family who supported us through this difficult time.

Things were looking up and life began to return to normal, thankfully. In February 1999, we were blessed with the arrival of Lydia. We were thrilled with four, healthy wonderful children – we were complete.

Yet, relations with my Mum and Dad were still strained. My older brother Andrew was having some personal difficulties. My younger brother Bradley wasn't speaking to him much at the time and neither was I.

I'd tried to help him but he'd been pushing me away. Bradley is very black or white on things like this and he'd chosen to give Andrew a wide berth; living in Grimsby, who he was playing for at the time, only distanced him further from the situation.

Lisa had spoken to my Mum about the domestic tensions and suggested getting everyone together at their house for tea in September 1999 to celebrate my Dad's birthday.

Lisa and I turned up with the kids. Andrew had his back to us and didn't even turn around when we arrived. Bradley and Hayley turned up shortly afterwards and he did the same to them.

Bradley couldn't take it and started calling Andrew out on his behaviour. I backed up Bradley. It went completely pear-shaped after that.

And all the while, Dad just let it happen. Olly was old enough to understand what happened and after getting the kids back home, he was very upset. I called Dad and told him if Olly relapsed into illness over this, I'd kill him. I didn't mean it, of course, but I was furious and extremely upset too.

My kids were the pressing concern. Olly's illness had caused us all kinds of stress in the previous years while Edward was suffering with severe asthma, also spending spells in hospital. Relations with Mum and Dad were put on the backburner and it festered in the interim period.

Lisa is a people-pleaser and she tried to rectify the situation three months later in December, when we organised a pre-Christmas gathering.

Lisa invited Bradley and his family down after a Grimsby game to spend some time with us. She also asked Mum and Dad to come but they only wanted to know if we'd spoken to Andrew. He'd treated us so appallingly at the September gathering – on top of several other incidents – that we decided not to.

Dad therefore said he wouldn't come. Mum took the middle ground by stating she would pop up for a cup of tea but wouldn't come for lunch.

She did just that. My sister-in-law Hayley and Lisa had bought angel outfits for the two babies – our Lydia and Phoebe – and I think seeing these and chatting about our plans to celebrate the millennium with all our family and friends in a marquee in our garden brought the emotion of the family squabbling home to her.

She got upset and went to leave. I followed her out onto the driveway.

'What's the matter, Mum?' I asked.

'I'm going to stick by my first love – and that's your father!'

I think we both knew at that exact moment that a line in the sand was being drawn.

'Mum, whatever Dad decides, don't let it stop you coming here. You are always welcome here to see us and the children.'

From that day, Mum came to the odd party over the following few months but then she gradually stopped sending cards at Christmas and birthdays to us and the kids. They had no further contact with us nor Bradley, Hayley or Phoebe, which is very sad.

The exact impact of Olly's illness on his sporting career is difficult to measure. It must have done something to his physical development to not play regularly in his early teenage years, a crucial period in the growth of any young player.

Still, he captained Essex in cricket at junior levels from Under-9's to Under-16s and was also showing plenty of promise as a footballer in the youth system at West Ham.

In all honesty, as a fine wicket-keeper batsman, he probably should have chosen cricket. But instead he focused on his football. The opportunity for a scholarship at West Ham was there and he went all out for it.

Despite showing great potential, they decided not to offer him a professional contract. There's a lot I'd like to say about it because a lot was going on behind the scenes at West Ham during that period but let's just say it didn't feel like an even playing field.

People might say that sounds like sour grapes – and ultimately I'm just like any other parent – but these things happen in football sometimes. Some players don't get what they deserve.

Instead, Steve Bruce offered Olly the chance to go to Birmingham on a professional contract and he spent two enjoyable years there. He scored regularly for the reserves before getting a serious knee injury which required surgery and meant he never made a first-team appearance.

His knee was never quite the same after that. Olly went to Barnet then Stevenage Borough, before a brief loan spell at Crawley Town and then one game at Thurrock.

He told me he was sat on the bench and one of the other players asked him something about the game.

'And when he did, do you know what, Dad?' he said. 'I didn't even know the score. In that moment, I knew I was done. I wasn't interested – the love had gone.'

That's quite a realisation aged just 23. Not long afterwards, he played in a game and ended up in a block tackle which damaged his knee again. I went down to see him in the treatment room and he just said: 'I can't do this anymore.'

He took it upon himself to get an interview for a broker's job in the city. I had no idea he was even pursuing it.

'I've known I was finished for a while,' he told Lisa and I back at home. 'My knee has gone for good, I'm not going to play at the level I want to so that's it. I gave it a go but that's that.'

The following day, I drove him into London for his interview.

'Dad, what happens in an interview?' He'd never had one.

'Olly, I have no idea.' Neither had I. All I could say was 'good luck', 'be yourself' and a few other platitudes.

An hour later, he came out and we began the journey home.

'How was it?'

'It was great. We chatted about football, cricket and golf. The guy who was hiring is a big Spurs fan so we talked about you,' he said. 'After about 20 minutes, I had to say "This is great but can we talk about the job?" He just said "Oh, don't worry about that – the job's yours."'

And he's never looked back. Olly's made a success of himself in the city and I'm immensely proud of him for reinventing himself like that. He did well in maths at school but had no specific qualifications. He just made the most of the opportunity he was given.

I was devastated for him when his playing career finished. The life football has afforded me was something I wanted for him. Of course, I'm biased but he had ability. He could score goals but at the end of the day, he had the Allen name.

Like me with my Dad, he was always going to be compared, often unfavourably.

In a lot of ways, I was like my Dad with Olly. I was hard on him because it made me who I was. Lisa had a completely different approach and it caused a few arguments between us because she'd seen how my Dad's attitude had affected me and our relationship. She didn't want this for me and Olly.

When he moved into a completely different walk of life which I had no frame of reference for, I couldn't give advice and he quickly became his own man. I'm glad about that.

Olly now plays golf more than anything else. We play together but I think Ed might end up being better than both of us. We all play sport – the girls are into their hockey and netball too. It is what we do.

We differ in mentality, though. Lisa hasn't got a competitive bone in her body. And win, lose or draw, Ed and Lydia have a great day. In a way, I can't relate to that. Amelia is the world's most competitive person on a netball court and she follows after me. It is amazing how kids take on different traits. Lisa and I compliment each other well in that regard – it is probably a reason why our marriage has endured like it has.

I worked for Sky for nearly eight years. The best thing about it was George Best. We were both on the very first *Soccer Saturday* show together. At the start, we would go on air at 11.45am for 15 minutes as a teaser to what was coming that afternoon. There was usually a live game at around midday so we would all go off for lunch and come back at 2.45pm, when the original show started. For those couple of hours, we'd all sit in the canteen and George would regale us with his catalogue of stories.

There were a few different guests who came in and out but George was always the star attraction, not that it ever went to his head. He was such a genuine, decent fella. Spending time with him was an honour.

Soccer Saturday ballooned in popularity in the same way the Premier League did and is now a staple part of the sporting weekend.

People still say to me today, 'I haven't seen you on Sky recently.' I haven't been on Sky for 15 years but people remember that period when it really took off.

Each pundit was on a rolling contract every season. Usually, we got to a couple of months before the end and renewal talks would begin, but as we neared the end of the 2000/01 season, for whatever reason, they didn't.

Nothing had been said to me about continuing. I was beginning to fear the worst when ITV Digital approached me with a view to joining them in a similar role. ITV fancied going head-to-head with Sky and were in the market for experienced broadcasters. Brian Barwick, later chief executive of the Football Association but at ITV then, called me to ask my situation.

I told him I was waiting on Sky but my contract was nearly at an end. Two days after my Sky deal ran out, I went to see Brian at Gray's Inn Road. He sold me the vision of ITV.

'We are terrestrial,' he began. 'I would never knock Sky for what they have done but Sky are division two. Working for ITV, you'd be in the Premier League. Where would you rather play? Sky have 500,000 viewers for *Soccer Saturday*. You'll get five million on ITV.'

I'd arrived at the meeting with an open mind and knew Brian was a big player in the media world, but his speech won me over. We agreed a deal and I shook hands.

As my foot hit the pavement leaving ITV's offices, my phone rang. It was Andy Melvin, the Sky *Soccer Saturday* producer.

'Hey, it's Andy. What the fuck do you think you're doing?'

I started looking around thinking someone must be watching me. 'I've been at Sky for a long time but I'm now out of contract,' I replied. 'I'm disappointed it hasn't been renewed.'

'What do you want then?'

'It isn't really for me to make demands – I was hoping you'd tell me.'

'I fucking hate you footballers.'

'Andy, I was a footballer for 17 years. For the last eight, I've worked for you.'

'I still fucking hate you footballers.' And he hung up.

Sky never made me a counter offer. ITV upped my salary and gave me the security of a three-year contract. It was a no-brainer from that point of view.

I had no idea whether Sky were planning to get rid of me or revamp their shows but Andy's reaction suggested they had just been slow on the uptake.

I worked on *The Goal Rush*, mainly with Ron Atkinson and John Barnes. It was the ITV equivalent of *Soccer Saturday* and I enjoyed it for six months or so. Until ITV Digital collapsed.

That security I mentioned earlier evaporated in an instant. Or so I thought. I must confess I never fully understood the contract I signed with ITV.

Completely by luck, my contract was with 'ITV Networks' and not ITV Digital. It meant I carried on with ITV on the World Cup, the Champions League and other rights they had for the length of my contract.

I was extremely lucky. Financially, things would have been difficult for us otherwise. It was our main source of income.

By early 2004, however, a chapter I thought might have closed forever suddenly re-opened. Tottenham were about to come back into my life in a very big way.

CHAPTER EIGHTEEN

Tottenham Calling

TOTTENHAM WERE IN A MESS WHEN DAVID PLEAT RANG ME. Glenn Hoddle had been sacked as manager in September 2003, a decision which triggered a slanging match between the pair, emanating from David's level of influence as Director of Football, a role to which he had been appointed five years earlier.

There had always been a degree of tension between those two, even during Glenn's very successful days as a player.

The best Spurs team during my time there in the 1980s owed a lot to David devising a system that suited me but also one which took all defensive responsibilities away from Glenn. He would tell us to get the ball to Glenn whenever we had it, such was the respect David had for his ability in possession.

I'm not sure Glenn ever quite appreciated that but then again I won't ever take sides here because he was the best passer of the ball I ever played with and David was one of the cleverest coaches in maximising the strengths of the players he had.

There was clearly an understanding on some level because David got so much out of Glenn as a player, but they never saw eye-to-eye and it turned particularly sour when they worked together in this new setup as manager and Director of Football.

Glenn was quoted shortly after his departure as saying David was 'so obstructive towards me, never working in harmony with me and always working to his own end – the job will be made just as difficult for any new manager coming in. This is the reason why I believe he [Pleat] should have the job on his own.'

I was watching all this from a distance but I'd heard the communication between them was poor. That sort of role seemed a perfect position for David given his passion for – and understanding of – the game but Glenn didn't want to work that way. Right from the beginning, the dynamic was awkward.

David was the first person to hold that title in the club's history, in fact one of the first in English football as a whole. Managerial omnipotence was still the preferred model and this move towards a more continental structure didn't sit well with some traditionalists.

Results eventually did for Glenn – Spurs had the worst points tally of any team in the calendar year of 2003 to that point with just 22 from 23 matches – and after a summer spend of £12million, chairman Daniel Levy made the change.

David took charge on a caretaker basis initially but after an upturn in results – seven wins and two draws from 12 games – Daniel decided in December to keep him on until the end of the season.

I had kept in touch with David since the end of my playing days but his call a few months later in spring 2004 was still something of a surprise.

He asked how I was but quickly moved the conversation on to whether I had any plans to go into club coaching.

His timing was impeccable. My contract at ITV was coming to an end and I had no chance of going back to Sky. There was about two months until the end of the season and David admitted he had no idea what would happen that summer.

'Just come in, work with the reserves, see if you like it and we'll go from there,' he said.

It felt like a good opportunity to test out what I'd learned during my time at the FA but also my experience in France. I'd picked up methods of improvement at Bordeaux which weren't around when I was coming through.

The endless repetition in practice which I did as a kid does not quite happen anymore. It is much more limited and controlled within the academy setups. They spent so much more time working in France, too. These kids were at it all day long, focusing on their technique, and they were more advanced at a younger age as a result.

I saw the benefits first-hand during my time in Bordeaux, playing in several games with the youngsters as part of a reserve team which competed in the French Third Division.

Those matches would be against reserve sides from other professional clubs or amateur teams and there were a lot of potential stars, not least left-back Bixente

Lizarazu, who went on to great success with Bayern Munich and France, winning the 1998 World Cup and Euro 2000.

I told David I'd give it a go. I felt some trepidation before I arrived but the moment I walked back into the training ground, I knew it was where I was meant to be.

David told me to experiment from the outset. 'Get your ideas into practice,' he'd say. 'You develop them in your own way and over time, they will develop you as a coach.' It was great advice.

Taking my own sessions was a big step forward for me but in truth it wasn't really the time for grand plans. The club needed to appoint a permanent manager and it was clear the summer had to bring significant change.

Speculation had reached fever pitch over the identity of Glenn's permanent successor and completely overshadowed the end to the campaign – the first-team finished in fourteenth place.

Eventually, the reshuffle began. Frank Arnesen was appointed as sporting director, taking over from David. Frank had a decade's experience in the role working at PSV Eindhoven and wanted Martin Jol on board. Martin had forged an impressive reputation during a six-year spell at RKC Waalwijk and came in as coach. Many people felt Frank was keen on making Martin manager but my understanding was the chairman thought he wasn't ready.

Instead Jacques Santini, who had taken France to the quarter-finals of Euro 2004, took charge, coming in alongside his fitness coach Dominique Cuperly, with Chris Hughton and Hans Segers completing the backroom staff.

This new setup began pre-season. Jacques was aware of me from my time in Bordeaux. He asked me to help him initially because I spoke a little French and he wanted an insight into what was happening at the club.

I took the reserve group on a regular basis but also briefed Jacques on the first-team players and the club's infrastructure. This continued for four weeks but I had still not been offered a contract. So with David Pleat, the man who had initially brought me in, having left the club when Santini arrived, I requested a meeting with Frank.

We talked generally about football for an hour – Spurs, French football, the England team, everything and anything – before Frank got down to business.

'What is it you want, Clive?'

'What's my position here?'

'As it has been.'

'Okay, but I don't have a contract. David brought me in and since then there have been a lot of changes so I just want to clarify my role.'

'Don't worry, we'll sort that out. What have you been doing?'

'I've advised Jacques but also taken the reserve squad, which sits between the first team and the academy.'

'Okay, do you enjoy that?' Frank asked.

'Yeah, I love it.'

'Great – carry on doing that.'

'Okay, fine but I need a contract.'

'Don't worry, you will get one.'

And that was that. The sum total of the meeting was basically letting a guy who had been at the club coaching for a couple of months take charge of the reserve team setup. They had no idea what they wanted and also because it all came together with Jacques and Martin so quickly, anything away from the first team was not considered a priority. I was formally given a contract with the job title 'Development Coach'.

One of Frank's biggest assets was supposedly that he knew how to manage the relationship between sporting director – or technical director as some people call it – and manager or head coach, but things quickly turned sour. Roles were unclear. I had no involvement with the first team yet Frank occasionally sought my opinion over signings.

A trusted scout of his from Holland had watched Michael Carrick prior to that summer transfer window at West Ham and concluded that he wasn't good enough for Tottenham. I was asked to give some input because my son Olly was with Michael at Upton Park.

'What's the situation with Michael?' I said to Olly.

'Well, he's had injuries and is struggling for form but there's a good player in there.'

I relayed that to Frank.

'So would you take him?' said Frank.

'Yes, I think I would,' I replied. 'It is like any transfer though – the price would have to be right.'

'Okay, what do you think he's worth?'

'Probably about £5million.'

'We might be able to get him for £1.5m.'

'Frank, in that case we have got to take him.'

'But my scout says he can't play consistently.'

'He's had problems but, honestly Frank, he'll return your £1.5m in no time.'

Frank decided to go for it and although the fee ended up being slightly higher – £3.5m – it was still a bargain and we signed him. In virtually the first training session Michael played in, he got injured. I couldn't believe it.

The catalyst for Michael's progress was a change in manager, something that occurred just 13 games into the season and although that constituted the shortest reign in Tottenham's history, it was a long time coming.

Both Jacques and Martin Jol were unhappy almost as soon as the season started. About three weeks into the season, Jacques and I sat at the training ground having breakfast.

'Everything okay, boss?' I asked.

'No.'

'What's wrong?'

'The chairman… this is not what he said it was. It is not going to work.'

He was very calm and clear. Neither expected to work with the other and they had been sold a vision of life at the club that was very different to the reality.

They had no relationship to speak of. The atmosphere around the place wasn't good as a result and the manager's departure shortly afterwards didn't come as a surprise. Martin, who had done very little during Jacques's time in charge, took the helm.

Michael got injured again after that initial problem but once he came back, Martin wanted to get him in the team and he just took his game to another level. By then I had my group and felt I knew what I was doing. While I was in France, I decided to write down the different training drills and techniques I'd been exposed to and they were working wonders on the Spurs kids.

The reserve team was ticking along well enough. Martin took Chris Hughton from a scouting role and made him assistant coach.

Martin wanted to oversee everything and engage with the youngsters. Consequently, there was now a pathway from the academy, through the reserves to the first team. Compared to the darkness of before, it was lit up like a runway.

One of Martin's greatest strengths was that he understood English football, having played here with West Bromwich Albion and Coventry City in the 1980s.

He understood the mentality. He knew what it took to get through to players and how to win. The Spurs boys liked him as a result, now free to impose his methods with Jacques no longer on the scene.

Initially, I remained in my role as development coach but also performing supplementary duties, which including scouting potential players. I was abroad on one such assignment for Martin's first Premier League game in charge: the November 2004 derby at White Hart Lane.

No match encapsulated the organised chaos Martin was trying to bring like this. Noureddine Naybet gave us the lead before Arsenal quickly went 3-1 up. Jermain Defoe scored only for Freddie Ljungberg to restore their two-goal advantage. We fought to the end, trading blows, but the scoreline finished 5-4 in the visitors' favour.

Spurs had lost but this game was a model for what he wanted, in an attacking sense at least. Martin focused on the tempo of the team, the way we moved the ball. Especially at home, the plan was to try and get on the front foot as early as possible and push teams back. There was an obvious Dutch influence there, too, but he felt that was well suited to England. It was also in keeping with Tottenham's traditions. At their best, Martin's teams could be devastating.

And Martin was a coach. He wanted to be out there with the players, influencing them on the training field. He had a very organised plan of the training regime – it was too early to see that have an effect against Arsenal that day – and the players very quickly bought into that.

He started well overall – winning Premier League Manager of the Month for December 2004 – and on New Year's Day a turning point arrived for me.

The first team had a game against Everton and Martin spoke to me about possibly giving a chance to Dean Marney. The games come thick and fast at that time of year and he was keen to rotate. Dean, an industrious central midfielder, was with me in the reserve squad and had played in our last game before Christmas – a 2-2 draw away at West Ham.

'I'm thinking of playing Deano, what do you reckon?' he asked me.

'I think he's ready, boss,' I said. 'Stick him in and he won't let you down.'

Dean had come through the youth ranks and made a few first-team appearances in the 2003/04 season without pulling up any trees, but I just felt he had reached a stage where he could do well.

Martin threw him in. I was a little nervous watching on so you can imagine my delight when he scored the opening goal and later added his second in a resounding 5-2 win.

Martin patted me on the back the first time I saw him afterwards and his nephew Robert, who worked with him at the club, told me how superstitious he was. If the team wins and he likes the people involved, he keeps them around. That was evident in his treatment of me.

He saw that I was going to give him an honest opinion, whether he agreed with it or not, and that was something he valued, plus Dean had given me some credibility by playing so well. More opportunities to have an input into the first team followed.

I continued as development coach but in the same way he would come to reserve matches, I began travelling with the first team as the second half of that season unfolded.

I had the best of both worlds: day-to-day involvement with the reserves and a degree of control before having the chance to watch Martin manage the first team at close quarters with only partial personal responsibility.

Chris Hughton was one of the most professional, thorough and detailed coaches imaginable. The way he carried himself was a lesson for everybody, me included. He was clearly on the path to becoming a fine manager and I never felt he would do anything other than succeed given the time and effort he put in.

Chris was Martin's most trusted ally. He was tireless in the way he worked and for me as a younger coach, it was a great example to follow.

The rest of the campaign was a mixed bag – league wins against Manchester City, Newcastle and Aston Villa offset by defeats to Charlton, Arsenal and Middlesbrough – and Spurs finished in ninth place.

Yet everybody felt that we had something to build on. Frank and Martin got on really well and everybody seemed to be pulling in the same direction after months of internal wrangling.

That was until Frank left in controversial circumstances. New Chelsea owner Roman Abramovich was searching for greater football expertise and you can understand why they wanted to take Frank from us; he was comfortable in the role and had an excellent network of contacts. Daniel didn't let him go without a fight – there were media reports at the time claiming compensation was anywhere between £3m and £10m – but eventually Frank got his way and moved to Stamford Bridge.

As staff, you have to accept it, but it felt like a blow to lose him because the club had the intention to move forward in this direction and Frank was the right man to make it work.

Everybody liked him. He was a football man and he understood the game. The whole structure of the club was destabilised by having to look for a new sporting director.

Damien Comolli, a former Arsenal scout and later technical director of Saint-Étienne, was confirmed as his replacement.

Damien set about overhauling the academy setup and for that he deserves a lot of credit. He had a great insight into what we had to do in the wider development of the academy. John McDermott, who is still there now, along with Under-18s coach Alex Inglethorpe, bought into Damien's philosophy and they all helped make it a reality.

The quality of the young players coming in also improved. Damien built up a talent identification network that was far greater than anything that existed before. It was global in scale, which represented a massive undertaking. His contacts were very important in that. You had to appoint the right scouts to identify those players at a young age and then develop that talent in an effective training facility.

That took a long time to come to fruition. Spurs now have one of the best programmes and facilities in European, if not world football, and they owe some of that to Damien.

At this point, I was enjoying taking what I'd learned from being around the first-team setup and applying it to the reserves, especially enthused by the knowledge both Martin and Damien were keen on producing our own first team players.

The most enjoyable time for me was when I coached alone as I could really get my hands dirty. Most development coaches have to learn on the job because it involves different numbers every day, often with very late changes if the first team want to take a player or two. Most reserve groups are made up of senior players and kids – a real mix. You are often thinking on your feet and that helped me develop as a coach. I really enjoyed that challenge.

Having an impact on young players is immensely satisfying. In the summer of 2005, Aaron Lennon joined us from Leeds and he initially found it difficult to establish himself.

He played for me a few times in the reserves and I like to think I helped him develop. I still enjoy catching up with him whenever our paths cross now. In fact, I had a decent relationship with the vast majority of the players. Jamie O'Hara was another one we developed who went into the first team and did well.

Aaron went about his business quietly. We knew he'd had a tough upbringing in Leeds and came to us saying he wanted to play as a centre-forward or number 10. But his lightning pace and small frame demanded he played out wide. Once he appreciated his strengths and his teammates recognised his quality, they gave him good service and he went from strength to strength.

He wasn't the best finisher or very consistent with his delivery but he'd get into dangerous areas time and time again. We just tried to give him the confidence to express himself. We'd often split off into small sessions tailored to encourage him to take on defenders, devise drills to develop the right angles and method of attack that would help maximise his talent.

The reserve group often contained other notable players including Tom Huddlestone, Wayne Routledge, Charlie Daniels and Lee Barnard. Results are not everything for the club in reserve matches because each individual has their own goals, but part of your job is to combine that into a collective and things were going better than I could have hoped for.

We lost in early October to Arsenal and again in November to Leicester but we'd only lose one more game all season, winning 20 out of 26 matches to win the 2005/06 Barclays Premier Reserve League South title, with Barnard scoring 19 goals in 19 games. It was right up there with the proudest moments of my entire career. I loved every minute of it. My only regret is we lost the Play-Off Final at Old Trafford to Manchester United in early May but it didn't take away from the consistency the team had shown despite an ever-changing cast of characters.

Reserve team success in itself doesn't lead to anything, of course. The whole setup was geared towards training homegrown players to make an appearance in the first team. Once they did so, that would also trigger bonuses for them and us.

Besides, what happened with the first team three days later overshadowed it completely.

*

The first team had got to the final day of the 2005/06 season needing to beat West Ham at Upton Park to qualify for the Champions League. It would be the first time Tottenham had qualified for Europe's premier club competition in 44 years.

A win against the Hammers would guarantee finishing above Arsenal – our fiercest rivals who had secured a higher league placing than us for 11 consecutive seasons – to hold on to fourth place and the final qualification spot. The top four was a barrier Spurs had been aiming to break for years and here, finally, we were 90 minutes away from doing it.

Martin Jol always liked to take the team away the night before games even if we were playing in London and this time we were in the Marriott hotel in West India Quay, next to Canary Wharf. The Gunners were staying at the Four Seasons just around the corner.

I wasn't there because I'd been taken ill and on the advice of the medical staff, I was told to stay away from the team to ensure there was no risk of spreading infection. That was a standard decision for anyone who comes down with a sickness bug but the irony of it turned out to be remarkable.

A buffet was laid on for the players with most of them choosing to eat lasagne. Just after midnight, players began falling like flies.

Michael Carrick could hardly walk. Edgar Davids, Michael Dawson, Aaron Lennon and Robbie Keane were among those to fall ill with food poisoning.

On the morning of the game, Daniel Levy phoned Premier League chief executive Richard Scudamore to ask whether a postponement was possible. It wasn't.

The bus came to take the squad to the ground but Martin and Chris were still going around the group seeing who was in any kind of condition to play. There were about six players who wouldn't have been anywhere near the starting line-up in normal circumstances.

Some were just about up to it, others weren't. Some probably lied and said they were okay when deep down they were struggling. That was the character they'd shown all season to get to the brink of Champions League football.

Within ten minutes, Carl Fletcher gave West Ham the lead. Arsenal were winning against Wigan. Everything was slipping through our fingers. Jermain Defoe equalised to give us hope but Yossi Benayoun restored the Hammers' advantage with ten minutes remaining and there was nothing left in the tank.

Arsenal won 4-2 in the final league to ever be played at Highbury and our misery was complete. It was a massive disappointment. We'd geared ourselves up for the whole season to reach the top four. We couldn't have gone into that last game in a worse state through something completely unforeseen.

Of course, during the season we'd dropped points we shouldn't have here and there but nobody could account for those circumstances on the final day.

Everybody on reflection felt it was terribly bad luck. Wrong place, wrong time and so, so costly. But that conclusion wasn't reached before the club tried a number of avenues, contacting the Premier League to explore the possibility of the game being replayed and speaking to environmental officers at Tower Hamlets council to see if the hotel had a case to answer.

I was even examined to see whether the illness I had at the time had contributed to the players' condition. I had a flu bug and to miss West Ham away on the final day of the season was the last thing I wanted but it was completely the right call. That said, I was surprised when the doctor came to me one day the following week to say I needed to go for an examination. They tested everybody to get to the bottom of what went wrong: every player, the staff, even some non-football staff.

I wasn't worried – I knew there was no correlation whatsoever and this was a case of the club following a rigorous internal examination – but I can honestly say I'd never been tested in this context before.

That summer, Michael Carrick was sold to Manchester United for £18.6million. He'd become a great player for us and I was sad to see him go but it only gave me more confidence that I could spot players at a young age. I'd played a part in making the club a huge profit and this was Daniel and Damien's preferred model: buy young talent, mould them into proper players and sell on for a significant sum.

The plan obviously relies a lot on talent identification and this is where Damien, to my mind, claimed undue credit.

He is an extremely clever man. He presents himself as a fountain of football knowledge but his greatest skill is aligning himself to people who understand the game and absorbing their expertise. He had a very effective network of contacts and the academy system was excellent. But I felt he overstated his own eye for spotting a player and his overall importance to the club in first team transfers.

He's forged a very successful and lucrative career for someone who, in my opinion, doesn't really have a feel for the game.

His 'Moneyball' mentality of developing players and turning a profit in the transfer market was very attractive to Daniel given the way he operates but how much did he really achieve?

In many ways, Damien was a forerunner for a lot of what we have now. Everyone thinks they can analyse a player with facts and figures to find the answers. I don't know whether it's because I am a dinosaur but for me there are certain principles that still apply. You cannot use numbers alone to identify whether someone is a good player or not. How do you measure someone's commitment or their capacity to develop with age? Damien always believed those intangible qualities could be quantified. Real football experts don't think that way. Football is not a clinical, cut-and-dried sport. Players can always surprise you and equally their numbers might be great but that doesn't guarantee success. All top clubs have analytics departments nowadays but there wouldn't have been a set of numbers in the world that would have told you at the start of his career that Harry Kane would become the player he is now.

That's not to say analytics have no place or that signing players on instinct can work in isolation; I worked with Harry as a teenager and I have to hold my hands up and say I never thought he would turn into a world-class striker.

But the best recruitment departments allow both aspects to shape their transfer policy. There is no magic formula you can write down on a piece of paper. On reflection, there are reasons why Harry did kick on. It comes down to all the fundamentals you need: the work ethic, the character, the determination, the self-belief – not just natural ability. None of these are quantifiable by a number and that would always be my argument.

Damien did a job for the club which was way beyond his capabilities and subsequently he's been to Liverpool and Saint-Étienne where it has not worked out for him. That's because what he believes in doesn't work in isolation. He would, of course, argue otherwise.

I like him – he's a good guy – but he is a businessman in a football world. If someone had assessed me on my numbers alone as schoolboy, I doubt I would have had the chance to make a career. Would I have been physically strong enough? Maybe not. They would have been able to quantify my lack of pace. There are a lot of factors that would have gone against me.

And I feel things happened on his watch which unfairly enhanced his reputation. The summer of 2006 saw Dimitar Berbatov arrive at White Hart Lane and that transfer is often cited as one of Damien's finest moments. But the truth is Dimitar was tracked for a long time before Damien was at the club.

Spurs' chief scout Eddie Presland and his staff were on his case and although Damien obviously helped to get the deal over the line, that deal wasn't his success story alone, far from it. It was the same with Luka Modrić, who was signed two years later.

Damien's relationship with Martin Jol began to deteriorate over time. The first team finished fifth in the 2006/07 season, eight points behind Arsenal in fourth. The style of football meant Martin still had the fans onside and a strong end to the campaign – losing just once in the league from 21 February – was supplemented by a run to the UEFA Cup quarter-finals, where we lost to Sevilla, managed by Juande Ramos.

It wouldn't be the last time Juande would get one over on Martin, who began to feel Damien was pursuing players he wasn't interested in signing.

He gradually believed he was being undermined. It didn't help that in August, pictures emerged in a Spanish newspaper of Spurs officials with Juande while Martin was still in job. It got worse.

In late October, Tottenham were playing at home in a UEFA Cup match against Getafe. I was in the crowd. We were in the lower level of the stand behind the dugout and we heard a rumour sweeping through the ground: Martin was getting sacked that night.

We weren't far from the press area either and you could sense from the amount of movement, phone calls and general atmosphere that the journalists knew something was up.

Martin's brother was alongside us and he got a message during the first half. I don't know for certain what happened at half-time but Martin reportedly became aware during the break that his time was up. Maybe his brother told him.

The atmosphere was surreal. Nobody had any hard facts as to what was going on. All I remember was at the end of the game, the players were kept in the dressing room while Martin disappeared to go and see the chairman. John Alexander, club secretary, came in to tell us Martin was in a meeting and we had to stay put. Only then did we know something definitive had happened. I've never experienced a managerial departure quite like that. You accept that at the end of games sometimes there is speculation and certain managers are under pressure but never that a decision would be leaked or circulated during the game.

We'd had a bad start – one win in ten league matches was Spurs's worst return for 19 years – but Martin never acted like he was under greater strain than usual in the days and weeks leading up to that moment.

He always conducted himself in exactly the same way whether the team was winning or losing. There had been speculation but I don't think anybody thought it would end in the way it did.

So began another sea change. Juande was appointed but not in time to take charge of that weekend's home game against Blackburn. I was given the responsibility and it was a fantastic experience to have that control. You can't do too much in that situation though. You are just trying to pick a team to win one game because you don't know what the future holds, even with your own position. We lost the game 2-1 in stoppage time – always the worst way to lose. We just didn't take our chances and it was a difficult atmosphere for the team given there were supporters protesting against Daniel's handling of Martin's departure.

Martin had taken an active interest in me and the reserve players I was working with but a new manager can always bring a fresh approach so I went to see Juande after he took over to find out if he viewed things in a similar way.

'What's your philosophy? I've been working with the younger players and also more recently with the first team,' I said. 'I'm really enjoying both roles.'

'Clive, you will not be with me. I have Marcos [Alvarez], my [fitness] coach, and I will have my first team group.'

'Okay, well I have some players working with me who have potential and could break into the first team.'

'I don't want to know. If I want a player, I will tell you. But you have your group and I have mine.'

'In that case, what do you want me to do with them? Under Martin, the reserves ran parallel with the first team in terms of the work we did and the style of play we tried to pursue.'

'I don't want to know.'

I had to ask more questions. 'So, what about the young players – do you want recommendations for possible options?'

'No. I have my group and in fact I will give you players. There are players I don't want. You deal with them.'

You couldn't ever divulge that lack of interest to the reserve group but the fact Juande was so rarely around was a clue in itself.

Some of them had very little, if any, first-team experience but there are always examples of lads who go on to have good Premier League careers after not being given an opportunity. Tottenham had that with Charlie Daniels and Adam Smith, who both ended up in the Premier League together at Bournemouth.

Those players on the fringes should always go out on loan at the earliest possible opportunity. You are playing men's football then. You are playing for points.

The further you go down the leagues, the more bonuses matter to players. For Premier League players, bonuses are just the icing on the cake of their basic wage, but these lads in the lower leagues need them to pay the bills in some cases. Fans are unforgiving too.

Young players are not going to be exposed to that primal hunger in an academy setup as they currently exist. I'm not saying it isn't competitive but the experience is completely different. You are in a cocoon in an academy. Lower-league football is the real world.

It is tougher with the more established players. There was a first team squad pre-season camp ahead of the 2008/09 season in Spain. Seven players were left out, including Steed Malbranque and Teemu Tainio.

'These seven players are yours, Clive,' he said.

'Okay, what do you want me to do with them?'

'Whatever you like.'

I asked Marcos whether he had a programme he wanted me to follow with these players but aside from a few drills, they gave me free reign.

Juande wasn't a cold man by nature. He was just clinical in the way he worked because once those players were out, they had no chance of getting back in.

The effect Juande's approach had on the first team was clear to me. Chiefly through that fear of being kicked out of the club, so many of them were playing scared. They saw what he did to other players he perceived weren't pulling their weight or not proving effective enough.

I drew on my past as a player. For Steed and the others, they knew they were moving on. They had a pre-season to get themselves fit and earn a move. I'd been there myself, working in isolation at City to revive my career. I put myself in their shoes and could sympathise.

'Make sure you do everything right,' I'd say. 'The training is geared towards getting you fit for the start of the season. If that isn't here – and it doesn't look like it is – then you'll prove to other clubs you have the right attitude for a move.'

They responded impressively. Morale was still sometimes low among the reserve squad because the young players are also quick to work out chances will be limited. If nobody is being called up to train with the first team, let alone making matchday squads, the writing is very much on the wall.

It was difficult at times, especially because there was no end game for them or me. People in my role were often judged on getting one or two youngsters into the first team or resurrecting a player whose career looked finished but, in a polar opposite approach to Martin, Juande made it clear there was no chance of that.

Looking back on that period, it was a very useful experience to be given such responsibility, but also daunting at the same time. Many players felt stuck or suffocated.

Our 2007/08 reserve team season produced reasonable returns. We finished fifth out of ten teams, eight points behind winners Reading having won eight and drawn six of our 18 matches.

The first team won the 2008 League Cup, coming from a goal down to beat Chelsea in extra time. It was Spurs's first trophy in nine years but in some ways it was also the worst thing that could have happened.

The majority of the players were having difficulty with Juande's methods because every mistake was punished in the extreme. If you messed up, you were out. There was a culture of fear.

But winning a trophy reinforces what managers believe in. If you succeed through your methods – and a win over Chelsea was undoubtedly a big achievement – you are never going to change. The board are less likely to ask questions too. I wonder if he thought the League Cup was enough.

You have to give that group of players a lot of credit because even when they didn't agree with what the manager was preaching, they got there and won it. It is very hard for players to express themselves in that environment though, again a far cry from Martin's style. And it got worse after the final.

Spurs won three of their last twelve Premier League games after the final, against West Ham and Portsmouth at home and Reading away, finishing eleventh – 30 points behind Liverpool in fourth place.

That summer saw a big turnover of players with Luka Modrić, Roman Pavlyuchenko, David Bentley and Heurelho Gomes among the arrivals while

Robbie Keane, Teemu Tainio, Younès Kaboul and Steed Malbranque were among those to leave.

The biggest departure, however, was the one most people expected yet took the longest to materialise.

Dimitar Berbatov is a genius. I absolutely loved him. He was an introvert but had an incredible love and knowledge of the game. He knew my record at the club and often wanted to talk about football in general, being a striker. I loved working with him. He could see and do things other players couldn't.

Just before he went to Manchester United, he had been alienated from the first team. I had the group on a Saturday morning while the first team were away. Everybody knew he was going but they were still finalising the transfer fee. Daniel had even released a statement condemning United manager Sir Alex Ferguson's 'sheer arrogance' in claiming he was confident of getting the deal done, branding it 'one of the worst [tapping up] offences by any manager in the Premier League to date'.

Things were at risk of getting ugly and Daniel, as ever, was playing hardball. Dimitar came to see me on the Friday.

'Coach, are you training tomorrow?' he asked.

'I am, Dimitar, but I've got a mixed group – a few young ones, the reserve group and a couple of senior players coming back from injury. I'm happy for you to come and join us but you have to do it right.'

He gave me a deathly stare in response. 'Coach, what do you expect?'

'All I'm saying is you have to train correctly even in your circumstances.'

He was devastated. 'What do you mean?'

'Because of who you are, I can't have you influencing this group in any way.'

'I would never do that.'

'I'm not saying you would, I'm just telling you now: don't come in and be silly.'

He walked away mid-conversation. I decided to let him go. The following morning he came in and was absolutely impeccable. He was great with the younger players, stopping to help them. We played a few small-sided games, some physical work and then running. They were in three groups moving around between each. He never questioned anything and was fantastic.

At the end, we were all warming down and he walked over to me with his arm outstretched to shake my hand.

'Coach, fantastic session, I'm done.' But he hadn't warmed down properly.

'Shit, what am I going to do now?' I thought to myself. The kids were sitting there and I had a decision to make: call him back and risk a scene or let him go but set a bad example to the young ones. I let him go and made an excuse for him, saying he was off to get a massage.

I asked one of the youngsters: 'What was he like today?' The kid looked at me and said: 'He was unbelievable.'

I replied: 'What does that tell you?'

'He's a good professional.'

'Yes, and? What's happening with him?'

'Well, he's going to Man United.'

'So, do you think he's come in here today to just go through the motions?'

'No'

'Right, so what did he do?'

'He was flat out.'

'Why has he done that?' They weren't getting it. After a pause, I continued: 'When he goes to Old Trafford in a few days or a week, is he going to be up to speed and ready to go?'

'Ah, yeah.'

I tried to give them a message – getting myself out of difficulty at the same time given he walked off – that he's a model pro.

I went in to see Dimitar.

'Are you okay? Why did you walk in?'

'I needed to stretch out and get into the warm.'

'But you didn't warm down with the group.'

'Oh, coach, I'm really sorry!'

'Don't worry, its fine.' He'd made his point and so had I. I thought Dimitar and United were a match made in heaven. I thought he'd be a megastar. It was a brilliant move by United and the stage was perfect for him. Whether he couldn't handle it, I don't know. Having spoken to people at United, I know they found him a bit strange. They couldn't quite work him out. He was very insular – but what a talent. Dimitar and Luka were the best two players I worked with as a coach. They would still play the game the same way no matter how much they got paid.

Luka came into a difficult atmosphere, however.

The failure to effectively replace Robbie and Dimitar had put Damien under considerable pressure and the relationships between Juande, assistant Gus Poyet and the players had become tense in the extreme.

The start of the 2008/09 season made for painful reading: two points from eight games, seven defeats in ten across all competitions. Bottom of the Premier League.

Damien's last throw of the dice was to get rid of Eddie Presland and several other backroom staff including Tony Book, Bryan King and Alan Hill. It didn't save him.

And so, in late October, Juande was sacked with Damien following behind him. It was an admission that the director of football structure had failed.

'Now is the right time for us to move back to a more traditional style of football management at our club,' Daniel said upon Juande's departure.

The shift from manager to a wider infrastructure has taken a long time to evolve. Arsenal moved towards something similar following Arsène Wenger's departure in 2018 but Manchester United have struggled with changing in the post-Ferguson era.

At the time, this model was in its infancy in England and it caused barely-concealed friction. Who's buying the players? Are they liaising? How important is the academy? On a more extreme level – and I'd never level this at David Pleat, Frank Arnesen or Damien Comolli by the way – who is picking the team? There are so many situations which can cause confusion in decision-making that prompts a breakdown. And then, ultimately, who takes responsibility? That's why it has taken years for the English game to adjust.

After Juande was dismissed, Spurs abandoned the process. It is amazing what the threat of relegation can do. Instead, they turned to a man who was probably the antithesis of that shift towards a continental approach: Harry Redknapp.

CHAPTER NINETEEN

Coach Journey

THE ALLEN FAMILY'S RELATIONSHIP WITH HARRY REDKNAPP GOES back a long way. Both my Dad and uncle Den – Martin's Dad – used to coach Harry when he was at school. They were professionals at Chelsea and Charlton respectively but Harry told me they would take sessions in their spare time to help out.

He always said he liked them both and I like to think that level of respect carried along the lineage into my playing career, having worked under him with my cousin Martin at West Ham.

Although we usually chatted whenever our paths crossed, we hadn't actively kept in touch in the intervening years to 2008 and in a sense I was introducing myself all over again, certainly in terms of my ability as a coach.

Harry arrived with his trusted lieutenants Joe Jordan and Kevin Bond. They had more experience than me but I felt I could add something to the setup given my knowledge of the group and history with the club.

I also believed I was ready for regular first-team involvement having learned about the realities of life in the dugout at the highest level.

I felt my passion for the cause would be a useful asset to Harry, even if it occasionally got me into trouble on the touchline during matches.

I always used to chirp away at referees during my playing days. You never know if you'll get anywhere.

But you know they are human beings, prone to second-guessing themselves. When I started under Martin Jol, the fourth official had a microphone to communicate with the referee and you hope anything you say can have a bearing because the man in the middle is listening.

So, if he's given a bad decision against your team, you start asking questions. You want to put doubt in their mind that he might have made a mistake, whether he might decide to even it up.

I've stood there and said to the fourth official 'you wait until you see that on *Match of the Day* tonight – you've all got that horribly wrong. It's going to be embarrassing.' It is part and parcel of the game.

Harry decided to take me on but I knew I had to learn from a few previous incidents. I was almost never abusive but I'd keep going until the official drew a line. In my day as a player, the referee would say 'that's enough, I don't want any more of it' and you'd stop. You knew the boundaries. As a coach in that technical area, you are just trying to put uncertainty in their mind over a big decision, especially in the first 45 minutes, because you know they are all going to discuss it at half-time.

Three days after successfully recommending Dean Marney to Martin Jol, I was asked to travel with the first team to Old Trafford for their game against Manchester United.

It was the biggest match I'd been involved in as a coach and one that went on to become arguably the most infamous: in the 89th minute with the score at 0-0, Pedro Mendes launched an audacious right-foot shot from just inside United's half.

It was a ridiculous waste of possession at a key point in the game. Roy Carroll stood underneath the flight of the ball, waiting to catch it and launch another United attack. Except he fumbled it, pulling the ball behind him before diving backwards in vain, failing in his attempt to scoop the ball away. Our players celebrated. So did we. But play continued.

Mark Halsey was the fourth official and I still have the same discussion with him today when we work together in the media.

'Mark, you know it was a goal,' I'd say. On the night, we jumped up straight away. You could see it live. We ran down from the dugout, past the monitor located on the left-hand side just in time to see the replay which confirmed it.

Mark just stood there and we started screaming at him.

'Look, Mark, you can see it is a goal,' I said frantically. 'Tell him. Tell the referee.'

'I can't, I'm not allowed.'

'Do you know how costly this could be at the end of the season?' (I'm removing the expletives here as there were too many to mention).

No matter what anyone said to him, he wouldn't turn his head.

The linesman genuinely didn't see it and I don't blame him because he's running with his head down for that split second when Roy spills it.

It was absurd, though. It wasn't even close. That's why the monitors were removed from the dugouts the following year because they caused all sorts of animosity on the touchline. It only made people shout at fourth officials more.

The Mendes incident triggered another debate about goal-line technology but too many people were still resistant to change.

Whenever I'm asked the question about technology in football, my experience tells me it is always a good thing. I saw how it was used in the NFL and football has to use everything reliable it has at its disposal because they have to get these big decisions right. Goal-line technology, finally in use in the Premier League as of 2013, would have ruled Pedro's shot a goal immediately.

There were times when I would just want to vent at someone and the fourth official is the obvious target. But I was often coming at it from a tactical angle. I was trying to influence their decisions. I'm not alone in that, by the way.

There are always referees you don't like, some you feel consistently call tight decisions against you in matches.

In recent years, I often saw referees act with the feeling 'I've got to give that decision' rather than 'this is my decision'. They were fearful of repercussions from decisions they didn't give. Every referee is assessed and they seemed to live or die by those scores. They refereed by the book because they had to rather than apply any common sense.

Under the guidance and pressure from Professional Game Match Officials Limited (PGMOL) and the Premier League, they were taught to second-guess themselves.

Whatever club you support, you will have a referee who you remember for giving decisions against you. Mark Clattenburg was one we got the rough end of the stick from. He was the referee for the Mendes goal, and when Nani scored what even Harry – usually mild-mannered towards officials – described as a 'scandalous' goal against us on the same ground a few years later in 2010. We lost 2-0 but the second goal, six minutes from the end, came after our goalkeeper Heurelho Gomes rolled the ball out for a free-kick we thought had been given after Nani had clearly handballed it. Instead, he wasn't penalised and so the play was still deemed to be active. Nani turned around, collected the loose ball and rolled it into the empty net as Heurelho stood in disbelief. Mark Halsey was the fourth official then too.

I don't know if Clattenburg was pro-United. I've certainly called him 'Mark the Red' before. Martin Atkinson was another who was never a favourite of ours either.

Everybody is always trying to get an edge. Harry would do it by not making a fuss. Brian Clough would famously never question a referee and people said he got them onside because of it.

I was more combative and it wasn't always well received. The worst incident was in August 2005 when I reacted to Mido being sent off against Chelsea at White Hart Lane. It was a straight red card in the 25th minute for what referee Rob Styles deemed was a forearm blow to Blues defender Asier Del Horno's head. From the sidelines, I didn't get a chance to talk to Rob until half-time. For 20 minutes I stewed on it, winding myself up and as we headed down the tunnel together, I let rip. This was an occasion I did cross the line. I abused him terribly. He took offence to it and rightly so.

He reported me to the Football Association and I had to attend a hearing alongside club secretary John Alexander.

The FA then sent a report back to Tottenham and the club chose to fine me. I was warned over my future conduct and it was a realisation to me I had to calm down. But that was all part of the learning curve of being a coach – taking those emotions, that passion, and using it in a constructive way to help the team.

As if to underline the point, when I look back I can't even think of an occasion when all that cajoling of officials actually got my team a decision. I suppose you never know for certain whether it ever had a bearing – and maybe with more subtle things in the odd free-kick here and there it did – but when I reflect back on all the things I said over the years, it's a bit embarrassing really. Referees have actually said to me since that they were almost inclined to go the other way because of how vociferous I could be. Family and friends have argued the same point, telling me if I acted like that around them I almost certainly wouldn't get my way.

If I go back into coaching or management now, I still think I would ask the question but hopefully in a more considered, reasoned way. I'd definitely be more restrained.

The funniest thing is before going back to Barnet again in 2018, my cousin Martin spent a period assessing referees on behalf of the Premier League. I've seen him at a number of Spurs games and on one occasion, my other cousin Paul was also there. All three of us used to give refs hell and what does Martin say to us?

'Bloody hard job, they've got.' We all laughed together.

'You stood in that technical area ranting and raving and now you say that?' Paul said.

'I know. But now I analyse every decision they make, you realise how tough it is.'

Appreciating that and dealing with referees is an important part of a player's development, too. I've refereed practice games in first team sessions, with the reserve and youth teams at Tottenham and deliberately given decisions against my better judgement just to see how players react. You create a situation to test their resolve. The players used to hate me refereeing five-a-sides, eight-a-sides, whatever it was. I'd give a decision and they'd say: 'You must be joking.'

'Well, you have to deal with it,' I'd reply. 'It's going to happen.'

And you'd mention a referee, adding 'that's probably how he's going to do it this weekend'.

'You are rubbish.'

'The referee might be rubbish on Saturday. What will you do then? Complain to me?'

I also wouldn't give obvious fouls and shout at them to play on so they learned to keep going to the whistle. Switching off like that when you don't get a decision can be the difference in conceding a goal on a Saturday, the difference between winning and losing.

Not everything is going to go your way, no matter how blatant you think a foul is. The ones that deal with it well do so on a matchday as well because they have the right mentality. I have wound a few people up along the way but it is a useful trick in helping identify a player's character and also tackling dissent if that becomes a problem in the team. When I think back now, Dario Gradi did the same thing to me as a player at Crystal Palace.

Graduating to working with the first team meant my peers changed. Generally speaking, I didn't have a problem with any opposing staff or managers but former Arsenal boss Arsène Wenger was an exception.

The whole issue dates back to a game at Highbury in April 2006. Arsène was furious we didn't put the ball out of play after Emmanuel Eboué and Gilberto Silva ran into each other in the build-up to Robbie Keane scoring the opening goal. He went doolally to the fourth official and then squared up to Martin Jol on the touchline. Thierry Henry equalised and the game finished 1-1 but that was just the beginning of it.

Martin was doing his post-match media while Chris Hughton and I went and had a chat with Arsène's backroom staff, as we would do with most opposing teams at full-time.

There was a little manager's office opposite the home team dressing room. As we walked in, Pat Rice was there alongside goalkeeping coach Gerry Payton. I'd played alongside Pat and he was captain at Arsenal when I was there briefly. It was all very amicable – they offered us a glass of wine and we began exchanging pleasantries when all of a sudden the door slams open and in comes Arsène.

'I am not drinking with you,' he said. 'You are cheats.'

I took offence to that and turned to Chris.

'I'm out of here, I'm not having that,' I whispered to him. Chris told me under his breath to stay put. Nobody said anything out loud so Arsène's words hung in the air. I was adamant I wanted to leave. As I went past Arsène, I looked him in the eye.

'Don't call me a cheat,' I said. 'I was sitting eight rows back in the dugout. I didn't cheat.'

'You are all cheats,' Arsène said.

I walked out. Chris told me I shouldn't have said anything.

'I'm not being called a cheat, Chrissy, it's not on.'

Arsène came out of the manager's room a few seconds later and I decided to have another word.

'You know what? If that had been your team and they'd kicked the ball out, you'd have gone mad they didn't play on. The referee said play on to whatever conclusion.'

'No, no, no,' he said. 'You cheated.'

From that point on, all I wanted to do was shake his hand as a winner.

We actually beat them twice – once thrashing them 5-1 in the 2008 League Cup semi-final and again in the league in November 2010 – but Arsène just walked off.

It ended up third time lucky. In October 2011, Rafael van der Vaart and Kyle Walker scored as we won 2-1 at the Lane.

I was wrong to do it but at full-time, I jumped up and went straight to see him nose to nose.

I stuck out my hand to shake but he just walked past me because he'd lost. That's the way he is. I chased after him down the tunnel.

'Come on Arsène!' I shouted. 'Are you a man or a mouse? Shake my hand.' He wouldn't. At that point, I lost it. The tunnel area was teeming with stewards, press and the players, who were beginning to make their way off the pitch. I couldn't believe his attitude.

'Where are you walking off to? You're a mouse!' I screamed at him. I was ready to blow. 'Just because we've won for once!' I called him a few choice names. He kept looking at me, edging away. I was ready to punch him.

Just as I went to swing for him, reserve goalkeeper Carlo Cudicini saved the day. He threw his arm over my shoulder.

'Clive, what was the score?' he said smiling. He dragged me away and into our dressing room.

The biggest mistake I made was speaking to a couple of reporters when I walked past the press room.

'We hear you had words with Arsène,' one said.

'He refused to shake my hand,' I confirmed. 'He says he didn't hear or see me. But he's two-bob.'

As soon as I said that, I knew I'd gone too far. Arsène said in response that I'd tried to make myself the story. 'How many people do I have to shake hands with? Is there a prescription?' he told the press afterwards.

The club were furious with me. They told me to write to Arsène offering an apology. I refused and I don't know to this day whether they ever held that against me.

The press and Spurs support were all with me for standing up to him but that wasn't why I did it. He called me a cheat for no reason. He cannot deal with defeat. It isn't in his make-up. He hasn't got a gentlemanly bone in his body when his teams lose. He is the worst loser I've ever encountered in football by a million miles.

He can only see it his way. His decision or no decision. The football his teams have played has been as good as we've seen. He's been phenomenal for the Premier League and Arsenal – that's hard for me to say as a Tottenham man.

But I lost respect for him the moment he did that. People can think what they want but for me – and you can talk to anybody in the game – you have to have that mutual respect. I just wanted him to be human. If he'd respected me, I'd respect him. But he couldn't do it. He couldn't handle being human in a difficult moment.

He made a complaint about me to the Premier League and Tottenham. I wasn't fined but they gave me a slap across the wrists.

They didn't like what I'd said, which was right – I hold my hands up for that. But I'll never take back that moment. All he had to do was shake my hand in the right way but he couldn't do it, even after all the years we'd done it in defeat.

I've never spoken to him since. I don't need to. I'm sure he feels the same. He's not worried about me, that's for sure.

Other managers I know have described his handshake as a 'wet fish'. He never meant it. He'd never look you in the eye. There was no warmth or respect there at all.

There are a lot of people in football who have been adversaries – Peter Reid for example – but a mutual respect has developed down the years. Arsène Wenger, no. I wouldn't give him the time of day as long as I live. It is not about football, it is the way he behaved. People might think it is childish but he's not for me. You have to take defeats on the chin. He can't and won't. That's one of the reasons why he's had so much trouble with fourth officials: touchline bans, fines and the like. And that stubbornness is why Arsenal drifted in his final few years at the club before Unai Emery replaced him in the summer of 2018.

My disagreements with Arsène sat neatly within the rivalry between Tottenham and Arsenal. Many people interpreted it as an exhibition of my love for Spurs and that genuine sense of affection for the club was something Harry wanted to bring back when he took over. If anything, it may have aided my cause in Harry's mind.

In addition to keeping me on, Harry brought in Tony Parks as goalkeeping coach to replace Hans Leitert. Tim Sherwood and Les Ferdinand began working with the juniors, as did Pat Jennings a few times a week, and suddenly there was a real Tottenham pedigree to the backroom setup again.

Tim and Les worked alongside John McDermott, Alex Inglethorpe and Chris Ramsey with players coming out from the academy. It was a big opportunity for them and Harry was always keen to give people a chance.

Juande Ramos had created a void between the academy and the first team so to develop players through the period following his departure was very important. I know Tim felt that a lot of it could be done by sending the younger players out on loan.

The whole thing had flipped right over. It was a more traditional philosophy and Harry was keen to integrate some of the more advanced youngsters.

Pat was a magnificent example to everyone. He helped Harry get that feeling of a Tottenham spirit inside the club. It all contributes to making the players feel they are part of something greater. Harry understood that and he could feel it. As a result, Harry was the right fit at that time.

It was night and day compared to Ramos. There was no room for error under Juande and football is not like that. People make mistakes.

Wherever Juande has managed, I'm sure it's been exactly the same. He's had some success but at that moment in time, Harry's approach was far better suited to what Tottenham needed.

David Pleat had a similar understanding and appreciation for the club's values. Mauricio Pochettino has taken that on now. The foundations were laid over a number of years.

You want them to buy into the historical journey and understand what it means to be playing for Tottenham. Perhaps doing that effectively gives you just a little bit of an edge. Jürgen Klopp has identified something similar at Liverpool. It can be a very powerful force.

When new signings come in, you hope it is within their character that they want to find out. And Harry wanted players who loved the game. Sometimes they are hard to find. Dimitar Berbatov was a scholar. Michael Dawson and Robbie Keane knew the history of the game too. Luka Modrić just loved playing football. They were four characters in the dressing room who had that passion and you need that so the one or two who don't are influenced to think about it. That could make the difference in a game of fine margins. Therein lies Harry's skill in getting players to play for him. We were about to find out how far it could take Tottenham.

CHAPTER TWENTY

Bottom Three To Top Four

HARRY REDKNAPP TOOK ONE LOOK AROUND HIM ON HIS FIRST morning as Tottenham manager and said, 'Clive, what the fuck has been going on here?'

We were stood together on the training pitch as the players filed out from the changing room before I introduced him to the group.

'How can we have two points after eight games? Look at the players we've got!'

'They are all petrified, Harry,' I said. 'They know if they step out of line or make a big mistake in a game, they are gone.'

'Don't worry, we'll sort that out.'

He brought all 34 pros together on the top pitch, something that never happened under Juande Ramos – in fact, the first team group had become pretty small in his final few weeks.

'Right lads, I know what's been going on,' he began. 'I can only play 11 but you have all got a chance. I'm not interested in what's happened before. You've all got a clean slate.'

And to a man – not just the ones who had been alienated but those in the team – they breathed a huge sigh of relief. It was a like a weight had been taken off their shoulders. They had a chance to express themselves again.

That's where Harry was very clever – his approach released all the fear and tension immediately. He wanted to know about the kids, told the academy lads they were old enough for the first team if they were good enough and brought everyone together.

The whole atmosphere changed. It became a team that had licence to play. He liked good players strutting their stuff and that was exactly what Tottenham needed at the time.

I took charge of one game as interim manager – a 2-0 win over Bolton at White Hart Lane – although Harry ended up sitting next to me in the dugout.

He really just let it go – the way we set-up, how the team played – but we talked as the game was unfolding. He asked 'should we do this or that?' He made observations but nothing major. From what I remember, he left it to me but you could tell right from the first whistle that he wanted to get stuck in.

The setting for his official opening game could barely have been more highly-charged: Arsenal away in the Premier League.

It would provide a sign of the rollercoaster ride that was ahead of us, and the opening goal that evening encapsulated the sense of freedom Harry had injected.

David Bentley picked the ball up in a central position 40 yards out, took one touch and hit an outrageous volley which beat Gunners goalkeeper Manuel Almunia to give us the lead after just 13 minutes.

That sort of attempt on goal was practically banned under Juande. Harry deserves credit for giving the players their self-belief but I took some personal pride in that goal too.

Before the game, I mentioned to David the positions Almunia would take up. He used to be a long way off his line and I knew David had the technical capability to take advantage of it. Of course, you never think someone's going to score from 40 yards in that way and it is completely down to David's ability that he pulled it off, but as a coach it is fantastic to affect a player in that way.

Mikaël Silvestre and William Gallas scored from set-pieces to put Arsenal 2-1 ahead, then both teams netted again before Robin van Persie struck 22 minutes from time to leave us sliding towards a 4-2 defeat.

Harry told the team to keep playing and as Arsenal poured forward in search of more goals, Jermaine Jenas got us within touching distance with a left-foot strike on 89 minutes. We could sense panic in Arsenal and a minute later, Luka Modrić hit the post and Aaron Lennon turned home the rebound. We were level at 4-4.

The way we came back and the football we played only underlined what this same group of players could have done before Harry arrived. That result endeared the squad to him even more and over the coming weeks he quickly worked out which players he wanted and who had to move on.

One of Harry's biggest skills is dealing with footballers. He understands their mindset, what makes them tick and with his vast experience, he goes about capitalising on that in the right way. If he thinks you are a 'player' – that's the word he uses – then that's it. He thinks he doesn't have to coach you, he can just manage you. If you are a player, he believes he can get the best out of you.

There were three coaches, so we would split the sessions into sections that either we took individually or as a threesome. I was never a specialist strikers' coach but when we broke the squad up into groups, it made sense that I worked with the forwards while Kevin used his experience as a defender to help the defensive unit.

Joe was vastly experienced and would construct a lot of the sessions himself, overseeing or sometimes taking a group off on his own when necessary. Harry very rarely came onto the training field and coached himself.

In fact, he pretty much had one session plan which he used whenever he wanted to take training: crossing, finishing and then a game where he'd go over a few patterns of play. He'd stand in the centre circle and play the first ball out wide before letting the group get on with it. I'd seen it as a player at West Ham and it was almost exactly the same session years later at Tottenham.

But he oversaw everything, made sure he knew what was happening and would sometimes ask us to do specific work if something needed improving, whether it be Kevin Bond working with the back four or me taking some time to develop the forwards. He would orchestrate that, asking for more crossing, finishing, midfield running or whatever it might be.

Sometimes it was difficult because he would walk out at 10.30am after everyone had warmed up and decide he wanted to work on something new for half an hour. That would blow our plans out of the water.

But as a coach, you have to be ready for that and adapt. Kevin and Joe Jordan had worked with him before and knew that was always a possibility. I became accustomed to it.

As a result of taking a step back from the day-to-day stuff, whenever Harry would take a player aside or deal with them one-on-one, it carried extra weight.

That was how he exercised his power. A player who might be unhappy with training could then go up the chain to the manager, who was detached from the specific sessions themselves, to argue his case. Harry, in response, could tell him what to work on or where he stood, with a degree of authority created by that distance. That's where he was at his best.

He is realistic about the players he can work with and those he didn't fancy were shipped out, a process made easier by Damien Comolli's departure.

Adel Taarabt was one he didn't want. He was a fascinating character, never short of confidence. During one of our conversations, he said: 'Tottenham should build the team around me. I am the new Zinedine Zidane.'

Adel was extremely talented but unfortunately unable to harness it in the right way. He was very difficult to work with and I'd rack my brains talking to everyone – anyone – for techniques to get the best out of him.

A few weeks later, we loaned him to Queens Park Rangers and they bought him the following summer.

AC Milan, Benfica and Genoa have all seen something in him but he'll never fulfil his potential. Adel has never got the best out of himself physically and won't apply himself to be as good in reality as he is in his head. In the games he played for me, you could tell within five minutes if he was in the mood to win it for you or he was going to be a waste of space. It was as clearcut as that with him. He would try to put it through someone's legs in the first minute and if it didn't come off, he'd try a more outrageous skill and things would go from bad to worse. But if that first trick came off, his confidence grew and he could do anything. Conversely, he could make himself look a fool.

Harry, though, tried for a short period to see the best in him. Sometimes he would attend reserve games hoping to see some consistency from him. On one occasion, he relayed a message to me to take him off after another over-indulgent performance. Then Adel beat someone like he wasn't there and Harry signalled to leave him on. Moments later, he gave the ball away again and Harry wanted to collar him. That was Adel. It was ridiculous but you knew at any moment he could suddenly turn it on. It was a case of how much you could tolerate everything else that came with it.

Adel was a strange character but that doesn't stop a player from being successful.

Benoît Assou-Ekotto, who joined the club in 2006, had no love or passion for the game but Harry still adored him. It was just a job to Benoît. He wouldn't remember who we were playing from one week to the next. Physically, he was very good but mentally he didn't invest in it. He always did the best he could but there was no wider interest in football. I don't think he derived any joy from it. He sought that in other ways.

One Thursday after training, I walked through from the coaches' room to the dressing room and Benoît was sitting in there on his own. The rest of the lads had gone for the day having been told to turn up on Friday lunchtime to train ahead of our mid-afternoon flight to Manchester for a Saturday game against United at Old Trafford.

'Benoît, what are you still doing here?'

'I've just been to the gym, coach,' he said. 'I always want to look after myself.'

'Good. Benoît, out of interest, what are you going to do when you finish playing football? I know you love your cars – would you continue buying and selling cars or do it full-time maybe?'

'I don't know, I don't know…' he said before pausing. I broke the brief silence.

'Any other ideas?'

'Yeah. I think I'm going to be a porn star.'

'Sorry, what? You are joking, surely?'

He was as calm as you like. 'No, I'm serious. Why not?'

I didn't know what to say. I tried to keep it light.

'Benoît, when you make your first movie, I want tickets to the premiere!'

He didn't realise I was joking. 'Coach, no problem at all,' he replied, absolute deadpan.

'Um. I'll see you tomorrow, Benoît.'

'Yeah, of course – who are we playing?'

'As we told the group earlier, we are playing a team that plays in red. Manchester United. They're not bad.'

'Oh.'

'Don't be late,' I said. Suddenly, his mood darkened. He was not happy at the implication he might be unprofessional.

'Coach, I'm never late.'

'To be fair, you aren't. I'm just reminding you – bring your overnight stuff too as we're flying up north.'

'Sure. Who are we playing again?'

'Seriously?'

'Yeah.'

'Manchester United.'

'Oh yeah.'

That was Benoît. It wouldn't affect his performance – don't get me wrong – there was just no natural enthusiasm for the game. It was a job to him and he always did it to the best of his ability. We could have beaten United 10-0 that weekend and of course he would have enjoyed it but the feeling would quickly pass with him. He was the same after a bad defeat which, actually, is a good trait for a player to have.

I couldn't relate to it but as a coach, you are always learning and this was an example to me of how football has changed in recent years. Professionals have got to be good to make a career but do they have to love the game, given the wealth they earn along the way? No. Would it make him a better player if he was passionate about it? Maybe, but its debatable.

Working with a player like that was a challenge. How do you get the best out of him? You can't affect his passion for the game because he hasn't got any. How do you make him a better player? Benoît was an excellent professional and he worked at his game, but I found it difficult to inspire someone like that.

Michael Dawson was at the opposite end of the scale. He would be devastated if he'd made a bad tackle that cost the team in a match. I found that mentality far more relatable.

The talent that Tottenham possessed meant an upturn in results was almost inevitable. Harry has said before that 'any fool could have taken that club out of the bottom three' and while I knew what he meant, it still required effective management.

And the improvement was rapid. We won eight of our ten matches in all competitions after the Arsenal game and reached the 2009 League Cup Final on 1 March against Manchester United at Wembley.

It was a strange day. United didn't let us play in the way we wanted to. It was quite a dull game and had a draw written all over it after the opening 10 minutes.

We were a shadow of the team that had played some good stuff to get there. The game meandered to a 0-0 stalemate and penalties. We had practiced penalties but there wasn't an air of confidence about them in the week leading up to the game.

The gulf between the teams – United had won the Premier League and Champions League in the previous season – was clear from the first three takers. We had Jamie O'Hara, Vedran Ćorluka and David Bentley. They had Ryan Giggs, Carlos Tevez and Cristiano Ronaldo. Only Vedran scored for us which meant Anderson struck the winning penalty for a 4-1 shootout scoreline.

Despite losing, it was an insight as to how far the team had come. But there was still a brittleness about Tottenham that had been around for years, exemplified by United's attitude towards us.

Roy Keane claimed in his autobiography that Sir Alex Ferguson's pre-match team-talk for facing Spurs once was simply: 'Lads, its Tottenham.'

We definitely got a sense that this perception of us being fragile existed far beyond United. Harry used to say to us: 'When we go, we really go.'

You might go 1-0 down and before you know it, it was 3-0 or even worse. There were many examples. Darren Bent and Luka Modrić had put us 2-0 up against United in an April 2009 Premier League game at Old Trafford. Cristiano Ronaldo won and converted a penalty after 57 minutes. Twenty-two minutes later, we were 5-2 down.

Harry used to despair at collapses like that. We would almost give up. It would give him sleepless nights. People called it 'Spursy'.

As a coaching staff, we did everything to try and tackle it. You look at the mentality of players and whether they began to disappear in matches. You learn as much about your players in those moments as you do when winning 3-0.

We studied matches repeatedly with all the statistical data we had available. We built up a profile of players, making notes of whether those occasions hurt them, how they reacted in the dressing room or in training the following week. Michael Dawson would come in after a defeat like that and it would feel like the end of the world. Others didn't care.

We had great players but some with a little kink in them, a soft underbelly. We tried to eliminate it in part by moving some players on. Sixteen players left at the end of that first season under Harry with only seven coming in. There was a concerted effort to streamline the squad and get rid of the characters at the heart of whatever 'Spursy' really was.

There were difficult decisions all over the place because you might be sacrificing the quality of a player for their character and vice-versa. That's where Harry's judgement is exceptional.

Maybe he didn't always handle it in the right way. In January 2009, Darren Bent headed wide from six yards out late on as we drew 1-1 with Portsmouth at White Hart Lane. It was a bad miss but there was more than that going through Harry's head when he conducted his post-match interviews.

'You will never get a better chance to win a match than that,' he said. 'My missus could have scored that one.'

He'd made his mind up by then that Darren wasn't for us in the long term. It is on record that Darren then rang his agent and asked to leave but we needed him until the summer so he stayed put.

In all honesty, Darren reacting like that only reaffirmed Harry's assessment of him. He saw Darren as fragile. He also believed Darren missing a chance like that was indicative of a character flaw. Darren didn't really fit into Harry's preferred style of football, either. He had to have the right kind of service into him; he would come to the corner of the box to receive it but wouldn't link the play up consistently enough. Get the ball into the channels and he can be a world-beater – one such performance for Charlton against Tottenham was the reason we bought him.

Martin Jol was in charge for a league game in October 2005 when the ball was played down the side of him time and again against us at the Valley. He killed us with his pace, scoring twice either side of half-time to put Charlton 2-0 up. Ledley King, Mido and Robbie Keane scored as we came back to win but afterwards Martin eulogised about Darren and said: 'I want him in our team.' It took well over 18 months but eventually we got him, for a club-record fee of £16.5million.

But for Harry's team, he wasn't right. Darren needed to be more of an all-round centre-forward for Harry. That's not his fault, he was just being asked to do something different. We didn't have players to give him the service he needed and he wasn't the type of character to be able to dig in to compensate.

But other strong personalities were beginning to emerge. We finished the season with six wins from the last ten games as Luka Modrić started to get a reputation as a really influential midfielder.

I knew Luka was a top player from the moment I started working with him. He never gave me any problems, no matter what he was asked to do. He loved every session because he is football mad. Everyone can see he is technically brilliant, but mentally he is so resilient. Arsenal looked at him but decided he wasn't physically strong enough and there were questions about that after he arrived in

England but Luka knuckled down, adapted and thrived.

The one aspect Damien Comolli deserves credit for on Luka is that he met his criteria in never giving the ball away. You could throw him the ball anywhere on the pitch and he would keep it for you. Whether there was one player near him or five, he'd make the right decision. But it was his mentality – again, an aspect you cannot quantify on a spreadsheet – that made the big difference.

Luka should score more goals than he does, not that he hasn't worked on it. He used to do shooting sessions almost every day but it never improved his finishing. It was terrible. The rest of his game makes him one of the best midfield players in the world as we've seen from his time at Real Madrid and when helping Croatia reach the 2018 World Cup Final, voted the player of the tournament and later the Ballon D'Or in the process.

However, as we went into the 2009/10 season, even Luka would eventually be overshadowed by the emergence of arguably the best player to represent Tottenham in decades.

✳

Damien Comolli called me at the training ground in the early part of 2007.

'I need you to come to White Hart Lane,' he said. 'We've got a meeting in one of the boxes with Gareth Bale and his parents.'

Southampton knew we were interested and the task was to sell Tottenham as a club to Gareth and his parents over his other main option, Manchester United. But I hadn't been involved in transfers at all up to that point and it seemed odd I was asked over the manager, Martin Jol.

'Why me?' I asked Damien.

'I want you to be in on the lunch to talk football. You've played for Spurs, you know the club.'

I accepted and the five of us met at the stadium, in the box overlooking the halfway line. Gareth's father said very little. His mother asked a lot of questions, all well-mannered and clearly motivated by wanting the best for her son.

I told Gareth: 'You've got a platform here to do whatever you want. You'll play every week whereas at United you'll be just one in a crowd. Are you going to realistically take Ryan Giggs's place straight away? You could be sat on the bench for years.'

You try to put those doubts in a players' mind when giving them the hard sell over other alternatives.

'London isn't too far from home, either,' I continued. 'It is easy for you to get back to your family and friends rather than going up north – where the weather is often terrible, remember – and uprooting your whole life.

'Obviously we want you living near the training ground but it won't be four hours back home like Carrington would be.'

Leaving that meeting, we still felt he was going to United, but a few months later we got a call confirming that he'd decided to join us. I wasn't the reason Gareth joined – Damien and Daniel got it over the line after that – I just tried to help.

He was a baby when he joined us and remained so for some time. He was young, inexperienced and had been mollycoddled at Southampton. We didn't find that out until a long way down the line. They very rarely made him train with even the slightest of issues. If he felt a little niggle, he'd be allowed to stay in the treatment room, no questions asked. He was never on a proper training programme.

Before the 2009/10 campaign got going, there was a discussion among the staff over whether Gareth should go out on loan. Harry has since denied this but I remember talking as a group about a temporary move to Nottingham Forest.

There was never any intention of selling him – that much is true – but he hadn't established himself in the first team and just wasn't progressing as we had hoped.

Part of the issue centred on Harry's view that Gareth wasn't a left-back. His defensive work wasn't good enough and he didn't have a natural instinct for sensing danger.

So, we had a choice: send him out on loan and hope first-team football would make him grow up or continue working with him internally, focusing on a positional switch to a more advanced role.

We went for the second option. His transition into a left-winger happened initially in the reserves. Over the course of several games, he began to get in more advanced positions on the pitch and started going past people like they weren't there. He started to grow up, heeding the advice of the coaching staff and knuckling down in a way we hadn't seen before.

He didn't play for the first team until late September, by which time we'd made a strong start despite losing Luka Modrić with a broken leg just four games into the season. Harry had also made several moves in the transfer market to help banish this 'Spursy' mentality.

Carlo Cudicini was someone who set examples for others to follow. He was a key signing for Harry because he could come in and help self-police the dressing room. He'd experienced that at West Ham with the big characters there and how they could do part of his managerial job for him. Carlo has an influence in the Chelsea dressing room even today as part of the staff and that's a credit to him.

We replaced Darren Bent with Peter Crouch, who was someone you could hit early with a forward pass, get around and play off him. And if you work it wide, his aerial threat gives you that other dimension. Crouchy scored more headed goals in the Premier League than anyone, including Alan Shearer. You aren't taking a chance with him, plus he was a great character who could thrive at Tottenham.

Kyle Walker and Kyle Naughton were also acquired and I don't think any of the coaching staff knew too much about that. Harry wanted one right-back and it was a surprise to all of us when two turned up. That double deal sums up Damien Comolli pretty well: he'd happily put his name to Walker after he moved to Manchester City for £50million in 2017 but not so much Naughton. Mind you, we all get them wrong sometimes. Kevin-Prince Boateng left for Borussia Dortmund on loan that summer. His first game at the club was a reserve match for me at Grays. The first team were away but they wanted him to play. On the back of his performance, I went back to the club and told them we'd signed a potential star. He was an incredible athlete and had all the attributes to be a top player. But he was crazy, mentally a waste of space. He couldn't apply himself. At least I wasn't alone in misjudging him – he's been at other top clubs since including AC Milan but never fulfilled his potential.

This more streamlined squad was showing great promise and although Gareth was progressing nicely in the reserves, he still had a monkey on his back: we had never won a Premier League game with him on the field. It was a weird anomaly not reflective of his contribution at all but Harry was conscious of the situation and it got to the stage where he wanted Gareth in the team to break the hoodoo.

It was threatening to become the thing Gareth would be known for, a point of ridicule that could stifle his development.

Finally, after 1,533 minutes of first-team action spread across two years and four months, he was on the pitch when we beat Burnley 5-0 on 26 September 2009 – his 25th league appearance. Harry put him on as an 85th-minute substitute for Aaron Lennon when we were 4-0 up.

The curse was broken and Gareth never looked back. He began to excel in training, using his pace and that magnificent left foot to devastating effect. Every player wanted him on their team in small-sided games.

Gareth became a regular fixture in the first team because it was impossible to leave him out. It was a vindication of the work we were doing with the development squad but you are never far away from another problem in the reserves and just as Gareth was proving he'd left all that behind, Alan Hutton and David Bentley were around to bring us back to earth.

Alan had arrived a year earlier in a £9m deal – the rumour at the time was we could have got him for a lot less so it was a strange one all round – but he hadn't featured much for the first team.

Aaron had overtaken David in Harry's thinking for the right-wing spot and both of them were short of match sharpness.

So, we organised a reserve game specifically for those two to get some football under their belts.

Alan turned up late. When he came out to warm-up before the game, the practice balls were lined up for the group to use as they got themselves ready and he smashed one of them all the way down the training field. As a coach, it quickly becomes a difficult situation when you've got a senior player clearly undermining your authority in a mixed group containing a few youngsters.

'You need to go and get that ball,' I said to him.

'Oh, fucking hell, what am I even doing here?' he shouted back at me. Everyone else fell quiet.

'Not a lot at the moment. If you don't want to play, I've not got a problem with it. Take yourself back in but as you go past Harry's office, just knock on the door and tell him you aren't playing.'

'Why am I even fucking playing in the first place?'

'Because the manager says you need a game. You either do it right or don't do it at all. It is your decision, not mine.'

'I'm going in.' He started walking off, in the opposite direction to the ball he booted away.

'Fine – just tell the manager.'

The rest of the lads went through their warm-ups and we returned as a group to the dressing room. Alan was sitting in there.

'Al, what are you doing?' I asked.

'I'm playing.'

'Right, well, you haven't warmed up.'

'So what? I need to play so I'm playing.'

'You aren't doing it right – you need to warm up.'

'Have you spoken to Harry?'

'No.'

He went out to warm up while I talked to the other players. The game started and Alan and David were a disgrace. Their attitude stank the place out. Early in the first half, Harry came down to watch as first-team training had finished, and he stood alongside me.

'Everything alright?' he asked.

'Not really gaffer. Hutton doesn't want to play. He's not warmed up and isn't interested. Bentley's the same. They are just messing about.'

'Right, get 'em off.'

I signalled to a couple of the kids on the bench to start warming up. All of a sudden, Harry changed his mind.

'Leave 'em on.'

I turned to the two youngsters. 'Sorry, sit back down lads.'

Harry continued. 'Get them all in at half-time. Don't say anything, I'll come in and have a word with them.'

'Fine, boss. No problem.'

I got them in and handed around a few drinks before leaving for the coaches' room. Harry went storming in and started to lose it. I walked back in behind him.

'What the fuck is going on here?' he said. 'And as for you, Hutton, you're an insult to this club.' Alan shrugged his shoulders.

'David Bentley – you're a disgrace.'

David responded by standing up, turning around and reaching into his jacket for his phone. He kept his back to Harry, who by this point was almost going to swing for David.

'What are you doing?' asked Harry, seething.

'I'm just ringing my agent to tell him to get me out of here.' He made the call, telling his agent to speak to Daniel Levy in order to get the club to sell him before putting the phone back in his pocket and sitting down.

'Who the fuck do you think you are?' said Harry, incandescent by now. David couldn't care less.

Harry vented his anger and substituted him. He banished him to the reserves for the next few days, training away from the first team.

I actually like David. He's a very bright boy and I remember working with him at England youth team level and he stood out as a real talent.

But when there was competition, David wasn't happy. Aaron Lennon had really kicked on and was a key part of a team going for the top four, meaning David's opportunities were limited.

He'd deny it and say he worked hard but he couldn't handle not being the main man. That was the root cause of an attitude which led to a situation where it seemed like he had no future at the club.

And yet, a few days later, Aaron got a groin problem which over time proved to be quite serious. And suddenly, David was required.

This is where Harry's man-management was excellent. Another manager would have told him he'd never play again but he was able to reintegrate him into a first team now threatening to finally break that glass ceiling of the top four.

And when David played, he was fantastic. He came in at the end of January and played eight consecutive games, then missed five but started six of the next seven including the FA Cup semi-final against Portsmouth at Wembley.

We lost that game in extra time, prompting more accusations of 'Spursyness'. Everybody wanted a trophy but the bigger prize in terms of the club's growth was Champions League qualification and it all came down to a match just over three weeks later at Manchester City.

Victory in our penultimate game of the season would guarantee us a Champions League place. Lose and it would be in City's hands on the final day at our expense. The stakes could not have been higher.

Harry often worked on gut instinct and it led to some baffling decisions at times. You wouldn't understand why some players were in from the cold or dropped without warning; sometimes I'd sit with Kevin and Joe, the three of us shaking our heads in confusion at what was going on.

The City game was the ultimate example of that. If you'd asked Kevin, Joe or I before the game how we were going to line-up, it would never have been the way we did that night.

We were in the hotel and followed the custom of going down early to sit in a room next to the pre-match meeting room for a backroom staff chat before the players turned up. The team meeting was always three-and-a-half hours before the game but ours took place prior to that over the course of an hour, planning tactics, discussing selection and finalising the message to the players.

Harry was agitated. We all were. We knew how important the game was and the desperation to get it right was etched on everyone's faces. It felt as though everything we'd worked for came down to this one game. We weren't sure what to do, in all honesty.

There was a long discussion about whether David or Aaron should play on the right. Aaron was finally fit again after being out for five months but David had done so well in deputising after that flare up with Harry at the training ground.

However, you don't manage more than 1,000 games by relying on sentiment. Aaron was back and the best man for the job.

The big decision was who would play up front. Crouch and Jermain Defoe? Crouch and Roman Pavlyuchenko? Pav did well in big games. Pav and Defoe? Maybe Eidur Gudjohnsen could play? He's got so much experience at big clubs. Should we play one up? Harry didn't want to play Jermain in attack on his own. We knocked it around for ages. Eventually, after a lot of agonising, the consensus was Crouch should start on the bench.

The players arrived and Harry began addressing them, spelling out the importance of the game, urging them to keep their heads and outlining general tactical information before naming the team.

'...and starting up front, Crouch and Defoe,' he said. The players got up and left the room.

Kevin, Joe and I sat on the back row and just stared at each other. I whispered into Joe's ear.

'Er, I didn't think it was Crouch and Defoe – has he made a mistake?'

Joe didn't say a word. Not one of us thought Crouchy would start.

I never felt a need to seek Harry out and ask why he made the decision he did. I assumed he just got a feeling and wanted to go with it. It was a big surprise and maybe the chairman wouldn't want to hear such decisions in games of this scale were made in this way but that's what you get with Harry.

Joe wrote up the set-piece details for all our players, making any necessary adjustments once we'd seen their teamsheet. Crouchy was detailed to pick up Vincent Kompany from corners. Michael Dawson was very vocal in geeing up the players. Benoît-Assou Ekotto, by contrast, was very quiet – he was waiting to come down from Mars to play just another game of football. These are the dressing room dynamics.

The game was tense. It was 0-0 at half time and still scoreless deep into the second half with both sides giving away very little.

It wasn't exactly going to plan but there was little need to change our approach. Harry brought on David for Aaron and then later Pav for Jermain – both like for like changes – and then came the perfect moment.

With eight minutes left, Younès Kaboul got to the byline on the right and fizzed the ball at Márton Fülöp's near post. He could only palm the ball out into a central position and Crouchy was there to head it home. The man who in all probability wasn't going to be on the pitch until Harry's sudden change of heart had won it for us.

City were done. They had nothing left. We saw the game out comfortably enough to spark jubilant celebrations. It was a mixture of elation and relief.

Harry gave a live interview to the Sky Sports reporter Andy Burton after the game. 'I'm so lucky to have such a good coaching staff – Joe, Kevin: fantastic. Clive...'

I'll never know what he would have said about me because he was interrupted by several lads pouring a bucket of water over him and his brand-new suit.

The ring leader? David Bentley. After everything that had gone on behind the scenes, David capped it off by wrecking Harry's designer suit, which he later auctioned off for a leukaemia charity. It fetched £2,000.

At the time, Harry was absolutely livid. David rubbed it in by putting his arm around Harry for a moment as they all jumped around celebrating. Harry gave him a look as if to say: 'I'll sort you out later'.

There would be time enough for that. The magnitude of the achievement was far more important. For many of those players, it felt like their time had finally come.

We'd shattered the glass ceiling. We'd been watching the Champions League on television for years, getting close to it under Martin, but finally we were there, securing a top-four place by winning the kind of match we were so often accused of blowing.

Tottenham had hit new heights, an achievement made all the more remarkable given where we were when Harry started 18 months earlier. But none of us had any intention of stopping there.

CHAPTER TWENTY-ONE

To Dare Is To Do

IF WE COULD HAVE HANDPICKED OUR CHAMPIONS LEAGUE play-off opponents from the options available, we would have chosen Young Boys of Bern.

Anticipation of the draw spread excitement throughout the club. We could potentially have faced sides with real pedigree such as Sampdoria or Dynamo Kyiv but you could drive yourself mad thinking about the permutations so we elected not to stop the training session which ran concurrently with the UEFA ceremony.

Instead, someone poked their head out of the training complex and shouted over: 'Its Young Boys!'

We celebrated on the training pitch like we'd qualified for the group stage. Harry dispatched me to Switzerland to compile a report based on their Swiss league match against Neuchâtel Xamax, taking place on the weekend before the first leg of our play-off.

Driving rain greeted me as I touched down in Bern and headed to the Young Boys Stadium, which looks more like a shopping complex from the outside.

I was sat with the locals. The stand housed one main concourse filled with people eating and drinking pre-match. I shimmied my way through the packed crowd, all sheltering from the rain, and found my seat to watch what was honestly one of the worst games I've seen in my life.

It was a plastic pitch, awful conditions, a game really low on quality and Young Boys lost 1-0.

I got back to London and saw Harry.

'What do you think?' he asked.

'If we do it properly, we'll get through.'

'No, no, no, Clivey,' he said. 'I want more than that.'

'Well, the centre-forward Tape Doubai is lively but we can deal with him. But, Harry, it is a plastic pitch.'

'It's fucking what?'

'It's a plastic pitch.'

'No! It can't be!'

The technology had improved dramatically over the years from my playing days on 'Omniturf' at Queens Park Rangers, meaning these surfaces were a lot closer to grass in the way they react and much less abrasive on skin and bone.

But we had a few lads with knee and ankle problems and the surface still created a different impact for the body to absorb when running, which meant many of them were not comfortable. They never wanted to train on our artificial pitch at Luxborough Lane, yet now we were facing a Champions League qualifier on the same surface.

Ledley King was the obvious concern. His fitness issues are well documented and I still can't believe the level he was able to reach every week with one knee in the state it was.

He couldn't walk some days, often in the 48 hours after a game. He did a lot of his fitness work in the pool, running with floats or swimming simply to protect the knee as much as he could while maintaining some sort of overall sharpness.

Sometimes he went to chairman Daniel Levy's house to use his pool and on occasion we wouldn't see him for a couple of days in a clear week leading up to a Saturday game.

That's where Harry was absolutely brilliant with him. He would say to Ledley on Friday: 'Yes or no?'

If Ledley said 'maybe', he'd say: 'Okay, you tell me tomorrow by 2pm when I name the team.'

On the day before a game, we often did some team shape work. Sometimes Ledley took part, other times he didn't. He might walk through it for five minutes and then go in or maybe 15 minutes at reasonable speed but then we'd tell him to stop.

We would have set-piece meetings at the meal on the day of the game and usually by then, Ledley would have told Harry if he could make it or not. If there was still some uncertainty, a replacement would be readied as well. If Ledley told us he couldn't make it at the last moment, Sébastien Bassong or one of the other lads would step in.

There was no animosity. Ledley never did it with any ego and in any case, they just knew how good he was.

Noureddine Naybet came in from Spain a few years earlier to play alongside him. He was a really likeable character and a very experienced player having been at Deportivo La Coruña for eight years, where he'd been part of the team that had won the club's first ever La Liga title and reached the Champions League semi-finals the season before he moved to north London.

A couple of weeks after he arrived, we finished training one day and I said to him: 'What do you think of the group?'

'The quality is very good. I am happy here.'

'What about the lads, do you think any of them could play in Spain?'

'Yes,' he replied. 'Only one.'

'What do you mean?'

'Only one who could play anywhere – Real Madrid, Barcelona – any club he liked. The King.'

And that was Ledley playing at 60 percent of what he would have been capable of granted full fitness. Tactically, he was brilliant. He had to be. His mobility was compromised but he read the game superbly and that was why he played in a holding midfield role for England at one stage under Sven-Göran Eriksson.

Earlier that summer, there had been a major disagreement about his recall under Fabio Capello for the 2010 World Cup. The medical and sports science teams at Spurs felt he couldn't do it.

He was barely able to play two games in a week for us but managed three right at the end of the 2009/10 season, lasting 90 minutes against Bolton, Manchester City and then Burnley on the final day. The England doctors looked at that and thought he could do it for them but Ledley only put himself on the line like that because it was the end of the season.

The Tottenham staff were certain he couldn't play a tournament and were subsequently, sadly, proved right. He started England's opening group game against the United States in South Africa but was substituted at half-time with a groin problem. It would prove to be the last of his 21 England caps.

Harry didn't want to deny Ledley his chance and that's why players like him. Ledley might have thought he could play a few games at the tournament if they could map out his involvement but in reality it just wasn't feasible. The games came too quickly and there was no hiding place in matches either.

He'd returned to us that summer needing to recover and get himself right. That couldn't possibly include a match on an artificial surface.

Ledley played in the opening game of our league season – a 0-0 draw against City – but we left him behind for the flight to Bern.

Once there, as is customary, we went to train at the stadium the night before the game. Within a few minutes of walking out, we could tell the lads were struggling to adapt. One or two didn't want to train. A couple more just wanted to walk through the session.

'I don't like this,' said Harry. 'I've got a bad feeling.'

We did a very light session before Harry asked us to do some team shape work, which was unusual – there were people from Young Boys watching us train and you don't want to give away tactical information before kick-off.

The ball was zipping about all over the place and the players weren't happy. A couple of them didn't train properly for more than about 10 minutes. Harry let them go because he didn't want to take any chances. I don't think any of the coaching staff slept well that night.

We went out for a stroll on the day of the game, the players had an afternoon nap and then we got to the ground for the match. Harry was nervous.

'You said it was going to be alright but I've got a bad feeling about this,' he said. We left Tom Huddlestone and Aaron Lennon on the bench because of the pitch and he agonised over the team as a result of how bad the session had been the night before. But we lined up 4-4-2 to give it a go.

After 13 minutes, we were 2-0 down. After 28 minutes, it was 3-0. It could have been five or six. Ledley's absence wasn't the sole factor but defensively we'd gone to pieces.

Harry was stood almost speechless in the technical area but at 3-0 down he turned to me.

'You fucking told me we were going to win this no problem,' he said. 'We're going out! We're not even going to get in the group stages! Everything we've worked for is fucked!'

He'd completely lost it and so had the team. We were a mess.

Harry pulled Assou-Ekotto for Huddlestone after only 36 minutes to try and give us a foothold in the game. It was damage limitation.

Bassong scored from a corner just before half-time which saved the team from the bollocking of their lives as it meant we had a chance. Harry would have been happy to get out of there at 3-1 and took off Luka Modrić for Niko Kranjčar at the interval to shore it up even more.

But Young Boys tired as the game went on and Roman Pavlyuchenko scored a second with seven minutes left, allowing us to escape with a 3-2 defeat and, somehow, a real opportunity to turn it around in the second leg.

It was a quiet dressing room afterwards. Harry was not happy at all. The pitch had given the players an excuse. He was sitting on the front of the bus when I got on and took a place about four rows back as we went from the ground to the hotel. I think he was on the phone to his son Jamie. This was another of Harry's traits: he deliberately started talking loudly enough so everyone could hear.

'Yeah, my fucking staff came out here and said, "We've won this, it's easy – no danger. Fucking hell, we're lucky to even have a chance. It's a fucking disgrace."'

I knew that was aimed at me. I reported on it and thought we were the better team.

'Don't worry, Harry,' I said when he finished his call. 'We'll be alright.'

He didn't reply but gave me a look as if to say 'you said that last time'.

There was a quick turnaround. After a weekend Premier League win at Stoke, we played the return leg at White Hart Lane the following midweek.

Ledley started. Crouchy scored after five minutes to settle the nerves. We were then ahead on away goals and the lads played at a tempo Young Boys simply couldn't cope with. We ran out easy 4-0 winners, going through 6-3 on aggregate. We did it right that time and thank God we did.

Not qualifying for the group stage would have been a disaster – imagine all that work from the season before being undone by a plastic pitch.

Grass pitches are so good – and many are hybrid surfaces now anyway – that there's no need for solely artificial pitches, except in extreme weather conditions. With the money involved in the Champions League now, they should be banned. I know I benefitted from a plastic pitch during my playing days but the game has moved on since then.

I got the blame but Harry wasn't one to hold a grudge. I don't think it affected our relationship. I didn't feel I needed to do anything different in scouting future opponents – something he would still trust me to do – and I'd say to this day, what I said was good advice. I put in my report that if the attitude was right, we wouldn't have a problem. But the attitude was wrong.

You always had to stand your ground with Harry and I always believed we'd go through. I don't think the players doubted it either in the second leg – they'd had their wake-up call.

Harry wasn't as confident and you can understand why but that first game taught us all a lesson not to underestimate anyone in Europe. They were a big side in Swiss football and while that league might not be high-profile, the Switzerland national team are strong and they were not fazed by playing us.

Champions League football was a fantastic carrot to dangle in front of prospective new signings. We'd strengthened the squad by bringing in William Gallas – a top defender with great experience – on a free transfer and tied Luka Modrić down to a new deal, an important pro-active move for the club.

William was a good pro. He knew what his strengths were and always looked after himself. He was an introvert but had a very strong mentality. Sometimes you had to let him do what he wanted because he was so convinced his way was right. His mistakes usually weren't costly – I've always thought that was the sign of a good defender. He used to speak his mind in team meetings, which we always respected, and always stuck to his guns.

We'd had an eye on him for a while and there were various other names linked with the club as the transfer window reached its climax but the arrival of Real Madrid forward Rafael van der Vaart on deadline day took everyone by surprise.

Rumour has it a move to Bayern Munich had collapsed earlier in the day and he was suddenly available for about £8million. Daniel pitched it to Harry and he didn't think twice.

I don't think anybody watched Rafa before he signed. Of course, you don't know about a player's character in those circumstances because you don't necessarily have time to perform due diligence in that way, but Harry always believed he could put an arm around players to get the best out of them.

Whatever problems someone had off the pitch, Harry would deal with them because the defining judgement for him is that the individual is a 'player'. Everything else pales into insignificance. Rafa was a classic example of that at

Spurs. He wasn't the best athlete and very rarely played 90 minutes. But he was a big-game player and a wonderful footballer, having established himself at Real and with Holland.

Harry handled him accordingly. He loved it at Spurs because he was allowed to play.

'Just go and do your stuff,' was invariably Harry's individual instruction to him.

He was taken off on occasions when Harry felt he could do a bit more or we needed someone more naturally suited to working defensively without the ball, but generally Rafa delivered for us.

Harry had a great feel in that regard. He valued players who could win games for him above all others. Whether they were nice or nasty, fit or not in optimum condition, Harry would find a way around it if they could win games. It was an education watching it.

The group stage draw was soon upon us. During training one Friday morning, we learned our opponents were Inter Milan, Werder Bremen and FC Twente. Everybody felt we had a chance, even with the European champions, Inter, in the group.

Adjusting to the extra high-profile games is a real challenge. Managing and preparing players required considerable change and we were all new to it. The Saturday-Saturday schedule is so much more relaxed than Saturday-Wednesday-Sunday, for example.

The Champions League requires you to be at your best all the time. And the pressure you are under in that one game to deliver is the nearest thing you can come to international football for your club.

No targets were set. The aim was to establish ourselves in the competition on an annual basis. Nobody thought we could win it so that had to be done through the Premier League. We viewed the Champions League campaign itself as a shot to nothing and every game was exciting as a result. The players revelled in it. I don't think they consciously saved themselves for those nights, though.

The league was still massively important to everyone at the club and if anything the extra games kept the whole squad on their toes. There would always be injuries and therefore the need to juggle it around a little bit. Harry was good at that.

We didn't do any more in terms of the amount of preparation but there was a real verve and desire to get it right. We gave the competition the respect it deserved. You play Premier League teams every week and know how they set up, tactically there are far fewer surprises and essentially you know all the players and have done for years. In Europe, we were educating ourselves with new managers, players and systems. It was a great challenge.

When you look at the players we had then and what they've subsequently gone on to achieve, you can see why they took to it so quickly. We gave them a platform, a template, and they rose to it. Gareth Bale came of age, Luka Modrić showed he was as good as any central midfielder in Europe.

Tactically, we learned a lot in a short space of time. A credible away draw in Bremen – for which Harry had allowed me to scout the opposition despite the Young Boys scare – preceded a resounding home win over FC Twente before we were handed a harsh lesson in the San Siro.

An awful opening 45 minutes against Inter left us 4-0 down and reduced to ten men following Heurelho Gomes's early red card. The home fans were baying for blood and we looked absolutely devoid of hope. It threatened to get really nasty.

Just outside the dressing room, Harry discussed his team-talk with us and also Tim Sherwood, who was sat up in the stands to provide a different perspective.

He opted to go into the players all guns blazing, telling them how embarrassed he was and accusing them of bringing shame on the club. He read the riot act. Every player needed to pull their finger out and step up.

The response was more than even he could have hoped for. Gareth probably announced himself to Europe that night. He took the game to them almost on his own, scoring a second-half hat-trick with three goals of unbelievable quality.

We still lost 4-3 but the belief we got from that game was incredible. With the odds against them and a man fewer than one of the best sides around, they fought like lions.

In that 45 minutes, they realised they could compete and mix it with the best.

We could have lost seven or eight-nil – Harry even said that to the players – but instead they came in almost feeling like they'd won the game.

Gareth's goals were all stunning, the type you'd see him score time and again in training yet he'd done it in the bear pit at the San Siro, albeit in a losing cause. He was very calm afterwards – he wasn't one to get carried away – but the fight they all showed was hugely significant for the bigger picture. They'd laid down a marker and Inter knew it.

In terms of experience and atmosphere, the reverse fixture two weeks later was the best I ever witnessed at White Hart Lane. I joined as a player in 1984 just after the UEFA Cup win so while I'm sure many of those games were special, that one against Inter was something else and a night I will remember for the rest of my life.

The place was electric from the first minute. We weren't overly confident but had conviction in our qualities, especially playing at home.

Gareth was out of this world. That was the night he surprised even us. He was unplayable. He was in the mood to put his full repertoire on show and proceeded to tear apart Maicon, the best right-back in the world at the time. 'Taxi for Maicon!' sang the crowd. I almost joined in.

Amazingly, Inter didn't seem to have a specific plan for him. That sort of thing was the basis of Rafael Benítez's managerial reputation and we anticipated in the days before the game they might double up or man-mark him yet instead they just left Maicon one-on-one.

It was unbelievable. If I'd been in the opposite dugout, we would probably have talked about putting someone as close as you can to him, to be physical with him and intimidate him. You then have to stop the ball getting to him.

So in the absence of any stifling tactics from Inter, the instruction was simple: get the ball to Gareth. Maicon didn't know what to do. He tried to get tight and Gareth would spin away from him. He would then give him a yard and Gareth just knocked it into space in behind and destroyed him for pace.

Roman Pavlyuchenko came up with another important goal after scoring at Young Boys to help turn the tie back towards us. The final score was 3-1.

Overall, Pav probably never fulfilled his potential at Spurs but that night, everything clicked. It was as good as it got. We felt we'd arrived on the European stage. This was where we wanted to be.

And yet, the following Saturday, we lost 4-2 at Bolton Wanderers. To some extent, it was inevitable because of everything they had put into the Inter game but, once again, another wave of 'Spursy' criticism hit us.

Harry went crazy in the dressing room afterwards. We'd capitulated again, 3-0 down after 76 minutes to two Kevin Davies goals and one from Grétar Steinsson.

'You do what you did in the week and then you perform here like that?' Harry said in addressing the players.

'It is unacceptable. You won't continue at that level if you can't come to places like this and back it up. You have to do it the right way every time. The rest follows.'

. A draw with Sunderland preceded victory over Blackburn before another dramatic occasion: the north London derby of 20 November 2010.

We were starting to get the feeling we were competitive with Arsenal after years of living in their shadow. They'd been better than us for years, finishing above us every season since 1995. It was a massive issue for the players and the staff. We had to break the back of it.

Arsenal had gone 2-0 up at Emirates Stadium through Samir Nasri – a great finish from a really tight angle, although Heurelho Gomes should have been stronger in coming out to meet him – and Marouane Chamakh, who converted Andrey Arshavin's cross at the near post. They smelt blood. A win would have seen them go top of the Premier League. At half-time, Harry was at his very best. As a staff, we knew this team were susceptible to going under and the Emirates would be the worst possible place for another capitulation.

He started digging out players over their attitude, telling them this could be an embarrassment (again), using all his experience to try to motivate the group. Harry brought on Jermain Defoe for Aaron Lennon at half-time to give it a go and positive substitutions like that only help send the message we want to restart on the front foot.

Gareth got us back in it five minutes into the second period. The players sensed an opportunity.

Luka began to influence the game heavily but it was Cesc Fàbregas who gave us the biggest assist, handling Rafa van der Vaart's free-kick in the box. Rafa converted the penalty and we were level. Arsène Wenger was furious but not as much as he would be. Rafa swung over a free-kick and Younès Kaboul guided it into the net. Arsène threw his bottle of water on the floor – what a great image that was.

It was the first time we'd won at Arsenal in 17 years – another tick mark on the checklist of things people said we couldn't do. We were in fifth place at the turn of the year, in touching distance of the top four, but the Champions League was always what would set the pulses racing.

December's draw paired us with AC Milan in the last 16, beginning in February. We'd had the experience of beating Inter Milan at home and although we'd lost in the San Siro, the stadium wasn't unknown to us and we knew we could perform there, at least in the second half.

In a way, you use a glamour tie like that to your advantage because the prospect of a knockout game in the New Year keeps everyone focused on working towards it, particularly in January.

We lost at Everton but were otherwise fairly consistent around the turn of the year before another one of those implosions, this time in the FA Cup at Fulham. Michael Dawson was sent off early on and they battered us 4-0. Harry had named a strong team and there was certainly no intention of taking it less seriously because of the Champions League. It was just another reminder of the work we had to do.

Harry tweaked the squad in the January window, finally shipping out David Bentley on loan and signing Steven Pienaar, who was a good pro and a snip at just £3million.

We won three on the bounce at the beginning of February so going into the first leg in Milan, we were confident. We had acclimatised to Champions League football too. We were ready.

We always wanted to go for it but this time the plan was based on being defensively disciplined and well organised. We knew we had a threat on the counter-attack which would cause even a defence as good as theirs some problems. And so it proved.

The lads produced a really mature display, controlling the game and keeping our balance throughout, capped off by Peter Crouch's winner ten minutes from time.

Aaron Lennon burst forward on the counter-attack and played the right ball at the right time to Crouchy, who had a tap-in.

The Inter performances were good but this was the best European away display we produced. It showed a different side of us: we didn't have to be gung-ho to win a game. It was also an absolute world away from Young Boys. We made some subtle little changes to the way we set up and the players implemented it superbly.

They learned from the Inter game, keeping their composure under intense pressure. Heurelho Gomes made several good saves too before Crouchy had his moment. Milan, by contrast, gradually lost their heads. With 55 minutes on the clock, Mathieu Flamini launched into a disgraceful two-footed challenge on

Vedran Ćorluka. It happened on the other side of the pitch from the dugout but I could see Flamini get up and throw his arms up at the crowd, demanding more energy. He was way out of line. Vedran was lucky his leg wasn't broken. Flamini was luckier still only to be booked. We had to take Vedran off but he came back out on crutches to watch the end of the game with a huge ice pack on his right foot.

Gennaro Gattuso put in a nasty tackle on Steven Pienaar 20 minutes later. He only got a yellow card too.

Probably the most memorable confrontation came later on when Gattuso squared up to Joe Jordan, twice getting involved with him on the touchline as Joe stood in the technical area.

I don't think Joe said very much although Gattuso claims he said a few choice words to him to rile him up. Whatever happened, he lost it.

Gattuso pushed him away by the throat as they came nose to nose with each other before at full-time he headbutted Joe, which prompted a few of our substitutes to get involved. The best part of all of it was Joe taking his glasses off and giving them to a sub as Gattuso came over the second time. Cool, calm but not giving an inch – Gattuso really messed with the wrong guy, not least because Joe had played for Milan for two years between 1981 and 1983. He warranted respect in that stadium.

Sometimes when things like that happen, you know you've got a team where you want them. Gattuso later apologised for the headbutt. We did a job on them that night in a way few thought we could.

And going from the sublime to ridiculous yet again, next time out we lost 3-1 at Blackpool. Charlie Adam scored from the penalty spot after Sébastien Bassong had fouled DJ Campbell and we were 2-0 down at half-time. The lads improved in the second half. We dominated it but didn't score until stoppage time and by then it was far too late. The result left us in fourth place, two points ahead of Chelsea who had a game in hand.

Harry was livid. The flaw was mental. Physically, they were more than capable and this time we had a week to recover from Milan. We'd tell them they had to have the same mental approach but sometimes the message doesn't get through. In those moments, Harry would decide on which players he wanted in the long-term.

The staff were all frustrated by it. Why couldn't we perform well week in, week out? Sometimes people don't quite appreciate the high you have going into those big games. The fans, players and coaching staff all experience a hunger for those occasions that is hard to replicate a few days, or even a week, later. Maintaining that level is difficult if you aren't used to it and we weren't.

The second leg against Milan soon came around and it was a really tight game. Some people thought we would try and roll them over in the same manner as Inter but you couldn't open up against Milan in the same way. We made a conscious decision to stay compact, just as we did in the first game. They took control in the first half with Clarence Seedorf pulling the strings. We improved after half-time but our fans were anxious as the night wore on. William Gallas kept us together at the back and we held on for a 0-0 draw. The relief in the stadium at the final whistle was huge.

By this stage, we'd exceeded people's expectations. Not many thought we could go this far and Harry had become the first Englishman to lead an English team into the Champions League quarter-finals in its modern-day format; Terry Venables was the last Englishman to reach the last eight, with Barcelona in 1986.

Nobody talked about winning it, even then. As a staff, we just kept thinking about the next tie. And in any case, the European run was by now clearly affecting our league form. Two 0-0 draws at home to West Ham and away at Wigan followed after we knocked Milan out and our grip on a top four spot was in danger of slipping.

The Champions League last eight draw pitched us against Real Madrid. It was a huge test of our credentials. We studied hours and hours of footage looking for possible areas of weakness, thinking about how we could possibly set up against them.

We came up with a plan and on the night and I remember standing in the technical area as the players warmed up feeling happy with the way the team was set up. Cristiano Ronaldo was at his peak and we reminded the players he would always shoot on sight, so they had to get close, show him outside if possible.

But we were dealt a big blow when Aaron Lennon got injured shortly before kick-off. It threw everything up in the air. Harry and the rest of us were thinking on our feet. We opted to bring in Jermaine Jenas and started Gareth on the right.

The tactical sheets and set-piece instructions had to be redrawn and while Joe scribbled furiously, Kevin and I went to each player individually to reinforce the messages.

In a game of that magnitude, it was the last thing we needed. Real were a better team so I don't want to make excuses but the disruption clearly contributed to the opening goal.

Jermaine was marking the space in front of Emmanuel Adebayor. Ade could be a world-beater on his day, which was usually when he felt like he had a point to prove, and being ex-Arsenal, facing us brought out the best in him.

He out-jumped Jermaine at a corner to head Real in front after just four minutes.

We responded well enough but Crouchy getting sent off just ten minutes later accelerated that feeling of the game running away from us. He has barely made a slide tackle in his life yet he lunged in twice, firstly on Sergio Ramos and then Marcelo in areas of the pitch where it wasn't necessary.

We knew then it was damage limitation after that. The Madrid fans were baying for a mauling. We were desperate to stay in the tie but in the dugout we were fearing one of those capitulations we'd suffered at smaller grounds, this time on arguably the biggest stage we'd played on. However, we had a few chances through Gareth Bale and Rafael van der Vaart and managed to get in at half-time just 1-0 down.

We'd restricted Ronaldo to a series of long-range efforts. Of course, he is capable of putting one in the top corner from 30 yards but if he does that, you just have to say 'fair enough'.

The team-talk was positive. We took off Rafa and put on Jermain Defoe to give us something going forward in behind them. It couldn't just be one-way traffic otherwise we'd be lambs to the slaughter with ten men in an arena as tough as the Santiago Bernabéu Stadium.

We held our own until conceding again from a set-piece after 57 minutes. Real worked a short corner to Marcelo who crossed and Ade rose above William Gallas to plant a header past Gomes. Could William have been a touch tighter? Should we have been more switched on to stop the cross? Perhaps, but it was a superb header.

At 2-0 we were still in the tie but despite out best efforts, it was starting to resemble the Alamo. Ángel Di Maria scored from the edge of the box – it was a great strike although Assou-Ekotto might have got a little closer to stop him – and that goal was a killer for us. We knew then we were out.

Just for good measure, Ronaldo got his goal three minutes from the end – Gomes beaten on the volley too easily at his near post – and it finished 4-0.

There's not a lot you can say to a group of players after a disappointment like that. We flew straight back to London after the game and the plane was very quiet. We didn't say much to Crouchy afterwards either. He knew what he'd done. There was nothing malicious in it – he was just so committed to the cause but jumping in again after the tackle on Ramos was silly.

He went some way to making amends by scoring twice in the first 34 minutes as we beat Stoke 3-2 on the Saturday before Real came to town for the second leg.

We felt like we had nothing to lose. We wanted to put on a show, although that always meant there was a risk we could lose by four again given how good Real were.

José Mourinho was comfortable enough to be planning ahead. Before the game, he left their dressing room early to stand in the tunnel. The dressing room doors were virtually opposite each other with the coaches' rooms a little bit further along the corridor.

He stood outside our dressing room for about five minutes waiting for our players to come out. He'd prepared his team, they were 4-0 up anyway and he obviously felt relaxed about the tie. As our players came out to line-up, he acknowledged a few but then made a big fuss of two in particular: Luka and Gareth. He was all over the pair of them.

I was standing there at the other end of the tunnel thinking: 'You cheeky bastard.' It was obvious what he was doing – even more so when you think about where they ended up playing.

He planted a seed in their mind that Real then exploited when they came to buying both of them. It was genius. I told Harry, who was still in the coaches' room. He was more concerned with the game itself.

And José had an impact there too. By making such a fuss of Luka and Gareth, the rest of our lot were probably thinking 'he doesn't fancy me'. José's psychology in dealing with players was fascinating and in that moment, you can't really say anything, as much as you might want to. It just isn't the done thing.

Real played within themselves that night. We started well and Luka could have had a penalty after Xabi Alonso brought him down, but they were always in control.

Gareth went over easily looking for another spot-kick. I would talk to him about that. Being labelled a diver is not only frustrating but it can also be detrimental – referees sometimes don't award free-kicks they should because of past incidents – and we made him aware of the risk he was running.

The criticism of him over diving was heavy at times. There were occasions when he went down too easily but some of it was wide of the mark – the slightest touch can knock you off balance when running at that speed and he was in any case the type of player who would inevitably get fouled a lot.

We had a few chances but never enough to truly worry them. Gomes made another mistake by fumbling Ronaldo's shot into our net just after half-time, making it 5-0 on aggregate. Over the two legs, he actually played well but two errors at that level cost you so dearly. 1-0 on the night was not a fair reflection but we didn't deserve to go through.

There was little time to dwell. We had to ensure the great Champions League journey we had been on wasn't just a one-off by qualifying again through our Premier League position. And a week after Real, Arsenal arrived at the Lane. They still had outside hopes of the title; we were in fifth chasing down Manchester City. Arsenal had the better end of three goals in the opening 12 minutes and we eventually came from 3-1 down to draw 3-3 as Rafa scored twice, the second a penalty.

There was a lot of fight that day but our results suffered thereafter. There was a physical and mental impact on the players after the high of reaching a Champions League quarter-final and the low of what happened in those 180 minutes against Real.

I hate to say we paid a price for our Champions League run but we did. People would argue as professionals, they should be able to do it no matter what but that ignores the human element. It is extremely difficult to turn it on three times a week and not for the want of trying. We took regular medical and sports science advice but we didn't have the biggest squad. The nucleus was really good but we could have done with two or three more players to back up the quality we had.

We lost at Chelsea, drew at Blackpool and, in a bitter irony, lost at Manchester City. That defeat at Eastlands ended our Champions League hopes, the same ground where we'd qualified a year earlier. Crouchy had scored the goal that night but this time he scored an own goal at the same end as City reached the Champions League for the first time. That's football for you.

We beat Liverpool 2-0 at Anfield to climb into fifth place which brought a return to Europa League football, confirmed with victory over Birmingham on the final day.

But we didn't want to be in the Europa League. The atmosphere, intensity and quality is nowhere near Champions League levels.

The aftermath of that season was a horrible time because we all knew the vultures were circling. Other clubs would look at our players, who performed so well in Europe's biggest club competition, and know we couldn't offer them that same experience again. The players may think differently, too.

They want to play in the Champions League every single year and the appeal of going to a club with greater pedigree where they are in it all the time was clear and unarguable. You hope in those moments for loyalty but football is generally short on that.

We sent them off with their summer programmes and I honestly wondered how many of them would return.

CHAPTER TWENTY-TWO

Harsh Realities

PEOPLE GET LABELLED IN FOOTBALL. I WAS JUST A 'GOALSCORER'. Harry Redknapp was supposedly a 'wheeler-dealer'. He hates that term to this day.

'Wheeler-dealer' is reductive and unfair. You can see from his career history he buys and sells players at a fairly high rate but the root of it is quickly identifying who he can work with, who he can't and what the team needs to improve.

That means there is often a high turnover, especially when he comes into a new club. That's the way he builds a team. He's managed almost 1,400 professional matches – you don't do that if you can't spot a player.

Harry wouldn't ask me to recommend signings but he did seek my opinion on targets. He has one of the best retentive memories of anyone I've ever seen. If he asked for an opinion, I might go and see a player but he would never want anything written down – it was always a verbal report. The question, every time, was: 'Is he a player?'

Whenever we travelled to away games, Harry would take the staff for dinner on the night before the match. On the table would be Harry, his backroom staff and a couple of guests – maybe an agent, a friend or a former colleague in football. We'd chew the fat over a couple of glasses of wine and a nice meal. It was always a group that was passionate about the game. I loved it. It was something I looked forward to because it felt like an hour or two of relief in between preparing the team and the pressure of the match itself. But Harry was unbelievable in remembering those conversations. This was something I learned over time: if you'd said two years before that someone was destined for the top, he'd always remember, especially if he was now playing in League Two.

Scouting players is always a tricky thing to get right. With Harry, I'd feed back with a 'yes', 'no', or a 'not sure' and he'd take it from there with the chairman. But if they signed a player you'd put your name to who later failed, internally it was your fault, whereas the successes he took credit for. That's a perk of being a manager.

I remember going to see Kevin Gameiro in France and I didn't think he was for us in the Premier League. I couldn't see him adapting effectively to English football but he's since had a decent career for Paris Saint-Germain, Sevilla, Atlético Madrid and Valencia.

I also went to France to watch Moussa Sow, top-scorer in Ligue 1 as Lille won the 2010/11 title with a team containing a host of promising talents including Yohan Cabaye, Gervinho and a youngster named Eden Hazard. I came back to speak with Harry, playing down Sow's worth to us but talking up Hazard. It was unavoidable – he was the star of that team.

'Ah, that's done,' Harry said. 'He's going to Manchester United.'

'What do you mean?'

'That's it, game over.' It was almost as if Sir Alex Ferguson had said 'hands off, he's ours' and Harry had given up.

Harry later told a story that he'd met with Hazard in a Paris hotel room for a few hours in a last-ditch attempt to sign him. Yet, despite his belief United would get the deal done, Hazard ended up going to Chelsea a year later in 2012.

Everybody was watching that Lille team at the time so it was no surprise competition was fierce but I felt I got Sow right. He hasn't had a great career since, taking in spells at Fenerbahçe and Al Ahli in Dubai. He's got a good record but hasn't gone on to big things.

It is hard to describe what you look for in a player. The subtlest little thing might convince you. If you have played at a high level – mid-table in Ligue 1, La Liga, the Premier League or the top of the Championship – you are already a decent footballer. But when you are talking about the very best, you have to have something special. One attribute, at least, that sets you apart. It could be explosive pace, great balance, vision when you are receiving the ball – these are the characteristics I try to identify.

Hazard was dynamic at a young age and would make things happen. Players like him are rare but easier to spot. You have to reinforce it by seeing someone three or four times and there would be other opinions thrown in from other scouts, members of the coaching staff and then, ultimately, Harry would look as well, whether it be on film or live in person. In that respect he was old school.

In any case, our main priority ahead of the 2011/12 campaign was keeping the players we had. I knew of Chelsea's interest in Luka Modrić and most people thought he was going to leave.

Luka had got it in his mind that Stamford Bridge would be his next move. From what I remember, Harry and the chairman spoke to him and they came to an agreement where he would give us one more year and see whether we qualified for the Champions League.

Manchester United were keen around that time too and so we'd done well to keep him for another season but the absence of Champions League football meant we had to lower our sights in terms of new signings.

That's the nature of the beast. We couldn't recruit at the level we wanted for financial reasons but also because we couldn't dangle the Champions League carrot in front of them.

We brought in Brad Friedel on a free from Aston Villa and Scott Parker on deadline day for £5.5million from West Ham. Scott had a great mentality and attitude.

We streamlined the group without Champions League football. Robbie Keane, Wilson Palacios, Peter Crouch and Roman Pavlyuchenko were among those to go out and we brought in Emmanuel Adebayor on loan from Manchester City.

We started the season terribly – a 3-0 defeat at United and then a 5-1 home defeat to City. Edin Dzeko scored four. We were fearing the worst at that point. We knew we didn't have enough and that had been reinforced by the results. To make matters worse, in comparison, City had spent big on Gaël Clichy, Sergio Agüero, Samir Nasri and Stefan Savić. Nobody was expecting us to match their spending levels but there should have been a greater desire to compete in the market.

*

Enthusiasm for a Europa League campaign wasn't high but Harry picked a strong team for the play-off first leg at Hearts and we eased to a 5-0 victory. That big advantage gave us the chance to blood some youngsters in the return game a week later, one of them being a teenage striker named Harry Kane.

Everybody knows Harry had a few loan spells and I'm not about to become the first coach who worked with him to suggest I saw him becoming one of the best in the world.

His rise has been remarkable and should serve as a lesson across the country both to players who think about giving up but also coaches that there are stars to be found in more obscure places.

The one thing I knew Harry had from day one was the right mentality. We are very similar in that regard.

I have to win at everything from ping-pong with the kids to an FA Cup Final. My wife can't understand it. I was the same in training. In a shooting session, I never wanted to get beaten, even when coaching someone less than half my age.

Harry was an example of that. We'd take part in finishing sessions together and until he turned 17, I made sure by hook or by crook I won that session. It was a way of injecting that competitive spirit into him. Some players walk away from it but Harry kept coming back, time after time.

'Can we do that finishing session after training again?' he'd ask.

'Yeah, fine, no problem,' I'd say. 'But you'll lose.'

He'd smile and walk off. As he got better, I would cheat or end it early – whatever I needed to do to win until eventually he beat me all ends up and I conceded defeat.

You hope they adopt that same mentality of winning at all costs and Harry certainly has. He wants to get better every day. Robbie Keane and Jermain Defoe had it too. Both of them always came back for more. I used to have regular conversations with Jermain about his finishing.

'That chance you didn't take on Saturday,' I'd say, 'What were you thinking?'

'Well, the ball was under my foot so I lost the chance to shoot.'

'Yeah but that's because you looked at the goalkeeper. The ball escaped you in that second and you miskicked it. Next time you are there, just look at the ball because that's the thing that's moving, not the goal. The goalkeeper will move but if you are looking at him, you won't strike the ball how you want to.'

He'd come back to me a few games later and say: 'You were right!'

'I know about it Jermain, I've been there – I know what it feels like.'

It was great to help these already good players find a little bit extra in their game. Jermain was like a sponge. Harry was the same and still is.

Harry has made himself a success but I like to think I gave him a little helping hand as I know from my career that you remember the coaches that identify small areas of improvement. The greatest compliment I can pay Terry Venables is that in whatever session you were in, he'd stop play and ask for your opinion on what had just happened or the situation you faced.

He had the gift of the gab but always sought feedback. He'd point out runs I should make, I'd then try them in a game and score. You'd think: 'Yeah, he's right'. If you can influence players like that – somewhere down the line the penny drops – you are a good coach. You earn their respect and they want more information.

Harry played in five of our six Europa League group stage games, scoring in the final match against Shamrock Rovers, but we hadn't done enough to qualify and having already gone out of the League Cup too – on penalties at Stoke City – the decision was taken to send him out on loan to Millwall.

We kept tabs on his progress but he wasn't exactly tearing up trees in the Championship. The reports came back that they thought he was a good kid but the jury was very much out on whether he could become a top player, hence why he went to Norwich and then Leicester before getting a chance at Spurs.

Tim Sherwood had monitored his development from afar at that stage so when he got the chance as Tottenham manager a few years later, he followed his instincts, threw Harry in and the rest is history.

At the time, we sent him to Millwall because, improbably, we were on the cusp of a Premier League title challenge and needed the finished article to help propel us forward.

Harry was great at bringing everyone together after those two early League defeats. He made us all take stock of the situation: anyone could lose to United and City, they just happened to be our first two games; we hadn't suffered any major departures, we were still a top side and this was the time to go out and remind people.

The response after City was great. We won 10 of our next 11 League games, only dropping points in a 2-2 draw at Newcastle thanks to Shola Ameobi's 86th-minute equaliser before the run came to an end away at Stoke on 11 December.

That defeat was only a blip, however, as we had a good run over Christmas, staying in touch with the leaders and well inside the top four.

But the turning point came both on and off the pitch in January. We faced City again on 22 January, this time at Etihad Stadium when they were league leaders.

United were in second place, three points behind City and two ahead of us in third.

It was a huge occasion but one that we all embraced. Harry had told the players they could achieve great things this season and a win here would put us right in the mix for the title with 16 games to play.

As was often the case, we tried to do things the hard way. Samir Nasri and Joleon Lescott put City 2-0 up but Jermain Defoe and Gareth Bale hauled us level, all four goals coming in ten crazy minutes early in the second half.

The real story involved Mario Balotelli. He had already been booked when he stamped on Scott Parker with six minutes left. Referee Howard Webb claimed he didn't see it and Balotelli stayed on.

It might not have mattered as Gareth skipped past Lescott in stoppage-time and crossed to the back post. Jermain was rushing to meet it but at full stretch he could only get a touch on the ball to take it wide of the post. Shades of Paul Gascoigne at Euro '96.

And to make it worse, Balotelli, who shouldn't have been on the pitch, won a penalty off Ledley King and converted to give City a 3-2 win right at the death.

Instead of being two points behind them with a win, we were now eight adrift. It was a killer blow to us and as a staff we feared the players would start to think that glass ceiling existed again.

But the one positive of losing was that Harry felt he could use the result to press home his demands in the January transfer window.

Harry told us during a staff meeting us that there were ongoing discussions with the chairman to sign Carlos Tevez from City. Tevez was a hugely talented player but also tainted goods at that time, having gone on strike after falling out with City boss Roberto Mancini following his refusal to come on as a substitute in a Champions League game.

City were demanding £25million for him, a valuation which had scared off AC Milan. Harry wanted Daniel to get Tevez either permanently or explore the possibility of a loan deal, something that might appeal to all parties given the need to restore his reputation.

Harry told us he said to Daniel: 'If you go and get Tevez, we will qualify for the Champions League – at least.'

There were concerns about his character, of course, but Harry being Harry, he felt he could manage any issues, especially on a short-term basis if it proved to be a six-month loan deal.

The other signing he wanted was Gary Cahill. Bolton Wanderers were willing to sell and Gary was talking to Chelsea and Arsenal at the time.

He was the centre-back Harry had identified to stop us having those meltdowns where we'd lose 4-0 at Fulham or wherever. His aggression, physicality and mentality were all perfectly suited to combating that.

Equally, Tevez had his demons but when a team needed goals in big games, he usually delivered. And on top of that, he was industrious, busy and a demanding character who would lead from the front in stopping the 'Spursy' trait.

Now it was down to Daniel. Cahill had conversations with Tottenham but a deal failed to materialise. Instead, he went to Chelsea for about £7m.

Talks with Tevez continued but City were apparently adamant a permanent deal was the only option and Daniel decided against it.

And so, instead of landing Tevez and Cahill, Daniel brought in two free transfers in Ryan Nelsen and Louis Saha from Blackburn Rovers and Everton respectively. Steven Pienaar went in the opposite direction as part of the Saha deal.

Both Ryan and Louis had their merits but this is where Daniel's understanding of football took us in the wrong direction.

I have no doubt Daniel wants the best for Tottenham but he operates with a cold business mentality.

Yet football is a unique business. Some transfers ask clubs to take an economic leap of faith. The financial logic may be questionable but the football reasoning is sound. If you can afford Tevez, you sign him. Almost any manager in the world would tell you that.

Opting against signing Tevez and Cahill was a sensible, prudent business decision but a crazy one from a football perspective.

The question I would ask is this: are Tottenham willing to do everything it takes to join the elite? There has to come a point where you make a decision that might be economically challenging but a football no-brainer.

Ryan and Louis were top professionals. This is not to lay any blame at their doors at all. Would they make us that much better? No, but they would reinforce what we had and would never upset the squad. They were no-risk acquisitions in that regard. But what we needed to do was take a bold football decision.

There is a chance history is repeating itself under Mauricio Pochettino now.

He urged Daniel to 'take risks' in the transfer market yet they bought nobody in the summer of 2018. When I heard Pochettino say that, it certainly sounded familiar. He repeated it once the fantastic new Tottenham Hotspur Stadium opened in April 2019, telling them they have to think like a big club to win titles.

Harry was disappointed once the transfer window closed and a look at the league table told you why. We beat Wigan 3-1 at the Lane on 31 January to move just five points behind joint-leaders Manchester City and Manchester United after 23 games. Liverpool were in fifth on 38 points, 11 adrift of us. Nobody really said it but the numbers showed a title challenge was not beyond us.

Yet that January window changed everything. From eyeing up the summit, everyone started looking over their shoulders at what a long way down it was.

We knew there and then we'd missed an opportunity. As good as this group could be on their day, there was always the risk of everything unravelling. And that's exactly what happened.

The second half of the season was a whirlwind for many reasons. Many people think Harry's court case had an impact but from my experience, it didn't affect him on a day-to-day basis.

The issue had been rumbling along for years and there was the odd occasion when he wasn't around or had to leave the training ground a little early but he always kept things professional. He never let his private life affect whatever was going on at the club.

On 8 February, Harry stood on the steps of Southwark Crown Court having been cleared of tax evasion and described the whole ordeal as a 'nightmare'.

We were sitting as a staff having a meal the next day and someone said to him: 'How did you feel when the verdict was read out?'

He said: 'Milan Mandaric [who also faced allegations of cheating the public revenue] had always insisted all along the process that we'd be fine but as we stood in the dock I turned to him and asked if it would be alright. Milan just said, "I don't know."'

Harry felt the night before that he would go to prison. He thought they wanted to make an example of him and stood there in the dock with Milan suddenly wavering in his belief, Harry was scared.

The relief therefore was huge but on the same day as we thought things would settle down, news broke that Fabio Capello had resigned as England manager. We all found out through Sky Sports News at the end of a staff meeting. He looked up at the television and said: 'Oh, I don't need this right now.'

Within an hour, the entrance to Spurs Lodge was swarming with camera crews. Speculation went into overdrive almost immediately – bookmakers reportedly stopped taking bets on Harry becoming England manager.

I knew he would have loved the job and was the right man at that time. He was exactly what those beleaguered England players needed – someone to inject some pride again. The public wanted him and the Football Association should have gone for him.

Over the next week or so, the training ground resembled a bunker. A couple of days in, Harry asked me after a morning training session whether I had any plans for the afternoon. I didn't.

'I want to play golf – can you arrange a round for the two of us?' he asked. I did so, dodging the media as we left Spurs Lodge.

We teed off and finally felt a sense of freedom away from the suffocating environment that had engulfed us. We were walking down a fairway to our respective golf balls when I asked the question every journalist at Spurs Lodge wanted to.

'Harry, have you been approached?'

'Clivey, no, I haven't. And I don't know what's going to happen.'

'But it is the England job, Harry. Surely if they offer it to you, you can't turn it down?'

He didn't answer. The timing of it threw him. There's no doubt he wanted it but Capello left four months before Euro 2012 when nobody thought there would be a vacancy.

There was a lot of talk that the compensation package Tottenham wanted was astronomical and the FA were looking to move away from an era of paying huge salaries for managers. Whether that was true or not I don't know, but we spoke about that behind the scenes.

I had no idea if he would have taken me with him. I sat at home and talked it through with Lisa, about the pros and cons of going to England. There's no doubt I would have loved to work with the national team, the best players around, with the end goal of making the country happy. I didn't have extensive experience but six years or so tasting everything at Tottenham was a pretty good grounding.

A lifetime in football told me you could never get carried away. Until the question is asked, you never know how you'll feel.

Next time out, we beat Newcastle 5-0 at the Lane which only seemed to underline Harry's credentials even more. That was a euphoric 90 minutes, the wave of goodwill towards Harry somehow carrying the team forward.

Yet all of a sudden, we began to struggle. We lost 5-2 at Arsenal – having been 2-0 up – then at home to Manchester United and away at Everton – three league defeats on the spin. We progressed in the FA Cup but it wasn't until 1 April that we won a league game again, 3-1 against Swansea. That result put us on 58 points, level with Arsenal in fourth place.

There had still been no FA approach but the media continued to speculate. None of it helped the relationship between Daniel Levy and Harry. Harry possibly could have ruled himself out of the running and reaffirmed his commitment to Tottenham but anyone who knows him is aware he always talks candidly about players, his future, transfer targets – whatever it may be.

And it was inevitable he would be asked about it every week at Tottenham press conferences as the FA worked out their next move. Perhaps he didn't handle it in the right way but the longer the FA took to make up their minds, the more strain it placed on everyone connected to the situation.

Chelsea thrashed us in the FA Cup semi-final at Wembley. We hit the post and had one cleared off the line at 0-0 but that game will be remembered for their second goal never crossing the line. Harry was incensed and we had every right to be frustrated, but they were too strong for us on the day.

Our season was on the brink of collapsing and the England saga took another twist when well-informed whispers suggested Roy Hodgson was in fact the FA's preferred candidate.

Whether or not the possibility of Harry leaving made other players look around at their options, taking their eye off the ball in the process, is debatable.

We prepared for each game in the same way as before and I didn't see too much of an impact. It was a distraction on some level but I honestly believe the bigger issue was physical.

The season was taking its toll and the lack of quality signings in January was having a real effect.

Ledley King began to struggle to defy the odds, too. Harry claimed in one of his books that Ledley pushed himself because he needed to play a certain number of games for contractual reasons but I wasn't aware of that.

Knowing Ledley, I doubt that was a factor in his decision to play whenever it was touch and go. I don't think he would ever have jeopardised the team for the sake of hitting an individual appearance target.

But it was obviously affecting him, even if shorn of full fitness he was still one of the best players I worked with. He was world class. But there is only so long anyone could pull off the weekly magic trick he managed in barely training yet playing to the highest level and it had a massive impact on the second half of our season.

Ledley played in seven defeats from January onwards. That isn't a criticism of him at all and some of those were big matches we weren't necessarily expected to win anyway, but he was so important to us we just couldn't afford the dip in form he had during that period.

In the end, it was too much – Younès Kaboul and William Gallas played the final four games, including a painful defeat at Queens Park Rangers where Adel Taarabt came back to haunt us.

As only Adel could, he scored the winning goal to beat us 1-0 before getting sent off for kicking the ball away just before the end.

'I knew we shouldn't have sold him, I'd never have sold him,' Harry kept saying to me on the touchline. Well, you did sell him Harry. You didn't want him. On balance, it was probably the right decision but it didn't feel like it that day.

We won three games at the end of the campaign but only secured fourth place on the final day of the season by beating Fulham, while Arsenal beat West Brom to stay in third.

A top four finish usually means Champions League football. But this time there was still an anxious wait because, against all the odds, Chelsea had reached the 2012 Champions League Final against Bayern Munich.

UEFA rules dictated only four teams from one country could qualify for the Champions League and therefore if Chelsea won, they would go into next season's competition as winners at our expense because we'd finished in the lowest eligible league position. Chelsea were sixth, one place below Newcastle United.

Had we finished third – and above Arsenal for the first time since 1995 – they would have been at risk and not us; we'd won just four of our final 13 league games but the match that cost us was QPR. Adel killed us in terms of finishing in third place.

Harry and the staff talked about it all week in the build-up to the final. And, suddenly, our fate rested in Bayern Munich's hands. Chelsea, under caretaker boss Roberto di Matteo, had ridden their luck to the final and had a poor season domestically but one game now stood between them and glory. And symbiotically, between us and failure. Nobody wanted the Europa League again.

The final started well for Bayern and Tottenham. Bayern dominated the game and created enough opportunities to put it to bed. As they kept missing chance after chance, I began to fear the worst but, finally, seven minutes from the end, Thomas Müller headed Bayern in front.

We were two minutes away from the Champions League when Didier Drogba headed an equaliser and the game went to extra-time. Bayern were still the better team but couldn't make it count. Arjen Robben missed a penalty. The more absurd it got, the more my guts were telling me this wouldn't be our night.

It went to a penalty shoot-out. When Drogba scored the winning penalty, my wife, who says very little during football matches, said, 'Oh, that's great an English team – one of your old sides – has won the Champions League.'

'That could cost me my job,' I replied.

'What do you mean? Don't be so stupid.'

'Just wait and see.'

Harry was in the stadium that night, a guest of Sky. He had to walk around the pitch after the game with Chelsea fans giving him terrible stick. They'd qualified for the Champions League and despite finishing in fourth place, we had not.

Missing out was a savage blow to all of us. Roy Hodgson had been confirmed as England manager and speculation over Harry's future turned to the fact he had only one year left on his Tottenham contract and we'd finished the season so poorly.

It was clear talks between him and the chairman over a new deal weren't going well and missing out on the Champions League only made things worse.

I thought there was still a good chance Harry would sign an extension. After all, we'd done a good job overall, albeit enduring a difficult six months or so. There were texts going back and forth on the morning of 13 June informing us he was going for a meeting later that afternoon. I heard nothing more all day.

Late that night, I was watching Sky Sports News when it flashed up that

Harry had been sacked. I was stunned.

I texted Harry asking if everything was alright. About an hour later, he replied saying he'd call me. Well after midnight, Harry was in the car driving home when he rang.

'Can you believe it? He's fucking sacked me,' he said. 'I don't know what's happening with you and the staff but for me it is done. It is all over.'

I didn't push it on my situation any further. Deep down, I assumed that would be it, but you just don't know. There was a lot of uncertainty, made worse for the fact I was up for renewal, not an extension. My deal expired at the end the month.

Quite quickly after Harry left, Joe Jordan and Kevin Bond were called to the chairman's office and they departed. I was left in limbo. It was a horrible situation. They hadn't said they wouldn't renew my deal and somebody new was coming in so I didn't know whether they would want me as part of their team, just as happened originally with Harry.

An agonising wait followed. I still had around two weeks left before the end of my contract when I attended Johnny Docker's funeral, a former apprentice teammate of mine at QPR. He was the same age as me and died of a heart attack. His son played for me as a junior at Tottenham. It was a very difficult day.

As I got in my car to leave, I saw I had several missed called from Darren Eales, Tottenham's Director of Football Administration. A solitary voicemail simply said: 'Clive, can you give me a call please?'

I returned his call and soon learned they were bringing in André Villas-Boas but couldn't say whether there was a role for me.

My contract expired and the situation dragged into July. Should I go back in for pre-season? Should I search for a new club? I didn't know what to do. June was always our holiday month so we went away but there was regular communication with the club during this period without any real progress.

It took three months before it was settled. I never spoke to Villas-Boas, who apparently impressed Daniel during his interview by revealing a portfolio of about 2,000 coaching drills.

In any case, the club's conduct had left a bitter taste. I ended up coming to an agreement that included a confidentiality clause.

Over that summer, I'd been advised not to speak to other clubs until my situation with Spurs had been resolved. In any case, I wasn't in a good place during that period. I didn't know what to do. Olly, who was loving life in the city, knew I was struggling.

'Every day I go into work and there are people around me who have a job at 8am one morning and then they are gone the next,' he said. 'It is ruthless. The people who make those decisions are the same type as the ones you are dealing with. They are businessmen. When you are finished, you are gone. They don't think ill of you. That's just business.'

And so, I was out of work and left to reflect on my time with Harry. To be honest, I always felt on the edge of his inner sanctum. Joe Jordan and Kevin Bond formed his trusted circle and while I know he appreciated my opinion, I served a purpose primarily as a connection with the club and its history.

Whether there was pressure on him from above to keep me on or he sincerely wanted me to join his staff, to this day I wouldn't know for sure.

Either way, it was a fantastic learning experience to see him work first-hand. He is a top football manager and has proved it for much longer than most.

I'll always be indebted to him for giving me the opportunity to coach, however it came about.

I loved every minute of it. It was a challenge. He made it that way and it should be like that. He demanded a lot from his staff and I gave him everything I had. It was a good working relationship. I would say we are friends, probably more so now than when we were working together.

Who knows whether that final season would have been different if we had acquired Tevez and Cahill, or two players of similar calibre. It certainly would not have been any worse.

One of the great ironies of the whole period is that a manager wrongly tagged as a wheeler-dealer was brought down in no small part by inadequate transfer business when the team needed it most.

CHAPTER TWENTY-THREE

Changed Lanes

IT WAS AT LEAST A YEAR BEFORE I WENT BACK TO TOTTENHAM IN any capacity. I felt lost. I'd set my heart on coaching, developing my skills and I loved the job. It consumed my life.

Every night I'd watch games, scout players, spend time thinking about opponents, go to youth games. It was all I knew. And that had been taken away.

Management was something I looked at for a while. I interviewed for the Gillingham job when, ironically, my cousin Martin got it. I spoke to a couple of other clubs but whether at a formal interview stage or just a chat over the phone, the conversation was always the same.

'Clive, we can see you've had extensive involvement with Tottenham in the Premier League and Champions League but you've got no managerial experience,' chairmen would say.

'We are going with a man who has greater experience.'

'So what you are telling me is you are going for the man with experience of failure?' Invariably, managers are only available because they were sacked somewhere else.

I understand the argument because it takes a brave chairman to appoint someone with no experience as a number one but following the logic through, no young manager would ever be given a chance if everyone had the same attitude.

That will always frustrate me. If I had been given the opportunity and failed, I would be on the managerial merry-go-round. But nobody will let me on the ride. I have not had ideas above my station and tried for big Premier League jobs. Yet it appears you have to drop down to a level where it is virtually impossible for someone like me to succeed – mainly because the game is so different at lower levels – and even if you do, you still need a bounce up at the right time where a club is prepared to take a chance on you.

However, I've got nothing but admiration for these guys who are so determined and thick-skinned to climb the ladder like they do.

I had some hope that Harry Redknapp would take me with him to Queens Park Rangers when he got the manager's job later in 2012.

During a short period while he was working out his coaching staff, we spoke on the phone and I made it clear I would relish the chance to join him.

QPR was where I grew up, where I learned my trade and it would have been fantastic to go back and pass on what I'd learned in the game. But the follow-up call offering me a job never came.

After that, I decided media work was the way forward. I never employed an agent to explore managerial opportunities on my behalf and I question myself on that: have I ever really had the drive for it? I certainly had it as a player. I always just wanted to play. Yet I guess if I'm honest with myself I haven't always wanted to manage at any cost. Maybe that's because I saw what my father went through.

I'll never forget my Dad sticking his head around my bedroom door as a 14-year-old telling me he'd been sacked at Swindon and the resulting effect it had on us as a family. I've known from a young age how tough it can be.

I don't have any regrets. I know what I gave in that six-year period at Spurs. I could not have done any more. Premier League finishes of fourth, fifth, fourth and a Champions League quarter-final. Harry was on the frontline managing but I played a part and I know what my contribution was. I believe people at the club know that as well.

Management was the next step after leaving Tottenham but it just never came to pass. I believe I have something to offer as a manager purely because of my passion for the game. I would love to be able to impart that on modern-day players. I know I'm a dinosaur, I know I'm old school. But I don't believe there are too many modern-day players who are in love with the game. They play the game – it is their business and they are 100 percent professional – but I wouldn't describe them as scholars or students of the game. That's just what the game has become.

I will never say never but I don't see me managing now. I still have the greatest passion for it but there's more to life than football for me. I get my fix but I enjoy switching off.

Through media work, I still have the drug of football and while its not the same pressure as working day-to-day at a club, I still hold myself to high standards.

It was media work that eventually saw me go back to Spurs in 2013. I saw Daniel and our first conversation was normal. By then, too much water had gone under the bridge.

I have a great relationship with the club today. I still work there as an ambassador and love doing so because I still get to be a part of things.

Sometimes I get stopped outside grounds like my Dad used to. They might ask for an autograph or refer to a particular game they remembered or a goal I scored.

And I'm proud to say I played professional football for 17 years. I loved it. I've got all my medals and individual awards on display at home. They are things nobody can take away and give me great memories.

As a coach, we broke new ground for Tottenham in the Premier League era. There has been a ten-year progression at the club from my time with Harry, climbing into the top four and now another leap forward under Mauricio Pochettino in achieving regular Champions League football and reaching the 2019 final.

What a journey that was. They were fortunate to get out of the group stage and again to progress at various points in the knockout rounds.

I went to both legs of the quarter-final against Manchester City and having won the first 1-0, you sensed sat inside the Etihad Stadium that something special was going to happen.

After Spurs lost 4-3 but went through on away goals – surviving a last-gasp Raheem Sterling goal after it was overturned by the Video Assistant Referee (VAR) – I didn't think I would see another match like it.

It was the most remarkable course of events in 90 minutes that I've ever witnessed, ebbing and flowing one way then the other with the stakes so high throughout.

But then there was the semi-final against Ajax. This time, Spurs lost the first leg at home before being 2-0 down at half-time in Amsterdam.

My eldest son Olly was with me in the ground and during the break, he phoned his wife to cancel the flights he'd booked for the final. He was due to fly from Edinburgh to Madrid.

'We're out, we're not going to Spain,' he said to her with disappointment and anger in his voice.

Out of nowhere, Spurs produce a stunning comeback to win 3-2 on the night – and progress 3-3 on away goals again – as Lucas Moura completed a hat-trick with what was virtually the last kick of the game.

Olly called his wife minutes after the hysteria had subsided.

'Em, you haven't cancelled those flights have you?' he said.

'Um, yeah, I have.'

'Re-book them!'

He ended up having to go via Hamburg and pay eight times the price of his original direct flights.

But the miracle of Manchester and that night in Holland emphasised the beauty of the game, why I love it so much.

The club took the matchday ambassadors and all the permanent staff to the final against Liverpool on a chartered flight to Madrid.

The final itself changed massively inside 30 seconds. Sadio Mané crossed into the box a fraction of second after Moussa Sissoko pointed to a teammate. The ball struck Sissoko's chest, then his outstretched arm and a penalty was awarded.

For Liverpool, it was the perfect start but it was very harsh. I can understand the decision from the referee because the handball law has changed with VAR but it felt wrong at the time.

Looking forward, that is something that I would be working with my strikers to exploit in pre-season. It almost feels like there is a loophole in the law. I kick the ball against your hand, your hand touches it, it is a penalty. There's an opportunity there to take advantage of if it is consistently applied. Defenders will have to change the way they defend, keeping their arms behind their back. You cannot afford to have your arms as a target and the whole issue will become almost as important as shooting at goal.

Spurs weren't bright or sharp enough on the night. They were too cautious until it was too late, losing 2-0 as Mohamed Salah scored the resultant penalty before Divock Origi struck a second near the end. It was a bad day at the office at the worst possible time.

Tactically, Liverpool were excellent. There were a number of games near the end of the Premier League season where Spurs faced a lot of teams who put men behind the ball and they struggled to break them down. Having got the lead so early, Liverpool executed a similar gameplan perfectly.

Harry Kane was an injury doubt having not played for almost eight weeks due to ankle ligament damage but I totally understand Mauricio's thinking in starting him.

In hindsight, you could say he wasn't 100 percent fit but knowing Harry, he would have done the necessary work and ultimately you have to trust him if he tells you he's ready.

You have to leave him on for 90 minutes, too, because regardless of his contribution in the game, he just needs that one chance. He didn't really get it.

Spurs have got to lose the tag of being nearly-men. They have to get over the line. And that next stage is their biggest challenge. Mauricio is hinting at that in what he was saying before and after the game. It is the balance between recognising the achievement but not being blinded by the reality of where they actually are.

I spoke to supporters coming out of the stadium and the overriding feeling walking away was: 'Blimey, they have played in a Champions League Final but you start again next season and how far away are they from getting back there?'

Real Madrid, Barcelona, Bayern Munich, Juventus, Manchester City, Liverpool – that's six teams that you think objectively have a better chance. Will this happen again?

They are going to need massive investment in the summer of 2019 and beyond. I'm not saying they will get left behind otherwise but the others will move forward again.

The opening of their £1billion stadium gave Spurs a lift at a vital stage and combined with the state-of-the-art training complex at Hotspur Way, the platform is there to go and challenge. I hope they can be successful now.

I was fortunate to have an early sight of the new stadium when helping Gary Mabbutt manage a Tottenham Legends side against an Inter Milan team named 'Inter Forever' in the final test event.

Mabbs called me in to help and I organised the logistics, which we treated like a first team game. The lads coming in from overseas stayed at the training ground on the Friday and then we went to the stadium by coach on the Saturday, just as Mauricio and his first team lads were coming in to prepare for their Premier League game at Liverpool.

Mauricio was desperate to play, and I think he would have done had they not had such an important match the next day.

Robbie Keane, Paul Gascoigne, Jürgen Klinsmann and Dimitar Berbatov were just some of the players involved and despite everything they'd seen in their careers, they were overwhelmed when walking into the training ground.

'Wait 'til you see the stadium,' I told them.

Each and every one of them was blown away. The home dressing room is incredible. If you were looking for the perfect dressing room as a player, a coach, a physio – whatever your role – everything is there. The shape of it is perfect to deliver your message as a coach or manager. The shower and hydro area, the relaxation room, the manager's quarters – I can't emphasis enough the attention to detail they have got right. It is absolutely incredible, simply the best football stadium in the world.

I had a chat with Daniel at the game and told him he'd done everything and more to give Spurs the best chance of success. He was both excited at the possibilities and relieved to finally get it over the line.

Sitting in the dugout was special. The spirit of White Hart Lane is still there. The memories came flooding back, the shiver up my spine that I felt when I walked out to play a game or sat and watched a big match. The atmosphere was five-fold what it was at the old ground because of the increased capacity and stunning acoustics.

The thing I like most of all is where they have positioned the golden cockerel, above the 17,500-seater stand. That will quickly become something iconic.

I stood for the team photo and there were tears in my eyes. It was in some ways as emotional as the last day at the Lane.

At the end of the game, I took my five-year-old grandson, Bertie, onto the pitch. So he has run out there now – another Allen generation to have graced Tottenham's home.

✳

I hope I am a has-been rather than a never-was. Dad has never told me one way or the other.

My parents are in their eighties now. Dad has got a heart condition in addition to one or two hip and knee problems but they are doing okay for people their age.

Our relationship has never been right since that innocuous falling out in 1999. It isn't something I discuss publicly very often. My career was inextricably linked to Dad's so we both know people in the game and when they would ask me how he was, it was difficult to reply 'I haven't spoken to him in years' or however long it has been.

We talk. I visit them regularly but they don't see Lisa nor the children, nor Bradley and his family. That's their decision and I can't change it, as sad as it is. I'm disappointed for my kids. Lisa's parents are very close to my children – they have the relationship I hoped would be replicated with my parents but it hasn't happened.

I'm a grandfather myself now and I always want to see my grandkids. I can't understand not ever wanting to. If they'd have knocked at the door, who knows what would have happened? Lisa has always insisted I should stay in touch to keep the door open.

I'm extremely proud of all the kids, their successes and as adults and individuals. Olly to overcome illness, adversity and injury and to carve out a new path – successful in his own right and with a beautiful family of his own.

Ed graduated from Loughborough University with an Economics and Finance degree and is now working in finance, but most importantly he is a genuinely thoughtful, beautiful person inside and out.

Mimi gained a First at Bristol University and then did a Masters at Cambridge. She is a teacher, strong and determined, fun-loving with a huge personality and highly competitive. Lydia is a kind, loving, beautiful soul now training to be a nurse at Addenbrooke's Hospital in Cambridge.

But they hadn't seen Olly since he was 13, Ed since he was eight, Amelia since she was six and Lydia since she was just 10 months old.

Until that one day at White Hart Lane in 2017, the final match to be played at Tottenham's famous old ground.

Before the game, most of the former players were scattered throughout corporate hospitality having lunch, myself included. My parents were sitting on a table with the Double winning team alongside Cliff Jones and several others.

My mother acted as if everything was okay when we both knew it wasn't but that's the way she is. She chatted away before I had to go out and meet a few people in one of the lounges.

It was an awkward situation as my parents and my children had not been in the same room for many years.

About twenty minutes later, I came and sat back down with Lydia and Ed. I had to tell them.

'Nan and Granddad Allen are over there,' I said, pointing in their direction.

'Yeah, I know,' said Ed. 'We went over to say hello.' I couldn't believe they had gone over off their own back like that, cutting through years of animosity and alienation.

'What happened?'

'Oh, nothing,' said Ed. 'We just said hello, gave them kisses, shook their hands and had a brief, polite conversation.'

I got up and went over to see Mum and Dad. Before I opened my mouth, Mum said: 'Who was that charming young man who just came over?'

'That was your grandson.'

She paused, both of them looking confused. 'What do you mean?'

'Mum, you know who that was.' She knew. Of course she knew.

I just couldn't get it. She was in complete denial. I don't think they could handle it because they knew what they've missed out on.

This was an opportunity to make a fuss of my kids – innocent parties in all this – and break down a barrier that had existed all Lydia's life but she acted as if she didn't know who they were. It upsets me to this day. The kids did it right – they were so mature and took the higher moral ground. I was incredibly proud of them.

After the game, I still exchanged pleasantries with Dad as we were in the tunnel waiting to go out.

A few of the other players being there provided a welcome distraction as we stood watching the stewards struggle to clear supporters off the pitch for the parade that followed.

The crowd cheered as I made my way out onto the pitch, waving and smiling to all four corners. What a moment. I'd barely taken ten strides when the PA continued.

'Talented and industrious, 370 games over eight years, FA Cup winner 1991, midfielder… PAUL ALLEN!'

I reached the centre-circle as Paul took his applause and walked to the other side of a central plinth from which world-renowned tenor Wynne Evans would later sing.

'The scorer of the first goal in that legendary double season of 1961, striker, LES ALLEN!'

With a crutch in his right arm, Dad made his way across the grass as the roll-call continued. Darren Anderton, Steve Archibald and Ossie Ardiles came next.

Ossie walked across the pitch and Dad took his place alongside me. The club's greats continued to file out and as 30,000 fans sang about Ledley King having one knee yet being better than John Terry, the rain began to fall and umbrellas were passed along the line to those of us already in the middle. Dad held his own umbrella, as did I. The weather did nothing to dampen the spirits, although it tried.

The names kept coming as the rain got heavier: Teddy Sheringham, Ricky Villa, Chris Waddle.

'Ladies and gentlemen, the great players who graced this pitch thousands of times between them. The Kings of White Hart Lane!'

The emotion of standing next to my Dad and my cousin while being described in those terms overwhelmed me. I looked across at Paul. He smiled back. I looked at Dad. Nothing.

The applause faded out as the London Community Gospel Choir began a slow but steadily quickening version of 'Oh When the Spurs Go Marching In.'

The current squad together with manager Mauricio Pochettino came out to take their applause and Wynne Evans started a rendition of 'Glory Glory Hallelujah'.

Everyone in the ground waved flags and created a cacophony of noise as the song sped up in repetition to a rousing conclusion. As tickertape was fired into the crowd and cheers rang out, nature provided the best special effect of all: the rain had receded to be replaced by a beautifully bright rainbow emerging over the skyline behind the west stand.

I looked at Dad again. A sensation came over me: in the eye of the celebrations around us, on the pitch we had both played on alongside my cousin with thousands of people celebrating our contribution, I wanted family to come first over football.

'The pitch isn't bad is it?' I said.

'Yeah, it is beautiful,' he replied.

'Look at all this,' I said with a tear in my eye. 'We did it.'